Enactments

EDITED BY

RICHARD SCHECHNER

To perform is to imagine, represent, live and enact present circumstances, past events and future possibilities. Performance takes place across a very broad range of venues from city streets to the countryside, in theatres and in offices, on battlefields and in hospital operating rooms. The genres of performance are many, from the arts to the myriad performances of everyday life, from courtrooms to legislative chambers, from theatres to wars to circuses.

ENACTMENTS encompasses performance in as many of its aspects and realities as there are authors able to write about them.

ENACTMENTS includes active scholarship, readable thought and engaged analysis across the broad spectrum of performance studies.

"To say Stanley Cohen lived a rich life would be an understatement. This charismatic man, trained as a lawyer at Harvard, lived several lives that started with a stint as the manager of a seaman's club in Yokohama and then brought him in contact with the Bohemian world of artists and writers in 1960s Paris and, eventually, with Hollywood. From the anecdotes, we get a sense of a person with fervent convictions about personal ethics and social justice. Underlying Stanley's drive and quest for his own identity has been a deep interest in literature: Joseph Conrad, Robert Musil, and Milan Kundera, whom he often met in a cafe without exchanging a single word, but who inspired an unforgettable imaginary dialogue about the very meaning of a memoir."

Dr. Joachim Frank

Winner of the 2017 Nobel Prize in Chemistry

"At times movingly introspective, at times lyrically descriptive (Paris! Yokohama! Manhattan!) and liberally studded with reminiscences of the great and the good (Kundera! Rothschild! Cartier-Bresson! Baldwin! Calder!) drawn from a lifetime of wandering and wondering, this candid and frequently funny memoir is as lively as one might expect from Stanley Cohen's long and richly endowed life. It will delight all who dip into it, and who then, enraptured, will likely wholly immerse themselves and, for as long as it takes, not bother to come up for air."

Simon Winchester

New York Times bestselling author of *The Professor and the Madman*, *The Map That Changed the World*, and *Land*: *How the Hunger of Ownership Shaped the Modern World*

I Never Made Love with James Baldwin

A MEMOIR

STANLEY COHEN

LONDON NEW YORK CALCUTTA

Seagull Books, 2026

First published by Seagull Books, 2026

ISBN 978 1 8030 9 665 0

Cover image: Stanley Cohen, age eighteen, working aboard an oil tanker en route to Japan. Courtesy of the author.

Cover design: Sunandini Banerjee, Seagull Books

British Library Cataloguing-in-Publication Data
A catalogue record for this book is available from the British Library

Typeset at Seagull Books, Calcutta, India

What motivated me to write my autobiography?

Of course it is an effort to recall joys and failures. And when one passes the ninetieth year with an immediate family substantially younger, there is a desire to share stories of the past that have remained untold.

Even more important, it is to acknowledge the gratitude that my wife, Carrie Chen, and my son, Paul, deserve. They have made my existence one of happy times.

With Paul an adult and leading his own life, the burden to make me, a cranky and moody senior, enjoy my final years with comfort far beyond expectations is a task that Carrie has undertaken with seeming ease, a testimony to her love.

I raise the glass and sound the toast.

To Carrie—accept my memory extracts that accompany my love and deep feelings for you.

Drawing of Stanley Cohen by Ann Geracimos, 1972. Photograph by Lisa Vollmer.

I shift about too much, I move too often.
You see me here, and yet I have already changed.
I'm already elsewhere. I never stay in
One place and that's why I have no style.

Pablo Picasso, 1963

Contents

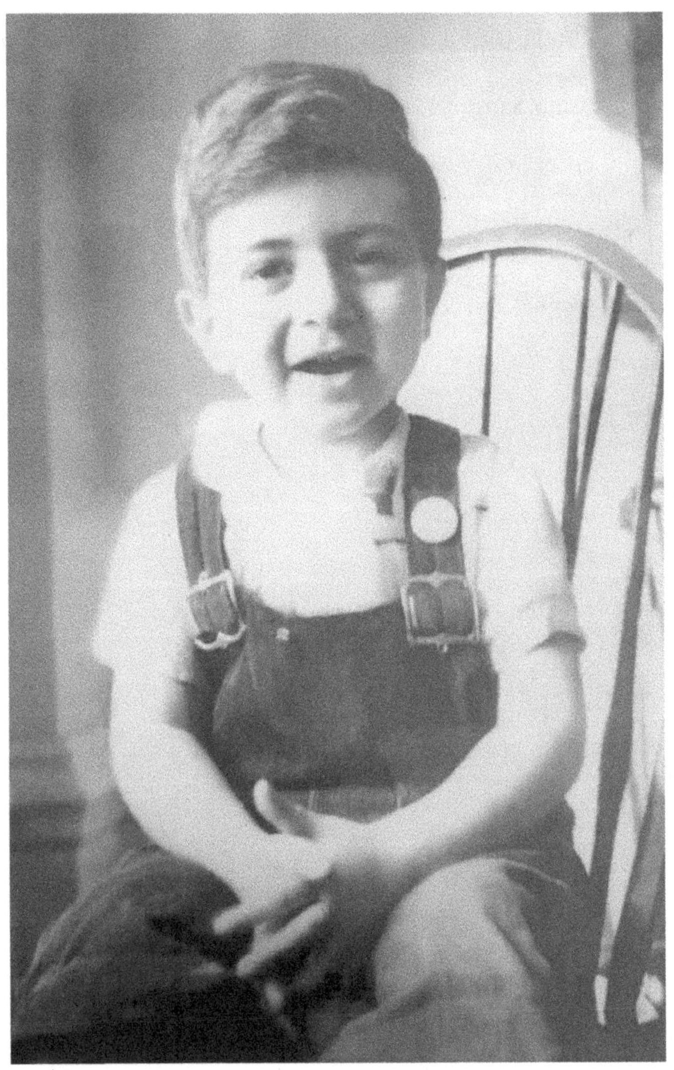

Fig. 1. Stanley Cohen as a toddler.

1

On and Off a Tanker

Someone was pounding on a door and yelling, "Wiper, Wiper, it's time to go"—a wake-up call too early for me to comprehend. Suddenly alert, I realized that I was on the floor in an unfamiliar space. I was not on the floor. I was on a thin mattress, a futon. I was naked. As was a girl still sleeping with her back to me. Black hair flowed quietly from her head to a tiny pillow: a still-life image of gentle repose. Strewn in disarray throughout the room were my clothes and shoes as if torn from my body in a sudden, agitated display. "Wiper, Wiper, let's go," I heard again, now as a command. I quickly dressed and ran out the door to join two companions waiting in a taxi. Off we went to meet our vessel. During our silent ride, still recovering from the shock, I was reluctant to ask how I ended the evening in that room. Was I still a virgin? That thought was quickly clothed in shame. I was not, nor could I ever be, a brothel boy. The need, already ingrained by imagined intertwining, of having a pre-coital talk, a kiss, a tender stroke, outweighed the drive to have a discharge in the dark.

Struggling to retrace events, I did a memory rewind. Halfway across the Pacific, we learned our destination was Japan. We arrived on a Saturday morning just after dawn. Civilian tankers do not remain long in port—discharging or loading oil is swift. Shore leave is rare. Due to a problem with some pumps, the engine-room personnel, including me, the lowest in rank, charged with wiping spills (which explained how I was addressed), were given an exceptional respite of twenty-four hours of liberty ashore.

Tethered to a dock some 100 yards offshore in an oil port about 30 miles south of Tokyo, I was anxious to leave the vessel and touch the land of my first foreign nation. Just after breakfast I hurried along the wooden passageway with a Brownie hanging from my shoulder. No passport control slowed our way; the official occupation of a defeated nation had ended, but American influence was still dominant in 1952. Taxis were waiting, seamen already departing. Hesitant to explore an unknown city by myself, I waited for my mates with whom I shared a fo'c'sle. They walked slowly, apparently less eager than I to view the sights. I waved to them to indicate that I was holding the last taxi. They returned my wave, signaling me to join them.

"Kid, we have plenty of time. Let's first have a beer." I had not noticed a small structure, a bar, at the end of the wooden passageway. I wondered if I should just take the taxi by myself? How much would it cost? What would I tell the driver? How could I abandon my companions who claimed they knew Tokyo well? It was only nine in the morning, so I assumed we had ample time to visit the Japanese capital. We entered the bar, and I sat in the corner, my camera at the ready. Consuming beers with a depth charge, a drink made by releasing a shot glass of rye gently into the stein so no liquid would stain the bar, my shipmates flirted with the bar girls. I could not hear their conversation, but they must have been telling funny stories as the bar girls often giggled, raising their hands to cover their mouths. From time to time they meandered upstairs. I assumed it was in search of the toilet, but then I realized that there was one just adjacent to the bar. Noon approached. "Soon, kid," I was told. "We still have plenty of time."

The bar owner loaned me a bicycle. I pedaled through the town, which seemed no more than an outpost in a jungle. I took no photos, saving my film for the trip to Tokyo. In the early afternoon I resumed sitting in my place. The owner tapped me on my shoulder, whispering the equivalent of "You don't belong here." I nodded. Leading me to a back room, he introduced me to a young woman. He explained that, inexperienced, she had just arrived to work behind the bar. Reluctant to let her mingle with seamen who might treat her roughly, he invited me to join his family for a special dinner and to stay the night with this novice. Initially apprehensive, I looked at her shyly. She was pleasant-looking, with a round face attached to a strong farmhand body. Offering a smile with no guile attached, she reminded me of a cheery full moon. She exuded a welcome. Should I, in the service of consumer fairness, confess my virginity? Was this a trap? Would I be kidnapped and miss my ship? Should I seek advice from my companions at the bar? Always unduly polite, it never occurred to me that I had a choice. I nodded, yes, thanking the owner. I returned to my chair. Tokyo was no longer a destination.

At just eighteen and on my first trip to sea, I was about to lose my virginity. Teenage sexual fantasies still preoccupied me, but the proposal just made was not one that I had ever imagined would become real. I sat there waiting, my stomach churning. How would the young woman and I communicate? How to begin? Should we kiss? Hold hands? Should we dance? How do virgins act on the first night of their romance? What would Dominick D'Orazio do? He was the handsome hero of my sixth-grade class who once called me a fag for the way I carried my books. It was a word I did not then understand. And what about Holden Caulfield, who had just appeared the year before in J. D. Salinger's *Catcher in the Rye*? Unable to engage in a casual sexual encounter when a prostitute came to his hotel room, he pretended to be unwell. Should I do the same?

My reveries were shattered toward three in the afternoon when my companions stopped drinking and sauntered up the stairs. As they approached me, I could smell their whiskey breath. "Okay, kid. Let's get to Tokyo." I murmured, "No, no, no." I was happy sitting there. I could not tell them what was awaiting me since I promised the bar owner not to divulge the invitation. I had a more significant reason preventing me from unveiling the invitation. Sex was still a mystery, a subject not to be discussed.

My shipmates were men of action, and, despite my protests, they lifted me by both elbows and carried me to the taxi they had managed to reserve. Perhaps I was secretly grateful to be relieved of a sexual obligation that was making me anxious. I had imagined first-time love as a passion, not a pre-arranged hookup. Memory of the dock and bar, the owner and the smiling, moon-faced young lady have remained vivid. What I fail to recall, or perhaps I've just successfully repressed, are the events beyond the initial taxi ride wedged between two large men. En route to Tokyo, my companions stopped at one more bar for a depth-charge drink. I tasted something for which I was unprepared. And then, at the sound of knocking, I woke up startled to find a stranger by my side, not the moon-faced girl in the bar by the dock who was to have been my start.

Returning to the dock with my companion, I tried to hurry past the bar when suddenly the door flew open. The owner and the young woman, who was meant to have been my companion, ran after me. She was in tears. He waved his fist. He gestured to the bar where I had quietly sat the day before and called me an American Tojo for refusing his hospitality. He swore at me in English before switching to Japanese. After listening to a few minutes of verbal abuse, I raised my hand and said, "You don't understand. I never had a date. I am a virgin from the Bronx." I thought of explaining further, but silence overcame me. I turned and swiftly ran along the passageway. As soon as I was aboard, mooring ropes were released, and we headed to Kuwait and Saudi Arabia to load our tanks with oil.

For weeks and more, sometimes at odd moments, and even years later, I wondered what would have happened if I had slept with that radiant, moon-faced girl. Perhaps I would have found some inner happiness, perhaps I would have remained in that hamlet, helping at the bar. More likely, it would have led to years of therapy. What the whole event did help me comprehend was my inability to convey my innermost thoughts to others. I had not revealed to my fellow seamen why I wanted to remain sitting in the bar's corner chair until closing time due, in part, to enduring years of silence in my childhood home. To communicate without fear of shame required a muscle that had never been exercised. I also sensed that I would not be able to overcome my personal deficiencies until I found the comfort of a moon-faced girl who truly wanted me.

2

My Son Paul and Milan Kundera

Seventy years later, Paul, my son, found half-faded photographs of me when I still had hair, lying idle and forgotten in a drawer together with currency that was no longer in use.

Fig. 2. Stanley Cohen, age eighteen, working aboard an oil tanker en route to Japan.

He was astonished to see me posing on the railing of an oil tanker or riding a water buffalo in Marajo, an island as large as Switzerland located in the mouth of the Amazon River. He was even more surprised to learn that I stayed in the work camps with those constructing the Trans-Amazonian highway. Knowing that I had started several times to write down stories I never told, he urged me to retrieve my drafts and provide a narrative that would be his inheritance.

Also left in the drawer were notes about characters who were my friends, names Paul knows from school lessons and from details I revealed from time to time. Travels with Joseph Heller, his wedding at my home. My son knows of my friendship with Alexander Calder and that I administered his estate, but he is unaware that Paul Strand, whose photographs line our walls, asked me to do the same, provided I first spend the day with his friend, Alger Hiss, and receive his blessing.

My son knows about my conversations with Hitler's aide, Albert Speer, and my effort to make a film based on his memoir, *Inside the Third Reich.* Paul has laughed at my account of a weekend with James Baldwin at his home at St. Paul de Vence and my rebuff of Baldwin's effort to test my bed. But I never disclosed that I became the lover of the woman whom Clancy Sigal, the leftist writer, claimed was the most beautiful in France. Paul knows that Betty Friedan often asked me to drive her to evening events when her eyesight diminished, but he does not know she advised me about aging gracefully rather than seeking to retain vestiges of youth.

In this book there are many other stories unknown to Paul—like my friendship with activist and socialist author Michael Harrington or my travels with Régine to open her discotheques. Nor have I ever mentioned Max's Kansas City, the hip joint of the

60s, whose opening night served as a celebratory farewell when I left for Paris, where Paul was later born. I had not meant to withhold these stories from him, but I only became a single parent when he was twelve, and I was nearly eighty. Our daily subjects were his schoolwork and playdates, rather than reminiscences of my youth. The narrative I have assembled discloses many memories. It reveals a darker side to the person I am, often indifferent and detached, weighed down by the silence that pervaded my childhood. My passivity may have caused harm to those who loved me.

The Czech novelist Milan Kundera believed that *living only one life, we can neither compare it with our previous lives nor perfect it in our lives to come.* I disagree. Responsibility for parenting a youngster offered me a second chance with knowledge of what empathy entails and enabled me to find the love of a moon-faced girl.

I explained to Paul why I had been reticent to record the stories behind the photos in the drawer. Toward the end of my twenty-year stay in Paris, I often dined alone at the restaurant Le Récamier. I would have a steak tartare, followed by a soufflé Henri IV with its mustard sauce. Kundera, all in black, was also a regular, sitting there by himself, perhaps seeking respite from hours at his writing desk. Although we did not speak out loud to one another, I would extend a wave and receive a gentle nod, as if he somehow knew I identified with Tomas, the protagonist of the book that assured his fame, *The Unbearable Lightness of Being*. Perhaps he surmised that we shared an admiration of Robert Musil, the author of *The Man Without Qualities*, whom Kundera considered his intellectual guide. Ulrich, Musil's main character in that novel, an introspective person who keeps all life options open, unwilling or unable to translate thought to deed, seemed to capture my own elusiveness.

When Kundera departed, he left behind advisory thoughts for me to savor with dessert, which I retain here between quotation marks. "Polyphonic" is the key. Mix imagination and memory, then add "anecdotes, stories, thoughts." Write a novel. "A novel is a meditation on existence, seen through imaginary characters. The form is unlimited freedom." And then Kundera was gone, his black-clad figure dissolved into the darkness of the Parisian night.

I was reflecting on his advice when Kundera suddenly returned to tell me not to lift weights, since that was how Musil died. As he turned to leave a second time, I shouted, "I am an imaginary character who keeps all options open. I can write about myself." That involuntary outburst stopped him.

"As soon as you create an imaginary being, a character," he responded, "you are automatically confronted by the question: What is the self? How can the self be grasped? It is one of those fundamental questions on which the novel, as novel, is based."

"Why not an autobiography?" I answered. If you write about yourself, he continued, you will place "an emphasis on plot and on all its trappings of unexpected and incredible coincidences. Nothing has become as suspect, ridiculous, old-fashioned, trite, and tasteless as plot. Tell an unlikely story that *chooses* to be unlikely!"

"But my life," I explained, "has had no apparent coherency nor continuity. The plot, if any, seems to change as quickly as a kaleidoscope."

He interrupted: "Man who desires his life to have a meaning forgoes any action that has not its cause and its purpose. All biographies are written this way. Life is seen as a glowing trajectory of causes, effects, failures, and successes, and man, setting his impatient gaze on the causal chain of his actions, accelerates further his mad race toward death."

Before I could summon a reply, Kundera added, with a grimace of dismay, "I suppose you are planning to begin with your birth and to continue in a chronological fashion?"

"Yes," I said, "but even then, there will be ample room for digression and contemplation, which you so often advocate."

Kundera shrugged and left, but not before taking a tiny finger swipe of my souffle. "Goat cheese and black cherry are the best," was his final admonition besides urging me to read his latest book, *Immortality!*

A few weeks later, I returned to Le Récamier to enjoy smoked salmon and blini. Kundera was seated in his usual place. It seemed he had forgotten our exchange, or he may have thought it was merely imaginary. Unable to resist more than a dozen minutes of quiet, I finally turned toward him and mouthed, in a friendly way, "I read *Immortality!*" To which he immediately responded, referring to his work and extolling the novel form: "A novel shouldn't be like a bicycle race but like a banquet of many courses... A completely new character... enters the novel. And... will disappear without a trace. He causes nothing and leaves no effects."

"That's my experience," I rejoined. "Indeed, what you extol in a character, born from a sudden gesture and fading without a proper farewell, is how I dealt with those who crossed my path. And I am now ashamed to have treated friends and lovers so casually, leaving no effect. Each chapter of my life seems as distinct as in your novel form. A bicycle can stop and start and yet not continue in a straight line. You define a novel as a prose form in which an author thoroughly explores . . . some great themes of existence."

I insisted that it could also be done in a memoir; one starts to write, uncertain of the path distant memories illuminate. In an expressionless tone, Kundera added, "The autobiography invades the novel, and everyone wants to write. The modern passion of each and everyone is to speak of the self. This passion for a compulsive urge to write is sanctified, whereas, in my view, it is the most grotesque and pathetic desire for power today: to impose one's self on others."

"But *Speak, Memory* is autobiography," I replied, surprised at his critique, knowing he respected Vladimir Nabokov. He closed his eyes, as he seemed to murmur, "the wound of . . . emigration." His effort to deter me from pursuing a chronicle of my life made me understand—I was not Nabokov. His critical commentary continued: "The world has become a right of man, and everything has changed to rights: the desire for love to the right to love, the desire for rest to the right to rest, the desire for friendship to the right to friendship, the desire for happiness to the right to happiness, the desire to publish a book to the right to publish a book, the desire to scream at night in the streets to the right to scream at night in the streets."

Perhaps I should have explained to Kundera that my tale is therapy—to endure waning years contemplating faults, a trail to self-discovery. Should I have raised Doris Lessing's praise of autobiography? The autobiographer has to be truthful, she wrote, or "[a]t least the attempt must be made." Novels need not be burdened with that effort or with sorting memories between truth and falsehood. Autobiography, mused Lessing, was a struggle to recreate memories of the past. "You sit there for hours, wondering. Is that true? Did I make it up? . . . Why do you remember this and not that? And what should be left out, so the work would not be too long?" Nabokov also praises the reach for memory as a "meeting point" of art and a personal life story, obliging the writer "to stick to the truth through thick and thin," a task perhaps more arduous than composing fiction.

But I did not say this out loud, nor did I allow Kundera to taste the blini on my plate as he departed. He left behind only his repeated admonition that the novel form grants freedom. Freedom? Should I have said freedom in my memoir means coping with derelictions of the past, a charge more challenging than living with the flaws of invented characters? Discouraged by Kundera's reproach that my proposed memoir was an attempt to "impose one's self on others," I postponed for years the arduous effort of exploring what Annie Ernaux would later describe as "an ethnological study of myself."

When I related this mythic exchange to Paul so he would understand why I had avoided relating the stories behind the photos in the drawer, he simply said he had not yet read anything by Kundera and pressed me to begin. After all, seven decades separated us, and my stories could bridge the gap. Besides, Kundera had died, and I should not feel burdened with that author's opinion of what I had so long contemplated. "Leaving your life account in print when you are gone," Paul said, "you will continue to exist." He added that he was uninterested in the famous names that figured in my life; instead, he wanted to know: how did I *feel*? He urged me to include flaws and faults, and the emotions aroused when confronted by memories and incidents from the past. "Tell me the story, right from the start." Although uncertain how much I should reveal, I nodded assent, pondering whether I should include incidents that caused and still engendered shame.

3

You Don't Belong Here

A Dropbox app has been inserted deep in my brain. Downloaded by God's malware, it remains sequestered there. The save button acts randomly and is difficult to control. The app comes to life at odd moments. Stray images stream through my head. Compelled to harmonize the bits of matter into coherence, my mind struggles to fill the gaps.

My genome kicked in as soon as the umbilical cord was cut. The influence known as family had not yet begun. Life was to be a contest for ascendancy and might never be resolved. Most of us accept our inheritance without a murmur. We become a communist or a Hasidic Jew, a Mormon or a Druze, and we never question why. My inheritance was silence in my home, although I did not recognize it as an encumbrance I would have to struggle to overcome.

I'll start with my first day of school. I was five, and the year was 1939. The Bronx building was new and modern. The room to which I was assigned was large and shaped as a perfect square. Each apprehensive child sat in a chair separated by a foot, sometimes two, and placed so that our backs were against a wall. Silence was the rule. I looked around. Who were these strangers sitting quietly by my side, sitting still without a babble or a buzz? Were they, like me, petrified?

The center of the room was strewn with imaginary hurdles to overcome to reach the teacher's desk. Within eye range was a freestanding wardrobe, a closet with a sliding door that was not completely closed. Its interior was dark and almost certainly housed a monster. I was frightened. The quiet of the room was so overwhelming that I wanted to shout to ensure I was still alive. Instead, I started to cry. I cried for a long time.

Crying was my weapon, my means of protest. I had already employed it the year before. My parents and I went to visit my brother, Howard, eight years my senior, who was spending part of the summer at a Boy Scout camp. En route, we stopped for the night at a small hotel. I slept in the same room as my parents. Perhaps I did not like the sound of heavy breathing. Or the squeaking of the bed. Most likely it was the odor of damp decay. The images on the wallpaper seemed menacing. I decided not to sleep. I began to cry. When asked what was wrong, I shouted, "The wallpaper." Distraught, my parents' only means of calming me was to leave our room in the middle of the night and spend the rest of the night in our car. On my first day of kindergarten, I thought I could use the same tactic and I would be allowed to leave, but the teacher just let me sob. A thought suddenly occurred to me. What was the worst that could happen? If either the monster or the teacher were determined to do me harm, would I cease to exist? I would probably enter nothingness. So what was there to fear? I stopped crying. The teacher came over to congratulate me. She reminded me of the hotel room with the unpleasant smell and the menacing wallpaper.

I was expelled from kindergarten a few weeks later, and my mother, Esther, was advised to take me to a doctor since each time the teacher neared my seat, I vomited on her skirt. The doctor was very understanding. He asked what caused my distress, and I told him that the teacher had warned I would be locked in that closet with the monster if I failed to sit up straight and behave. The source of my fear did not seem to register as important. My parents made no complaint and made no effort to have me readmitted. I spent the rest of the school year in my bedroom.

Sometime during that year of home seclusion, I answered the doorbell one afternoon to find a uniformed policeman standing on our threshold with terrible news. My grandmother, who lived with us, had died while walking to the local bakery. I have only a faint memory of her. The image that remains is the Friday-evening ceremony when she lit candles to signal that dinner was prepared. With her absence, I dimly understood the nothingness of death.

As soon as my grandmother vanished from our lives, my family's routine abruptly changed. Until then, Jewish traditions had become second nature to me. Dairy products could not be combined with meat dishes during the same meal. In anticipation of Passover week, our regular dishes, pans, and utensils had to be exchanged for a special set. The apartment was scrubbed to remove any crumbs of food not sanctioned by the dietary laws. Yom Kippur was a holy day when all adults fasted until sunset, and I tried my best to follow suit. Such rules, I thought, were immutable.

To my surprise, I found my father having lunch instead of embracing abstinence on that holy day. I was deeply troubled. "How can you eat on Yom Kippur?" I asked him. "Your grandmother is no longer alive," he replied. Our kosher ritual ended, as did my religious beliefs. We soon ate Chinese food. Bacon was introduced. I grasped that no convention could withstand the ring of a doorbell. I felt free to ignore any rule imposing conformity.

I entered first grade. Told that I was assigned to a special class, my mother asked no questions. She did not consider grade school any different from a daycare center, just a drop-off at the entrance.

I was placed in an all-boys class, which was odd in a co-ed school. Some of my classmates were struggling to learn the alphabet, which I thought was a bit strange as I had already begun to read. The teacher was pleasant. She didn't smell of decay or remind me of ill-colored wallpaper. My fellow students, some with distorted grimaces, often wandered aimlessly around the room. The teacher did not complain. Instruction was mostly one-on-one.

After a week or so, the teacher came over to my desk, bent down, and said, "You don't belong here. You will be moved to another class. It will take a few days for the paperwork." I nodded, wondering what that meant. She added, "When we go to the auditorium, I want you to guide the class and make sure all the boys remain in line and don't stray." I nodded once again.

The next day when we left our homeroom, I led my classmates through the halls. Arrayed by size, they were gathered in two rows. I turned around to ensure they were all still there. The angle of their heads sloped gently toward the sky. So gradual and graceful was that line that it could only have been drawn by a master with a pen that we sometimes mistake for God.

My mother was invited to meet the principal one morning before the start of class. She was fearful that I was to be ousted once again. The principal began with an apology. He explained that the school housed hundreds of students. Errors of placement were sometimes made. Since I had missed kindergarten, it had been assumed that I should start in a remedial class. The principal added that after a few weeks it was clear that I belonged in a normal setting. I was to be transferred at once. Only then did I begin to comprehend. The principal and teacher passively awaited an appreciative response from my mother. Or perhaps they thought she might be upset that her son had been placed in what was politely called "a slow class."

Esther did not immediately respond, but then she asked, "Are the hours the same?" Told that my new class began a half-hour later, she replied that the change was not convenient for her schedule. I sat quietly. Was I entitled to a choice? I wondered what schedule filled her day. My mother insisted that I remain where I was initially placed. After another silence, the principal no longer spoke of a "slow class." My mother finally understood. I was transferred to a classroom with desks placed in neat rows. After that meeting, neither of my parents ever came to school or asked any of my teachers about my progress. And I never considered seeking their aid.

Certain events in life stand out as noteworthy and impactful. Sometimes an incident will significantly influence how you construct your life. Often it requires a rear-view mirror to apprehend its significance. In that school meeting when I was six, I knew I was participating in one such moment. Something critical was happening, a message was being sent. I vaguely understood that I would have to fend for myself. A sense of isolation enveloped me; I entered a protective carapace.

And there was something else. Life seemed composed of elements of uncertainty. Or shall we call it chance? Was I going to be buffeted by unexpected episodes beyond my control? Suppose the teacher had remained unaware of me in the midst of those twenty-odd "slow learners"? Suppose she had shrugged and thought there had to be a reason why a Cohen had been placed there?

I lived in a family with little or no communication, few hugs or touches. That to me was normal. I would withdraw to my bedroom, an island in our flat, to be alone with fantasies of flight that I equated with escape, although I was still too young to fully grasp what that meant. Next to my bed I had placed a souvenir of a day spent at the 1939 World's Fair. It was a snow globe with a tower in the center. When shaken, the tower faded under the snow only to reappear when the storm subsided. I later realized that that tiny structure was the Eiffel Tower, not a make-believe artifact next to which I too would vanish, then reappear.

Other than that trip to Flushing Meadows, where I acquired the snow globe, few family events figure in the sparse narrative of my young life. Childhood memories? Did they exist? Or were they repressed for reasons long forgotten or ignored?

Harry, my father, was rarely home. No laugh disturbed his austere face. Smiles rarely moved his lips. Only one photo remains to prove his time on earth and his tie to me. He is standing on a beach in Far Rockaway. I am straddling his shoulders, holding tight, evidence of a rare moment of contact. When I now view children in a sandbox, a parent standing by to prevent a calamity, I cannot recall a protective gesture from his hand.

Esther, my mother, was kind, but aloof. Not one conversation with her remains intact. She was a queen of clean who pursued me down the hall if I unwittingly left a sock behind. Her obsession with a spotless apartment left a mark on me until I was thirteen, when I was sent to Boy Scout Camp for six weeks and assigned to Tent Two. Chosen to be its leader, my main task was to ensure that our bunk was neat and orderly, cots made, shoes shined and properly placed facing out. The tent that scored highest in complying with these rules was entitled to a campfire with marshmallows to roast at the end of each week. I was a relentless authoritarian. Tent Two won four weeks in a row. At the end of that period, several campers left, replaced by newcomers. As soon as they arrived, I gave them an orientation on how the tent was to function. I touted our reputation as the marshmallow-campfire leader and said that I expected that honor to continue. One boy in particular had a round, soft, very white face. I was fearful that he might not live up to Tent Two standards. I was right. He left his boots on top of his bed during the weekly inspection. We did not win that week's marshmallows. When I found out, I verbally assaulted him until he burst into tears. I pulled back quickly. It was a noteworthy revelation. I whispered to myself, "I'm my mother."

The incident had a profound effect on me. After apologizing, I instantly resigned as Tent Two leader. Neatness in the room and in the mind became elements of the past. This decision gave rise to frequent debates with my mother.

Dinner without a recount of the day's events became standard. I did not realize this was unusual. None of my schoolyard friends ever came to our home as guests. My brother, eight years my elder, was too senior to be a peer. In the army for several years, he had an early marriage and left home before we could share significant events to recollect later.

It was only after both of our parents had died that my brother revealed, almost as an aside, a bit of our family history.

Harry, my father, had a dream: to own a hardware store in the Bronx, not far from where I was born and raised. He succeeded. He was apparently gregarious by nature, the sort who savored a bit of gossip with his customers. I can picture him weighing a pound of nails or explaining with active hands the difference between a crowfoot and a lug wrench. Each morning, as he opened the store, he might have cast a glance around the shelves, surveying a small domain that was his.

My mother, born a Spigel, was a rank higher in society. Her family owned a series of stores comparable to Woolworth's Five and Dimes, which were started by her father, who died quite young, leaving inexperienced uncles I never knew to manage the business. Bank financing was soon required. My father, recently married to Esther, agreed to be a guarantor. Bankruptcy followed. My father lost his store, his prestige, and his dream. The uncles disappeared.

I can only surmise that Harry never forgave my mother. And as a form of punishment, he spent virtually no time at home. When he did appear, he rarely spoke. Years later, when my brother recalled this aspect of family history, a long-repressed image suddenly surfaced. One morning after shaving, Harry cupped water in his hand and flung it across the mirror, letting the slow drips spread and stain the glass. Although I was only ten, I understood that this was an act of retribution, comparable to what I witnessed played out among my friends in the playground. After he left, I wiped the glass to remove every trace of his unhappiness. Silence is a weight harder to bear than a sudden slap across the face. Indifference is its legacy; insouciance, a way of life.

We moved frequently, always within the Bronx. I recall a tenement apartment on Walton Avenue whose walls were fragile and no longer straight. My daily task was to haul an ice block into place for our non-electric fridge and to collect the milk and seltzer bottles when they were left at our front door.

My father finally settled into a job with the John Hancock Insurance Company. He sold life insurance policies to the lower-middle-class residents in his territory, also in the Bronx, along and below the elevated train, the IRT Number 6.

Not only did he have to convince people to buy insurance, but he also had to collect the weekly premiums, paid to him in cash. Since most of his clients worked during the day, his collections took place in the evening. That was another reason he was seldom home. Since he began his sales rounds late in the morning, he rarely emerged from his bedroom before I left for school. Until I was allowed to walk the streets by myself, my mother rushed me there in time to return home to prepare breakfast for Harry. Her reference to a "schedule" when she met the principal now made sense. She was fearful of being late and igniting Harry's temper.

Once a month Harry and Esther sat at a bridge table with a large black oblong book separating them. Each page was headed with a customer's name, together with a series of boxes that had to be checked to show the current payment status. My mother would count all the money to ensure the total from the boxes equaled the cash spread across the table. Often five or ten dollars was missing or in excess. My father got angry, his face a portrait of frustration with a job he did not want and a life he could not enjoy. If I had grasped this as a child, I might have reached out to stroke their backs to comfort them.

With my father's job as an insurance salesman, our family qualified for a housing project: Parkchester, in the northern Bronx. We were among the first residents in the development, which had been completed in 1942. Our two-bedroom apartment was airy, clean, and, to my amazement, came with a Frigidaire. There was an elevator, the first I had ever encountered.

I was too young to appreciate the revolutionary history of Parkchester, an experiment in communal living for a lower-middle-class population. Constructing affordable housing was fostered as a New Deal project to help reduce the widespread homelessness caused by the Depression. Regulations were relaxed to allow life insurance companies to invest in real estate. And the Metropolitan Life Insurance Company, the largest in its field, decided to build Parkchester, 130 acres of red-brick buildings, not as tenements but with open spaces and parks. The developers hoped to foster cultural education and social exchange through programs, sports, and shared amenities. Half of the development remained open for recreation, with gardens, fountains, shuffleboard, softball fields, and paddle tennis courts.

Numerous sociological studies have examined why that fraternal aspect of Parkchester living failed. The residents—white only—worked all day. At night, they were too worn out to make use of the available amenities. The shuffleboard and paddle-tennis courts lay empty. Friendships failed to coalesce. Residents remained divided into ethnic tribes, mostly Irish and Italian, with Jews in between.

Our move to Parkchester signaled the end of temporary housing for us. With a population of some 30,000, the complex reflected life in a suburban town, insular and uninterested in a world beyond its gates. Parkchester was an enclosed universe. We had a Macy's and a movie theater. A Chinese restaurant, where one could order two dishes from list A and one from B, sat conveniently just outside its perimeter. Red and green were the colors of my youth. However far I looked, red brick filled the space. But once inside, a dark hostile green shaded the elevator to our floor.

Due to our move, I had to transfer schools once again. It was the second year of World War II. My former school had established an evacuation plan. Each student received a number depending on the distance required to reach the safety of home. Since I lived furthest from the school, a "10" was inscribed on my record. My new venue, P.S. 102, had a different classification. A ten meant I belonged to a class of slow learners. That is where I was put. After a few months, the teacher came to my desk, bent down, and said, "You don't belong here." I was transferred to an advanced class. I was just adjusting to new friends when I was told that I had not been in that class long enough to judge whether I should skip a term, as was projected for the other students. I was transferred back to the lower-achieving group I had left a few weeks earlier.

Odd, what bits and pieces are permanently fixed in memory from early school days. In the fifth grade, my classmate, Jean Gherzih, suffered a singular moment of embarrassment in the music appreciation class. She identified the William Tell Overture as the "Lone Ranger by Tonto." The teacher made fun of her. I thought that was unseemly since she had recognized the music, if not the name of the composer. I wanted to speak out but remained a timid observer. As I had no musical aptitude, I felt a comradeship with Jean. Tested by the teacher who organized the singing in the auditorium, I had been told to move my lips but not utter a single sound. I was to be a listener. And so I was. That experience with Jean reinforced my concern that forces beyond my control governed the world that awaited me. What was to become of Jean? I did not know where I was headed, but I knew she would be left behind.

It was in this class that I began to feel that I was there and yet I was not. Floating in the clouds, I saw my seat was bare. The entire class was in view. I saw every pencil, every dab of gum. Carol stroked her hair. Stewart picked his nose. The teacher wrote notes. Meanwhile I felt disengaged from the dramas unfolding below, though I can still recall the names of almost every student in the photo, where they sat, and how they held a pen to write answers to exams.

Dominick D'Orazio was the hero of the class. Tall with broad shoulders, his light-colored hair flowing softly in the wind, he was already adored by the girls in my class. We all believed he would be a movie star. At first, I was invited to evening parties devoted to spin the bottle and brief kisses. But Dominick accused me of lack of interest in spin the bottle or clasping young ladies in my

Fig. 3. Stanley Cohen's school class photograph, 1946; Cohen, top row, second from left.

arms. After that indictment, I was no longer invited. At home the matter of sex was never raised; I knew neither porn nor smutty magazines. It was not until my high school biology class that I realized cats were not female dogs, as I had long believed.

Everyone has a favorite teacher. Mine, in sixth grade, was Louise Kirschner. She had graduated in the midst of the Depression and became a teacher to survive. She talked to students as if we were adults, pausing in the middle of a math lesson to reflect on Einstein. With tears of joy in her eyes, she revealed that Truman had defeated Dewey. It was my first experience with someone who could perceive my thoughts, a grownup with whom

I could explore nascent ideas. Since conversations at home were so limited, I relied on school, on lessons and conversations in the classroom, for my sense of the wider world.

Once, Mrs. Kirschner asked what newspapers we read at home. My classmates mentioned the *New York Times*, *PM*, and others. I raised my hand. "*Daily Worker*!" I blurted out. After a few seconds of silence, someone yelled that it was a Communist newspaper. Scorn ensued. I was clueless about this unfamiliar term. Communist? I did not know what that meant. Politics, news, or the arts were not topics I had had a chance to absorb. After that, unless compelled, I never spoke in class again, fearful of a mistake, humiliation, or failure. I became, instead, a listener, receding deeper into the shell I had constructed when I witnessed the exchange between my mother and the principal, as she sought to free me from the slow class.

Mrs. Kirschner stopped at my desk one day. She bent down and said, "You don't belong here," adding something to the effect that my score on an IQ test had passed an exceptional threshold. I was to be transferred at the end of sixth grade to a rapid-advance class at Herman Ridder Junior High, the only student honored by such a move.

Herman Ridder High, while still in the Bronx, required a trolley ride along East Tremont Avenue. It was my first solo travel experience. Each morning when I boarded, I imagined an unknown destination, the inculcation of an urge just to go, even if I didn't know where. I loved the trolley's lurch when starting, the clang of a bell warning cars from straying onto the tracks. I enjoyed the challenge of every stop when the wooden doors slowly opened and a hidden step flipped down to allow passengers to board or depart for their unknown destinations.

My new school was an odd place. Students selected for rapid advance gathered for classes on the top floor of the building. Other floors were meant for students from the immediate neighborhood, mainly of African American descent, a group that could not have walked easily through Parkchester without being confronted by its private police. Even though we were housed under the same roof, we remained separated by both geography and flights of stairs.

Although my family was no longer observant, I was expected to learn enough Hebrew to celebrate a bar mitzvah. After school, I would descend to a cellar synagogue for religious instruction, trying to avoid a sharp rap of the ruler Rabbi Katz held tightly in his hand. For reasons never explained, my father booked a backroom in an Irish bar for the reception after the ceremony. It was packed with relatives and family friends. In addition to the usual gifts of fountain pens, I received envelopes of cash, which I hurried into a toilet stall to open and count.

When my father realized what I had done, he was furious. He grabbed the money, upset since he could not tell who had given how much. I was allowed to keep the pens. His confiscation was less out of meanness than a need to pay for the event. He was careful with funds. Once, I took a quarter out of his pocket to buy a handkerchief for my mother's birthday. By the time I returned from the store, he had already counted all the coins and noticed the discrepancy. I was not punished, but the importance of a quarter has stayed with me. Even today, in a supermarket, I weigh my choices carefully—comparing size and unit cost, calculating whether I might save a penny, just as I did as a boy shopping for my family in the Bronx.

I went through junior high and high school so quickly that I have little recollection of attending classes. Nor did I form any friendship that endured. When I close a chapter, all those individuals who appeared as personae in that period simply disappear, filed in a memory folder, a habit that I started early and that has continued throughout my life.

I was unaware that specialized, academically enriched high schools existed when I completed junior high. Instead, I enrolled in Christopher Columbus, the neighborhood high school, from which I graduated in January 1951. I was sixteen. Other than a Boy Scout summer camp, day excursions to the beach, and a World's Fair visit when I was five, I had never left the Bronx. I was an innocent ready to explore, a Dickensian character waiting to be taken up by a benefactor.

4

Making Mountains into Hills

Years later, when I exchanged childhood memories with the poet Stanley Moss, who was born and raised in Queens, I learned that he often skipped school to go to Manhattan to stroll through museums and galleries. He would spend a morning at the Public Library on 42nd Street or an afternoon at the Apollo Theater to see foreign films. To take the initiative to leave the Bronx for Manhattan would have been inconceivable to me when I was growing up. Even more inconceivable was Moss's assertion that, at the age of seven, he informed his teacher that he would be a poet. Moss had discerned that there was an outside world in which he would play a role, whereas I had few expectations other than to get through the day. No one at home had ever asked: "What would you like to be?" If the question had been raised, I would have remained perplexed and silent, as I had no ready answer.

On a shelf in a bookcase in my bedroom, I found a volume titled *Best Short Stories Ever Written.* I never knew how it got there. Perhaps it was a bar mitzvah present that had arrived by post. One story was of particular interest. Now that years have passed, I realize I may have embellished it. It was about a soldier who fought in World War II. Discharged from the army, he returned to his small-town home. As he entered his house, he was greeted by shouts and cheers. Family and friends had gathered to welcome him. He raised a hand for silence. "Folks," he said, "I am grateful for this wonderful reception. I joined the Army in 1941, just after Pearl Harbor. After training I fought in North Africa and endured the hardships of the desert. I went ashore at Normandy on D-Day and was lucky not to be killed during the landing on the beach. I fought in the Battle of the Bulge and nearly froze. I crossed the Rhine as part of the Third Army and was pinned down in the bridgehead. Only one thought kept me alive and brought me safely home. I dreamt of getting into my bed to feel its warmth and enjoy the quiet of the room. I hope you will understand if I just go upstairs."

The guests left without a word. The returning veteran remained in bed for several days. His mother brought him meals and other items. She gently suggested that he should at least come down to have dinner with his family, or to see his girlfriend, who had come to visit several times. But his mother retreated into silence when he recited a litany of what he experienced, stories of battles fought with bullets whizzing past his ears and dead men laid out each night on the dark earth. This pattern was repeated week after week. His mother, having reached the limit of her patience, raised her voice. She wondered how he could remain immobile on the bed and why boredom did not impel him to leave his den. Finally, he explained that his days were fully occupied with a task that consumed him. "Look at the bottom of the bed," he told her. "See that large mountain resting there. Now watch." He spread his legs. "You see, I made two hills, and soon I'll return them to form a single peak. That undertaking saps my strength and seems as productive as any of my tasks over the last five years."

That story was a revelation for me. There was no need to do anything; no ambition had to be pursued. I was not obliged to *become* anything or anyone. I entered my single bed, my feet stretched some six inches apart. They protruded gracefully through the blanket as two small hills. I slid them to rest side by side and admired the single peak. My aspiration was limited to making mountains into hills with the intensity of that soldier who had returned home uninjured from the front. Joseph Conrad, whose works I would soon discover, confirmed the validity of my goal when he wrote that "a consummate capacity for doing nothing" was among the greatest of gifts.

Although no one spoke or encouraged me to attend college, I assumed I would. No school counselors existed at that time, and neither my parents nor my brother raised the subject. I knew the cost would be mine to bear. College sports reported in the *New York Times* was my guide. Cornell had a decent football team; its name, The Big Red, was certainly appealing. A tuition-free School of Labor and Industrial Relations had just been created. I decided that was where I would go. If I did not earn enough for my living expenses, I would continue to work until my savings could cover the costs.

I was unformed and culturally unaware. I had never been to a museum, to a concert, or to a theatre, but I did have access to the well-equipped Parkchester library. Each week I wandered through the stacks, hoping to find an escape from life's trajectory. That is where I discovered Joseph Conrad. *Heart of Darkness*, *Lord Jim*, and *The Secret Agent* were soon markers on the path. Was I Marlow in my youth? Was I Jim? Of all the works I took home to read, Conrad's *The Secret Sharer* replayed the most obsessively in my head. I identified with the young, inexperienced captain who decided to stand watch "in those solitary hours of the night to get on terms with the ship of which I knew nothing, manned by men of whom I knew very little more."

According to a biographer, Conrad had been influenced, at the age of ten, to go to sea by reading Sir Leopold McClintock's book about the Arctic, *The Voyage of the Fox*. Conrad recorded that he had placed a finger on a map and "said to myself, with absolute assurance and an amazing audacity which are no longer in my character now: 'When I grow up I shall go *there*...' And of course I thought no more about it till after a quarter of a century or so an opportunity offered to go there—as if the sin of childish audacity were to be visited on my mature head."

Sitting on a Parkchester bench, just before my seventeenth year, I revealed my ambition to a companion, Stephen Bender: "When I grow up, I shall go to sea." He suggested that his neighbor, a cartoonist for an oil company newspaper, who had many photos of seagoing ships on his wall, could advise me on how to make my wish come true. I insisted that we promptly visit the gentleman and that Steve should join me in my effort. His eyes widened. He seemed tempted by the idea, but wary of working on a vessel or even departing from the confines of our Parkchester sanctuary. At my urging, we rang his neighbor's bell. The cartoonist cordially welcomed us and explained that we needed Coast Guard papers to work aboard a ship. He agreed to furnish us with a letter from his employer, Socony-Vacuum, forerunner to ExxonMobil. That letter would include a promise to hire us, the sole prerequisite for a Seamen's Card to be issued as soon as we turned eighteen.

In the meantime, I needed a job, as I knew I would remain responsible for my keep if accepted at Cornell. I was hired to work in the mailroom of Van Raalte, a manufacturer of high-end women's silk gloves and underwear. My commute, to what we called "downtown," was about forty-five minutes by subway after a lengthy walk to the station. I loved working in an office and chatting with the staff, an antidote to the silence of my home. My resolution to spend a life converting mountains into hills began to waver.

I decided to take an aptitude test, convinced that its scientific formulations would yield a life path inexorable and rewarding. The advertisement that intrigued me read: "Just like scientists use data to make predictions, aptitude testing can help you predict the types of careers you'll thrive in. Our work is rooted in the scientific study of human abilities and the mission of our founder, Johnson O'Connor, who believed that everyone has natural talents that should be nurtured and used." I made an appointment at the Johnson O'Connor Foundation and was greeted by a pipe-smoking specialist with a white lab coat. Since 1922, I was told, thousands of people had taken their tests to find direction or choose careers "that fit their minds." It would cost twenty-five dollars—a very large sum for someone more accustomed to extracting twenty-five cents from a pocket. But since I was now a professional mailroom clerk, I could set aside a few dollars each week.

During lunch hour on three successive days, I underwent a battery of tests. They included everything from putting squiggly blocks together to comparing rows of numbers to determine if the eight digits placed in parallel columns were identical. A month later I returned for an intimate conference with the white coat. I had hardly slept the previous night, knowing that I would soon learn what I would be doing the rest of my life. I thought of ancient Greeks consulting an oracle to whom they bore gifts. Should I bring pipe tobacco as an offering? The white coat seemed hesitant at first. After studying the results, he explained that a number of subjects do substantially well in all aptitudes. In such cases, it was not possible to find determinant traits. He had no recommendation for a career that fit my mind.

"I paid twenty-five dollars to find out what I should be doing with my life," I told him after a brief silence. "I want an answer." He studied me for an instant and then resignedly explained, as if I had not understood, that there was no one trait that stood out. I insisted on the return of my twenty-five dollars. Attempting to placate me, he pulled out from his desk a book by Johnson O'Connor titled *The Too Many Aptitude Woman* and handed it to me. Leaning back, he took a few puffs on his pipe, then explained that the book for men had not yet been written, but it would be much the same. I should take it home and read it. I raised my voice and repeated that I wanted my future told or my twenty-five dollars back. I could tell he was angry. He removed his pipe and placed it on the desk, then studied the test results a third time and looked at me with a subtle smile, "You will be an insurance adjuster."

I did not get my money back, nor did I become an insurance adjuster, although I often thought I would awake one morning so transformed. Only as years passed and efforts went unfulfilled did I grasp how prescient the white coat's conclusion was. With interests so diverse and widespread, finding an undertaking that fits my mind would be elusive. And yet, in retrospect, I realized how close the book's title came to an accurate prediction of my vocation. If only the last two words of the title were reversed and pluralized would I have known my future course: *The Too Many Women Aptitude.* An abundance of aptitudes was a burden, and I later came to realize that I had spent my life flirting with different opportunities, unable to settle on one passion. Fifty years would pass before I found a vocation that fit my mind.

I was reading *Amok*, a novella by Stefan Zweig. Virgin that I was, I wanted to absorb the emotion that had so overwhelmed Zweig's protagonist, a doctor. Working in a remote area of Indonesia, the doctor is visited by a white woman seeking an abortion to protect her reputation. Seized by an infatuation he cannot control, the doctor attempts to extort from her a promise of intimacy. The woman refuses. She seeks a native healer instead and dies when the operation fails. Honoring her last request, he issues a false death certificate. Returning to the West on the same boat as the body, the doctor relates the story to an anonymous narrator, then plunges into the sea clinging to her coffin. I thought: If only I could experience the passion that permeates this story, I would abandon my goal of turning mountains into hills.

My reputation as a mailroom star was enhanced by my acceptance letter from Cornell. The office staff threw a party. James Van Raalte, president of the company, personally congratulated me. Since I was headed to a college specializing in labor relations, he offered to send me to one of his factories in Dunkirk, New York, for a month before school began so that I could experience factory work. I am not sure if Mr. Van Raalte knew that I was just seventeen; my new factory colleagues certainly did not.

I showed up at the factory bright and early, neatly dressed. Welcomed by the foreman, I learned I was to be an industrial engineer, or more precisely, a time-and-motion study expert. I was given a stopwatch and all sorts of questionnaires placed neatly on a clipboard. My job was based on applying Fredrick Winslow Taylor's principles of scientific management. To help me understand Taylor's precept, I was asked how I put on my socks and shoes. Did I put on both socks before the shoes? When I said "Yes," I was told that my method was inefficient. If I was putting on a sock on my left foot, it was more productive to first put on the left shoe rather than switching feet to place the sock on the right foot. Now I was ready to go to work and make sure that every employee understood the shoes-and-socks theory of Taylor's scientific management.

Led onto the factory floor by the foreman, I was surprised by its extreme quiet, a silence disturbed only by the humming tick-tock of sewing machines. I was the only male in a large area housing some eighty young women, most no older than myself. These workers were piecing together lingerie. I was to watch their movements and improve their efficiency. Unduly awkward in the presence of young women, I now had a four-score in front of me. I had to choose a female each morning and hover over her shoulder in order to time the movement of her hands. The small hairs on the back of her neck stirred an instinct to bend and kiss the neck. The pheromones wafting around my clipboard filled me with longing to stroke her tiny breasts. From that moment on, the nape of a woman's neck has attracted me most.

At the end of the workday, I hurried to the rooming house where I was staying to recuperate from the female odor and relieve myself. Eventually, several members of the office staff invited me to share meals or sit in the local bars, although I declined to drink. What surprised me was that most of these new colleagues, born and raised in Dunkirk, dreamt of visiting New York City or other places they only knew from books. I would leave when my internship ended. The young ladies and their sewing machines would be left behind.

A few weeks later, after a brief stop in the Bronx to pack, I took the train to Ithaca. No one waved goodbye. I did not see my father before I left and never saw him again.

5

Cornell, Then the Sea

I entered college with the belief that everyone there had come from their own personal Parkchester, shaped by the same middle-class experience. Placed in a dormitory suite, I lived with a pair of cousins. It was my first experience having a bathroom of my own, as well as proximity to individuals of a different economic class. Toward five every afternoon, the cousins would start to drink. They opened windows to yell obscenities about Franklin D. Roosevelt, dead for over six years. We exchanged stories. I touted Bronx public schools. The cousins recounted their years of boarding school. I did not know what that was. "Kent, Kent," they explained. And when I finally understood they had lived there rather than at home, I blurted, "You mean, you paid for high school?" They looked at me as if I had dropped from outer space. After the first term, I moved into an off-campus apartment.

Since I received no funds from home, I worked odd jobs to finance my living expenses. Sometimes I drank malted milk early in the morning and allowed a lab technician to poke needles into my blood vessels to see what nutrients I had absorbed. A better job was working as a bartender at fraternity parties. These houses were careful with their reputations "on the Hill," as Cornell was called. Success for the gathering seemed to depend on the quality and quantity of alcohol consumed.

My reputation as a bartender was enhanced one Saturday evening. Working at a cellar bar, I filled the glasses with much-appreciated rapidity. When the couples went upstairs for entertainment, the fraternity president congratulated me on my exceptional service. I alerted him to a problem—we had run out of alcohol. He was concerned about the house's reputation on the Hill. I assured him that I would take care of it. Before everyone returned to the cellar, I emptied into a pitcher all the remnants of drinks left in glasses strewn on tables, carefully extracting the cigarette butts. I added several cans of grapefruit juice and ice. I cleaned the glasses and wiped off the lipstick marks. When the guests and fraternity brothers returned, everyone was pleased with the quality of the punch. I received a bonus.

I'd always been an aficionado of want ads and read them every day to learn what the world was calling for and to determine if and where I might fit in. In the classified section of the *Ithaca Times*, part-time salesmen were being sought. What caught my eye was a weekly cash guarantee of an advance against commissions. Eight of us applied. The product was a salad-maker device with five exceedingly sharp cutting cones. Each cone would slice, shred, grate, julienne, or chiffonade the carrot or pepper or onion to beautify the salad to be served to guests. We were given a choice. Either forgo the paltry minimum, hardly worth the effort required to go from door to door, or opt to receive high commissions. Seven chose to be paid by commission, but as I was from the Bronx, the minimum was fine.

This turned out to be the right choice, since I could not make a sale, even with a well-practiced routine. Knock, knock, and here was Cohen with his five cutting cones. I mainly solicited married graduate students. Finally, I found a couple who were interested. Asked if the device would cut meat, I lied. Handed a chunk of brisket, I pressed it in the cone with my thumb and turned the handle with some force. Blood spurted across the room. I stuck my thumb in my mouth and asked if they wanted two. My thumbnail has never returned to its pristine shape. I learned then and there that sales was not my calling.

Since the Labor Relations School provided ample opportunity to attend classes in the Liberal Arts College, I studied European literature with Professor Collignon, who was visiting from the Sorbonne. He introduced me to Thomas Mann, Elias Canetti and Italo Svevo. *Buddenbrooks* became a companion. Collignon practiced the European method of teaching. Rather than exams, we were required to write an essay for each book assigned. Astonished to receive the highest grade in the class, I began to think I should substitute literature in some manner for insurance adjusting as my true vocation. I visited Collignon to receive his congratulations and encouragement. "Ah yes, Cohen," he said in a welcoming tone, "you seem so sincere and naive that I felt I had to give you good grades."

Disappointed by the coolness of my reception, I assumed my literary career was at an end. When I told the Collignon story to one of my friends, he encouraged me to attend the lectures of Vladimir Nabokov, who was teaching nineteenth-century European literature. I went as an auditor. Since his classes were popular and crowded, I pretended I was registered and secured one of the few empty seats, trusting its number would not be called. Nabokov's autobiography, *Speak, Memory,* was my introduction. I found it precious, pedantic. What I retained from my first perusal—more of a skim than a thoughtful scrutiny, I'm ashamed to admit—was that in his youth he and his family had fifty servants to cater to their every need. His prose was so rich with words I did not know—*phylogenetic, incunabula, couvade-like, plangent, mystagogues*—that I thought he must have swallowed a dictionary when young.

Nabokov bent over a podium to read his lectures. There was no improvisation, no deviation from his notes. Oral questions were not permitted. Inquiries had to be in written form. Nabokov never raised his head to see if we were still there. Véra, his wife, monitored each class. She stared directly at the back wall. Her eyes rarely wavered; no emotion flicked across her face. Students kept their heads down to avoid the ferocity of her glance.

A second reading of *Speak, Memory* engendered a wholly different reaction. This was not a school assignment. Instead, I took Nabokov's memoir of growing up into my hands to fill idle moments. While the early chapters were burdened with challenging Russian names, his poetic coming-of age language ("leaves mingle in my memory with the leather of her shoes—the discomfort of young females with shame and blushes—nostril of her snub nose running") was in contrast with the cultural desert of my Bronx upbringing. Here was an expatriate, forced to wander at an early age, writing, as Conrad did, in a second language, with a vocabulary, experience, and knowledge far beyond my own. True, my time was often spent foraging for money. Yet Nabokov's penury when young had not prevented him from knowing Tyutchev or Lamarck or writing poetry at age fifteen or "conducting several love affairs simultaneously," while I could only surf wet dreams or knock on doors to sell salad makers to housewives home alone.

A friend invited me to tea at Nabokov's home. The professor was cordial and friendly, unlike the formality of his lecture style. Self-assured, he seemed to be living proof that, as his French publisher, Maurice Girodias, would write, "no great writer can be less than a monster of egomania." Véra hardly participated in the conversation, but her presence was a silent force. They might have been brother and elder sister. Vladimir's face, unwrinkled and smooth, contrasted with Véra's austere appearance, her hair touched with gray. We were unaware that the manuscript of *Lolita* was soon to make the rounds of publishing houses, collecting nothing but rejection slips until finding its way into print with the Olympia Press, owned by Girodias, whom I would later meet. In his desperate drive to find a publisher, Nabokov was forced to make use of one known for publishing porn.

Intellectual to his core, Nabokov was the first person I encountered whose thoughts and ideas became part of a vast inventory for later use. The tiniest details could not escape his eye. Whether on trains or in seedy motels, including a stay in Uvalde, Texas, in pursuit of his beloved butterflies, he would summon the perfect word or phrase to be scribbled by pencil on three-by-five-inch cards or a pad. As I sat in his home sipping his tea, I understood that he frequented a country of which I was not yet a citizen. I was merely a visitor, one who might never fulfill the requirements for an upgrade in status. While that realization disturbed my self-esteem, the disenchantment faded when I received my Seaman's Card at term's end.

I was now entitled to work as a wiper, an ordinary seaman, or a messman. I rushed home to find Bender, and we began our search for a vessel, certain we were following in Conrad's footsteps. Our routine for the next few weeks was steady and unchanging. Leaving our Bronx apartments at eight a.m. sharp for the subway to the South Ferry station, Bender and I entered the Socony-Vacuum hiring hall precisely as it opened at nine. The rectangular room had benches on each side. At the far end, two clerks sat behind a counter, seemingly as remote and inscrutable as Franz Kafka's Klamm in *The Castle*. Upon arrival, we deposited our Seamen's Cards in a basket and retired to the benches to wait. We were participating in a ritual that had hardly changed since the days of the seamen who sought berths on *The Pequod* to hunt for Moby Dick. Job openings would be called and made available to those seamen who had been on land the longest. Every once in a while, a name would be announced. A seaman would rise from the bench and approach the counter. After a few minutes of whispers, he would leave the hiring hall for an unknown destination.

The hall closed at noon for an hour. With our sandwiches in brown bags, Bender and I took the Staten Island ferry, then a nickel a ride. The conductors did not make us leave our seats for the return trip, allowing us to enjoy a leisurely lunch while admiring the harbor, the Statue of Liberty, and departing seagoing vessels on which we hoped to embark. Then it was back to the hard bench until a bell rang, ending the day.

This routine was well into the third week when we realized that as newcomers, our names might never be called. That evening we explained our predicament to Bender's neighbor, who promised to help. Two days later, we heard the call "Bender Cohen." We were each given assignment slips, one to join a tanker in Philadelphia for a coastal run and the other to fly to Los Angeles to meet a vessel that would shortly arrive in the port of San Pedro. Bender and I looked at each other, disappointed that we would not be working on the same ship. We had assumed that our attempt to go to sea together was as simple as going to summer camp. Since he was responsible for the contact that enabled us to be hired, I felt Bender was entitled to choose. He was silent, so I handed him the Los Angeles voucher. The clerk advised us that we would be given formal instructions in a few days, but first we had to go into a back room to be inoculated, as this was our first trip.

The medical officer advised Stephen that since he had been assigned to a tanker that was headed overseas, he would need to receive, all at once, vaccinations for typhus, typhoid, yellow fever, cholera, and tetanus-diphtheria. Stephen replied that he was allergic to tetanus shots and had to be given the vaccine in small doses. The doctor was unsympathetic. Stephen and I exchanged jobs. A coastwise vessel required fewer vaccinations, and a tetanus shot was not compulsory. I detected Stephen's relief. He had been ill at ease since learning we would not be traveling together. From the start, my eagerness had propelled him to participate. He didn't aspire to a life at sea, but had merely been indulging my determination to imitate Conrad standing night watch.

Conrad was a perfectionist, favoring those who were highly proficient in all aspects of seafaring life. He would evaluate members of the crew. He could smell the competence of a new captain as he approached the gangway. "This stranger was walking up and down absorbed in the marked contemplation of the ship's fore and aft trim; but when I saw him squat on his heels in the slush at the very edge of the quay to peer at the draught of water under her counter, I said to myself, 'This is the captain.'"

I had less than a week to prepare to leave. Bender had already left for Philadelphia; he retired from service before the end of his first day. Life at sea was not for him, he later confessed. The smell of oil, a lower berth, a shared toilet, and working in a darkened engine room so unnerved him that he scrambled to flee the vessel before the gangway ladder was hauled up, so that he did not have to remain captive until the next port.

I was summoned to appear at noon at 42nd Street near Fifth Avenue, where I would await a ride to Idlewild Airport, then in operation only for five years. Arriving early, armed with a small suitcase of work clothes, I waited, uncertain what to expect. Four or five others drifted to our meeting point, just in front of a Schrafft's, part of the popular restaurant chain. There was little conversation, just a nod to acknowledge our common destination.

I was the youngest; the rest were seasoned crew. The silence was broken when one of the new arrivals suggested that we have a beer. En masse we entered Schrafft's, well known for its ice cream and desserts. Chicken à la king, lobster cocktail, and scrambled eggs were featured. These dishes were now being served to assorted tables full of middle-aged women, some with nets guarding their hair. There were no men among the clientele. Our entrance caused a stir, which grew louder as my companions sat down at the counter and ordered beers. When they learned that alcohol was not served, a shocked silence fell. The clientele resumed their meals, quietly appreciating the floor show unfolding before them.

We returned to the street to await our transportation to the airport. I was assigned a window seat and watched the sky throughout my virgin flight. I remained utterly calm, as if I were an experienced traveler, a professional seaman returning to a familiar vessel. Until then, I had not realized how chameleon-like my personality was, readily adapting to fast-changing circumstances without a moment's hesitation. I never even wondered where the tanker was heading or whether I would return in time for the fall semester at Cornell. An indifference to the future had been embedded deep in my character, and it would remain lodged there despite my efforts to remove its tenacious hold.

Since we arrived at the San Pedro docks at night, I had little chance to appraise the vessel other than to note it lay deep in the water, evidence that it was being charged with oil. Shown to the fo'c'sle, as our quarters were called, I was offered an upper berth. Aside from sleeping, little time would be spent in that fo'c'sle, which I was to share with three other seamen. Toilets were elsewhere, and I soon learned it would be my morning task to clean them. There was no small talk, no questions were asked, no "What was your last vessel?", no "Where are you from?" No one had a past—only a present on a piece of steel, soon to be far away from memories of land. I was told I could go ashore; departure was scheduled for the next morning at five a.m.; I was to be on duty at eight.

Conrad did not define departure as the ship parting from the dock. Rather, it was the last sight of land, the moment that required navigational expertise. I decided not to correct my mates. "What I felt most was my being a stranger to the ship; and if all the truth be told, I was somewhat of a stranger to myself. The youngest man on board . . . and untried as yet . . ." That was Conrad's diary entry, as if anticipating my first night in his world.

Whatever romantic fantasy I entertained about my first evening as a seaman was quickly dissipated. I was to be "the kid." Although I may have preferred to remain aboard and explore the ship, camaraderie with my new mates required that I accompany them to the nearest bar. I pretended to enjoy the fraternity hazing and did not reveal that I was too young to join the depth charge crowd.

I woke up early to get ready for my chores. Land was no longer in sight. I could no longer pull a Bender. I was sailing on a T2 tanker left over from the war, as were most of my fellow seamen. Some 520 feet in length, with a beam close to 70, the T2 class resembled a flattened container with large tanks buried deep within its hull. Two separate superstructures sat atop the deck. One was midships, housing the officers and the steering mechanism on the bridge. The second was the crew's fo'c'sle area in the aft. Just below its frame was the mess which gave way to an open area that stretched fifteen feet to the stern, where I often sat in the evenings, inhaling the salt sea air and enjoying the freedom of anonymity conveyed. Our speed averaged about twelve to fifteen knots. A catwalk linked the superstructures and then extended to the bow, where one held tightly to the rails when a storm battered the ship with heavy winds. To a professional mariner, the vessel might have seemed weary, but its defects I was yet to see. Years later I found an apt description by A. L. Liebling, the *New Yorker* correspondent: "A tanker is a kind of a ship that inspires small affection. It is an oil can with a Diesel motor to push it through the water . . ."

My duties included cleaning the fo'c'sle and the communal heads, and, after a hearty breakfast at a group table, I descended to the engine room for other tasks. I carefully eased my way down a metal ladder facing inward as other seamen did. On my first day I examined each rung coated with grime, wondering what universe I was entering. The engine room turned out to be an ecosphere divorced from reality. Noise was constant, conversation rare, just orders shouted out to be obeyed. Scraping rust, repainting, and wiping spills were my main responsibilities; I was also on call to respond to whatever the engineers needed.

Unlike the seamen who worked on deck—four hours on, then eight off, and four again at night—I was on duty throughout the day. Working in the bowels of the ship, I rarely saw the sun. After ten days we arrived at our first landfall, Yokohama. The story of my adventure there opened this book.

From Yokohama we headed to the Persian Gulf, a voyage of around 8,000 nautical miles, more than twenty days of sail. Unloaded, the ship stood high in the water and rolled more severely than it had during the initial crossing. After a bunker refueling in a small Malaysian port, we entered the Indian Ocean and were immediately struck by a typhoon.

Conrad describes an approaching storm: "A dense bank of cloud became visible to the northward; it had a sinister dark olive tint, and lay low and motionless upon the sea, resembling a solid obstacle in the path of the ship." For the first time I worried whether our aging vessel could withstand the wind and impatient sea. "Heavy sprays enveloped [us] from stem to stern, and instantly in the midst of her regular rolling she began to jerk and plunge as though she had gone mad with fright," Conrad wrote. "Once a vessel began to roll," he added, "you felt that she would never stop." As I lay in my upper bunk, knotted twine held me as secure as a lover's nighttime grasp. Conrad had warned, "There was no position where you could fix yourself so as not to feel a constant strain upon all the muscles of your body."

Eating was much more of a challenge. Chairs and tables were solidly clamped to the deck, but as the ship yawed from one side to the other, our plates slid to the table's end. We patiently waited for the ship to steady. When the food coasted by again, our forks were at the ready, and we impaled a morsel and ate it quickly. This was straight out of a cartoon or a slapstick comedy. The storm disturbed the Exocoetidae, the flying fish that sometimes glided above the waves. Lifted by a strong gust, the errant cod would land on the deck only to be grabbed by a seaman who would then race to the kitchen to turn the flapping fish into a midday snack.

There is a quiet among the professionals who go to sea. Stories I'd read about tensions and conflicts on board ships seemed exaggerated, and none arose on my voyage. Although I was not asked, nor did I volunteer that I was a college student sailing for the romance, I believed most on board understood a young Cohen was not in training for a sailor's career. I became the mascot. Victim to hoaxes to amuse the crew, I was often instructed to search for a tool that did not exist. I was even invited to the bridge by the captain. He directed me to take the helm and steer the ship, which he then released from automatic control. The course was indicated on the compass. The wheel controlling the rudder was difficult to keep steady, and I was soon off course. In a contest with the ocean's force, I struggled to navigate toward the directed compass point. Turning a heavy ship that's moving with speed takes time and space, an understanding that had escaped me when I had watched films of naval battles. Relieved by the captain with a nod and a smile, I returned to my bunk with a feeling that I had just advanced to higher rank.

Given names were rarely used. We addressed each other in terms of our respective positions. I had become "Wiper," and my special mentor was "Pumps," the pumpman, in charge of the mechanism to discharge oil. Unlike other seamen, he told me stories and chronicles of his life, a farm upbringing in Pennsylvania and wartime crossings of the Atlantic. His natural engineering aptitude was consistently on quiet display. In his hands, tools were not idle instruments; they fit like gloves. His open, craggy face conveyed the reassuring competence of which Conrad would certainly have approved. I did not know his age, though his demeanor suggested I add ten years to my guess.

Pumps shared a failure he felt deeply and one that bound him to the ship. Retired from earlier seafaring, he had taken his savings and purchased property in rural Pennsylvania. He made a careful study of his land, intending to find oil and minerals buried there. After all, Pennsylvania had been the origin of the nation's oil rush. Production had peaked a half-century before, yet Pumps was undeterred. After encouraging tests, he signed a drilling contract. Royalties for oil would be paid, but the prospector retained all rights to natural gas. That is what lay above the oil, an ample reservoir of gas with an extensive life that assured profits to the driller, but not to Pumps. Having no money in his purse, as Herman Melville wrote of Ishmael, Pumps once more sought refuge in the sea. His hands were roughened by work, and I watched his upright, steady walk, his robust figure burdened with fatigue. I thought of my father likewise suffering from events beyond his control. I imagined his face when the bailiff came to seize his bolts and screws and close his hardware store.

Pumps was not the only member of the crew whose seafaring was influenced by disputes or personal struggles on land. Some surely shared Conrad's view that "Once on board and far from land . . . the ocean calmed whatever was the nature of the pursuit." Stars above and the moon's reflection on the sea disarmed any sense of anguish shore life might engender. As I was the youngest member of the crew, I became the secret sharer and silent repository of countless stories and cautionary tales. Life lessons to be learned.

Jim, an able-bodied seaman, spent a good part of the year at his home in Panama City, Florida. But when his funds ran low, he returned to work on deck. He walked with self-assurance, and a coolness in his glance set him apart from the others pulling mooring lines at his side. Because I was, to him, the kid, he opened up. Neither romance nor pay had induced him to work on a ship. He was a professional poker player who had free run with a captive group of amateurs. Suggesting I sit at his side for the nightly game, I was astonished that he emerged as a winner of almost every substantial pot. Once, I saw that he had a better hand but allowed another player to win. I almost cried out but restrained myself. He later explained that the pot was small, and he wanted his opponent to expose a tell. When payday came, the line to settle debts to Jim was long.

The very thought of the Persian Gulf suggests a story hiding there, a Lawrence striding on the sand. On a vessel equipped only with rudimentary fans, the heat prevented sleep. While the ship was moving, the breeze was ample. Once we docked, first at Mina

Al Ahmadi, Kuwait, and then at Ras Tanura, Saudi Arabia, our fo'c'sle became unbearable. We carried our mattresses to the upper deck. I took my place at the end of the line, as suited my lowly rank. My feet edged out beyond the shadow of the bulkhead, and the rising sun tinged my toes red.

On a map, the Persian Gulf appears in close proximity to the Suez Canal. The distance from Ras Tanura to Port Suez, the gathering point to transit the canal, actually exceeds 3,000 nautical miles. We sailed past names I never knew: Bab-el-Mandeb, Seven Brothers Islands, and the Farasan Islands. I was beginning to wonder when our vessel would return to the United States and if I would arrive in time for the academic term. American flagships, I was told, must dock in a US port once a year. If we were going through the Suez Canal, most likely we would sail for home.

Arriving at Port Suez, we waited until enough vessels gathered to form a convoy. The canal is managed for one-way traffic with bypass lakes. At that time, its width approximated that of a football field. Moving at a slow pace, we appreciated the views of the desert and the villages on either side. At the northern end of the canal lies Port Said, where we anchored and added stores as ships had done for close to a hundred years. An artificial town built of sand from the dredging of the canal, Port Said thrived as the crossroads of Europe, Asia, and Africa. British ships halted there, a waystation en route to India. In 1913, Kipling disembarked for a visit to Egypt. He found an acquaintance who had chosen Port Said as his retirement home, content to sit idle and admire "the constant parade of ships." If one stayed long enough, noted Kipling, all friends and schoolmates would eventually pass by, but he was unimpressed.

Myself, it don't excite me nor amuse
To watch a pack o' shipping on the sea;

But I can understand my neighbor's views
From certain things which have occurred to me.
Men must keep touch with things they used to use
To earn their living, even when they are free;
And so come back upon the least excuse—
Same as the sailor settled near the sea.

I thought of Kipling as I composed a multi-stanza poem that began

Oh, ring the bells and sound the gongs
The men are going home again
To their wives and kids and everything banal.
Hurrah for the 100-mile ditch known as the Suez Canal.

As we anchored in the bay, I was instructed to close all portholes. High-pressure hoses were being prepared on deck. I was warned that we would soon be surrounded by a fleet of feluccas, the traditional wooden single-sail boats familiar from the Nile. Young boys would scramble up to test our portholes. If any were unlocked, the boys would shimmy through and swipe all items that they could fit through the opening. Suddenly, dozens of Egyptians appeared on the deck to both sell and seek souvenirs. When they refused to leave, our hoses forced them over the side. Once clear, the ship made a hasty departure to avoid the harbor police responding to complaints. We did not know that a revolution was taking place and that Egypt's King Farouk would soon be leaving, too.

The passage from the Suez Canal through the Straits of Gibraltar and across the Atlantic to a New Jersey port moved quickly—a smooth run. I had completed the first of several trips around the world.

6

Still a Sophomore

Two days after our landing, I returned to Cornell. I did not swagger nor boast of my exploits; that chapter was closed. Since I have the habit of quickly adapting to my changing environment, I accepted my role as just another sophomore. The school year passed without any major incident. With a midnight curfew in place and a ratio of five males to one female, I rarely dated. I declined to test my status as a virgin, uncertain if I still was one.

The highlight of the year was meeting Joseph O. La Follette, scion of the distinguished Wisconsin political family. We shared an apartment, and he became my closest friend. Our sense of humor aligned—without that, no relationship can endure. He never bored me. He taught me how to drive and tried to teach me how to sail on a boat we later bought together, but I preferred to watch him hold the tiller with a skill I could not equal. If I had any complaint, it was his habit of lighting a cigarette as soon as he woke up, even before leaving his bed. Tobacco smoke would drift to my side of the room as I slept just a few paces away.

Joe never talked to me about his family or Wisconsin politics. We were students, and the world was far away. He had a girlfriend named Joanne and claimed he was in love. We soon became an inseparable threesome; I often left the apartment so they could have some time alone.

The La Follette family, founders of the Progressive Party, dominated Wisconsin politics for generations. Joe's grandfather,

Robert M. La Follette, had been the governor, then a senator, and he sought the US presidency in 1924 as the Progressive Party nominee. Joe's father, Robert, Jr., also served as senator for over twenty years, only losing his seat when he was pressed to enter a senate primary as a Republican in 1946 rather than retain his Progressive label. He lost to Joe McCarthy by a few thousand votes. I did not focus on this political history until one morning in February 1953, when I answered the bedroom phone. It was a presidential advisor, Clark Clifford, calling with the news that Joe's father had died by suicide. A plane was being sent to Ithaca so Joe could fly to Washington to be with his family.

Joe's relationship with his girlfriend grew more intense when he returned from the funeral, and he seemed less cheerful. I did not think it was serious, not until his mother telephoned. Joe was out, but she explained she had called to speak to me. She asked me to fly to Washington; a ticket was being held in my name at the Ithaca airport. She added that I should not breathe a word about her invitation to Joe. I assumed she wanted to check on Joe's well-being and to talk to me confidentially.

The La Follette residence in D.C. was the largest home I had ever entered. There were separate sitting, living, and dining rooms, the size of which I had only seen in films. I had trouble reconciling that luxurious way of life—a style that had formed Joe's youth—with the close and smoky quarters we shared at school. Joe's mother went directly to the point. She offered a brief summary of the family's political history. Then she outlined the aspirations she held for Joe. He was to enter politics directly after graduation. He would advance from state office to congressman to senator, all through the power of his name. My first reaction was to explain that Joe had never expressed interest in a political career. What's more, I did not think he had the patience for either campaigning or compromise. Then, the real reason for my trip to D.C. emerged. Joe's girlfriend was a Nussbaum, and her religion would inhibit his rise. Since I was also Jewish and his closest friend, surely I would understand. My assigned mission was to explain to Joanne—his mother knew her name—the reason why their college romance had to end.

I was stunned by her request. It was a message I could not conceivably relay to a friend. Moreover, until that moment, I hardly thought of my Jewish identity. Antisemitism was not yet part of my experience. Parkchester friends were diverse; religious affiliation was never raised. No one on board the tanker had seemed to care. I was not even aware, until later, that there may well have been a limit to the number of Jews admitted to my college.

I never said a word about my covert trip to D.C. to either Joe or Joanne. Nevertheless, the pressure on her must have become severe. I don't know who might have intervened, but despite my efforts to save their relationship by assuring her that Joe was strong enough to stand up to his family, their affair was soon over.

Joe was devastated. He quit school for a year. Perhaps inspired by my own seafaring experience, he decided to work on a United Fruit vessel transporting bananas from Central America. His father had been a director of the company. Then he worked as an assistant to a public relations professional, Eddie Jaffe, whose office was a third-floor walk-up at 156 West 48th Street above Zucca's Restaurant. Eddie was one of the great publicists for films and theatre productions, and for their stars. During school vacations I would meet Joe there, usually late at night.

Joe was happy as Jaffe's assistant. He even produced a short film, *Mambo Madness*, about the dance craze of that moment. When he returned to finish his studies at Cornell, we spent good times together. After graduation, he worked for IBM, started a family, and seemed content with life. But I detected a lack of the intense joy that had infused our year as roommates. He died in 1997. Some years later I found a psychiatric portrait of Joe's father, Robert M. La Follette, Jr., destined to always be "young Bob." The author suggested that La Follette had been pressed into a political career he did not seek. The article ended with this statement:

> Around noon, on February 24, 1953, Bobbie committed suicide. He had appeared calm to his family and coworkers that morning and left no note. Days before he shot himself in the head, however, he expressed to friends "how he never should have let McCarthy beat him, how he had let his father down." The La Follette family cited depression brought on by ill health in his later years as the key to Bobbie's suicide. It seems likely, however, that Bobbie's death, like his life, was more the product of his early years, of incredibly high parental expectations, of a boy prohibited from exploring or even discovering his own wants and identity and who found temporary refuge in acute physical suffering. His suicide was a tragic end to a distinguished senator and the man who had been his father's pride and best hope.

The year of his death was McCarthy's apogee; the Senator's investigation of communist infiltration into the military, with Roy Cohn at his side, dominated the television screen. I wondered if the hearings chaired by his successor were a weight too heavy for Joe's father to bear. I also wondered about the impact of spending a life, perhaps mine, working in a career that did not fit the mind.

7
To Sea Again

The ILR school had been in existence for five years; its quarters were temporary, a Quonset house at the edge of the Cornell campus, ample for a student body of roughly 200. Its mission was "to improve industrial and labor conditions in the State through the provision of instruction, the conduct of research, and the dissemination of information in all aspects of industrial, labor, and public relations, affecting employers and employees." The courses, especially for the first two years, were broader than what the description suggested. Emphasis was placed on history, sociology, and economics. The initial faculty was exceptional and included Milton Konvitz, a constitutional law expert, and Maurice Neufeld, who had been a labor union organizer as well as a Greek scholar and translator of poetry.

Professor Neufeld introduced me to the joys of archival research, which much later would become my main pursuit. I quickly realized that sitting in an obscure library or repository of fading newspapers and documents provided satisfactions I had rarely felt before. Neufeld encouraged me to write a term paper about the influence of the Communist Party on labor unions, for which I received a prize. He also arranged an internship for me with the New York State Board of Mediation for the summer after my sophomore year. Meeting leading business executives, union heads, and aspiring politicians while attending conferences to settle labor disputes, I noted something new. I had no sense of hierarchy and felt no hint of intimidation. I interrupted to offer my own solution to avert a strike, as if the participants were companions rather than adults whose standing I ought to have respected. This habit often stood me in good stead, but at times I was firmly told to stand down.

Since I was now on a first-name basis with union leaders, I requested a berth on a ship after my junior year. The union was normally quite strict, but I received a message that my name would be placed on a special list. As soon as the term ended, I appeared at the Seafarers International Union (SIU) hiring hall in Brooklyn. I thought I could walk right in and obtain a berth. An African American gentleman housed in a box-like structure slightly larger than a telephone booth stopped me as I approached the entrance. He wanted to see my union card. I tried to explain my special situation. He made a phone call and told me to wait. As I waited, he told me his story. Even though he had been a union organizer, a change in leadership resulted in his exile, most likely because he was Black.

After ten days of waiting, my companion, still wedged in that shameful box, suggested I seek a different summer job. But I waited. On the eleventh day, his phone rang. He answered, looked at me, and shrugged. Then he pressed a button, and I went inside. I approached the desk at the far end of the hiring hall, knowing I was subject to a lottery system. I could be sent anywhere in the world and be absent for a period that might mean missing a part of my senior year and having my graduation deferred. I did not hesitate. I was to be an ordinary seaman on a coastal vessel that shuttled between New Jersey and Port Isabel, Texas. Advised that the trip would be a trial to determine if I could join the union, I was asked to pay an initiation fee of $1,500 (about $8,000 today).

I explained that I had no funds until I earned my first wage. I calculated that I would have little left over for my senior year.

The vessel on this coastal run was manned by Southerners, most of whom lived in Port Isabel. They could not be accused of seeking the romance of the sea. They were like the stokers Conrad had disparaged when steam replaced the sail. Most remained on the ship for years, touching home port twice a month. The ship was also a T2 class tanker, so I boarded her with a sense of familiarity, not yet grasping that my chores as a deckhand would be quite distinct from my prior engine-room experience. Assigned to the eight-to-midnight watch, I was sent to the bow after enjoying a hearty evening meal. I was instructed to follow Coast Guard rules and ring a bell to alert the steersman to ships that might be drawing near. Every time you spot a light, ring once for port, twice for starboard, and thrice for dead ahead—these were the instructions I was to follow.

We were sailing south along the coast of New Jersey. Abundant lights dotted the shore, all on the starboard side. Each deserved the two-bell ring. I was as conscientious as a Conrad disciple could be, proud of my first night watch. The sea was calm. The motor that propelled us gently through the waves caused the deck to vibrate. Toward 11 p.m., I sensed a stir at the bottom of my stomach. What started as mild discomfort quickly became an overwhelming urge to send the remnants of my dinner dead ahead. The wind that enveloped a moving ship favored neither side. Vomit covered my entire face. Moments later I was told that the captain wanted to welcome me. I went directly to his cabin, hoping he could not smell my misfortune. He merely thanked me for the bell-ringing concert. Shore lights did not count.

Since I had not endured seasickness during my previous trip, I assumed my episode of distress was a one-off incident. I was apprehensive during my second night's watch, but 11:30 p.m. came and passed without incident. I stood quietly, admiring the power of the ship, waves parting before its thrust. Alone in the dark, I felt I had assumed command of the entire universe. My contentment abruptly turned to shock when my stomach again revolted. When I was relieved from duty, I hurried aft to dispatch evidence of my plight.

On the third night, laden less with food, I managed to withstand the menace the ship's rocking motion caused. With humility toward the elements that composed the poetry of the night, I recited Virgil to prove I was well suited to be its companion. "Freshening breezes blow as night comes on and a full moon speeds their course." My single paraphrased line failed to capture the majesty of Virgil's epic verse, so I closed my eyes, hoping Virgil's words would flood back. "By now the day had slipped from the sky and the gentle moon was riding high through the heavens at mid-career, her horses pounding through the night." Leaning forward at the prow, I heard and felt the pounding as waves collided with the bow, stars so near I could touch their light. The wind, no longer an adversary, soothed me as if to say, "You have learned a lot." If allowed, I would have stayed at that spot until dawn and then given a James Cagney shout, "Top of the world, Ma', top of the world."

At 8 a.m. prosaic tasks replaced the magic of the night. Chipping rust and repairing the damage the salty sea air inflicted on the deck were my morning chores. After the morning shift, I had the option to continue working during the afternoon. Weekend shifts were also available. One Sunday I volunteered to enter the storage tanks that had been filled with the chemicals we delivered. I would be earning hazard pay. My chore was to hammer off the impurities that had formed on the sides of the tanks below deck. Although it was hard to breathe, the main danger was causing a spark in a gas-filled pocket that could, at least in theory, erupt right in my face.

Although no one made direct comments to me, I did have a fo'c'sle mate who was uneasy in the company of a Jew. He watched me as I shaved, expressing surprise that my beard grew fast. When we approached New York Harbor, he could not resist replacing *New* with *Jew.* He walked the deck with an aggressive strut that signaled he was ready for a spat. There was a meanness in his manner that became evident during my third round trip. I called him Red for the color of his hair that barely scraped his scalp.

The pumpman on that vessel had no Southern roots. He had come from Greece years before and spoke with an accent that sometimes made his speech difficult to absorb. Well respected by the officers whose mandate prompted speed, he worked with alarming dispatch and adjusted the pumps with ease. As we approached the Texas shore, clouds of immense mosquitoes stirred up from the swamps along the coast enveloped us. To avoid large welts, we coated ourselves with heavy, foul-smelling oil, and to ease the dryness of our throats, we hoarded cans of drinks and stored them under our bunks. The pumpman proposed a solution to ensure cold beverages closer to the deck. With permission from the captain, he installed a commercial Coke machine and stocked it with a variety of sodas. As with many plans that seem ideal in theory, there was a flaw in this one. Seamen work in shorts, pockets remain unused, coins are not stored. But when a drink was essential, a dime was needed. Pumps was called and asked to provide the key or a ten-cent piece; repayment was to be made at a later time. He awkwardly explained he would never collect such a minor debt. The drinks would then be free, and he would suffer loss.

At last, Red saw his chance to bully a weaker man. He started whispering that the Greek was un-American in refusing to provide a coin. The whisper turned to shouts. Union solidarity was evoked. One member was not allowed an advantage over others. Following union rules, all work was suspended for a meeting or, rather, a trial of the culprit whom Red had already found guilty of an infraction not yet framed. At first I thought this was a petty squabble that would soon be forgotten, but as the engines slowed and all members of the crew were called to gather in session, I knew that Pumps faced a quandary that went beyond the Coke. Ouster from the union was to be discussed, and that would mean the end of the Pumps' employment on a union ship. His livelihood was at stake.

Uncertain if I would be welcomed at a union meeting, I entered the venue at the last minute and sat near the door. No one objected. Red acted as the prosecutor. The charge was disloyalty to the men who shared the deck. Pumps' conduct was compared to treason in the war. Few men spoke, cowed by the vehemence Red displayed. The Greek man then rose to speak in his own defense. Tearfully, he promised free drinks for the balance of the trip. Upon arrival at home port, the offending machine would be removed and harmony restored. Startled by his tears, the seamen seemed to relent. I assumed, as others did, that the ordeal would now end, and all parties would file out sheepishly, ashamed that it had even begun.

Far from it. Red now rose to issue a proration more bitter than his initial charge. He was a Donkin harassing Conrad's *Nigger*, waiting for his death. "Yer nobody. Yer no one at all! He spluttered with such a strength of unerring conviction that it shook him from head to foot in coming out and left him vibrating like a released string." I decided that I, the sole elite, should respond to

Red and deter my mates from a vote they would later regret. Before I even cleared my throat and brain, Red ended his discourse with a gesture. I was the target of an arm with an index finger raised. Pointing directly at me as if knowing what was in my mind, he said, "Even the kid knows better. Ain't that so?" I was so shocked at being singled out, I merely nodded reflexively. The vote to remove Pumps from the union was later overturned by union headquarters. The incident was soon forgotten, except by me, ashamed of my silence, my failure to oppose a wrongful treatment.

One Sunday morning, just after dawn, we were awakened by a loud and urgent "Man overboard!" We rushed from our bunks to the deck and found we were in a narrow channel not far from our Texas docking station. Our tanker had rammed a smallish barge. Its two-man crew jumped into the water and quickly swam to shore. An inquiry into the causes of the incident prevented our immediate departure. Given a day of rest, a few crew members who were not at their home port planned to take a taxi to Mexico. The border was no more than 20 miles away. I asked to join them so I could buy some souvenirs.

Apparently, I had not learned the lesson from my last shore trip with members of the crew. My companions, not revealing their destination, headed first to Boys Town at the edge of Matamoros, just across the border. It was a tolerance zone. Brothels edged an unpaved square. We arrived at high noon. No shadows disturbed the deserted streets. Everything seemed closed. "This is a land of nocturnal animals," I said. "Let's just go to town." The clamor of empty whiskey bottles and discarded beer cans set flying by our taxi sent a signal announcing our approach. Suddenly, wooden shutters opened on the upper floors. Arms protruded slowly and gave an inviting wave. It was like a scene from a Fellini movie. The image still haunts me. A disembodied appendage seemed to float in mid-air within a window frame. It was the first time I uttered the word "surreal."

I found a bar and had a Coke while the others tested the stairs. I expressed surprise to the waiter that I was sitting in an otherwise empty square. He confirmed that it was rare to see anyone before 6 p.m. The heat was too severe. When I questioned how legal the establishments were, the response was swift. He said the last mayor who asked such questions retired with a bullet in his head.

Whether due to damage from the collision or for scheduled maintenance, the trip terminated at a dockyard in Mobile, Alabama, where the tanker was to undergo repairs. I received my pay and discharge papers proving I had worked on a union ship. I had so far avoided the so-called initiation fee. At each port, I had successfully argued that I had not yet received enough pay, and the union representative there allowed me to postpone paying. At Mobile, as the seamen began to disembark, I was told that three large men were washed on shore asking for me by name. Changing quickly into a jacket and tie, I waited for the officers to descend the gangway. I discreetly joined them. Engaged in conversation, I calmly walked past the reception party. It was not my proudest moment.

I decided to hitchhike to Miami, hoping to find a ship for a working return to New York in time for school. My scheme was utterly mad, for I had no map to guide me and no sense of how long the trip would take. Only secondary roads existed at that time, and the route meandered through the Deep South. I was soon picked up by a male driver who, after a few minutes of desultory talk, offered to unbutton my pants for $20. I kept negotiating the price until we arrived at the next town. I had reached $35 when I jumped out of the car.

I thought it best to leave as soon as possible. I boarded a local bus, which would allow me to progress a few miles down the road. With my small bag, I took a seat in the rear. The bus soon pulled off the road. The driver approached my seat and hovered over me. "You don't belong here," he said. The bus would not advance until I moved to the white-only section. I will not pretend that I am entirely color-blind, but I had not noticed that all the other passengers around me were black women, probably commuting to do their jobs in white folks' homes. In that instant, I realized there were no Negroes I called friends. I reflected on the absence of African Americans in Parkchester, or on the vessel I had just left, or in my classes, or in any part of my life. I had barely noticed the utter silence that greeted my arrival on the bus. The other passengers just stared straight ahead. Should I protest or acquiesce? We were in a forested rural area. I changed my seat. Whites could always get off the bus. At that time, in 1953, African Americans had no other means of transport.

When I finally arrived in Miami, I went to the union hiring hall in search of a vessel to New York. I assumed my discharge papers would vouch for my union standing. The local delegate, a burly man, asked for my Coast Guard card. He was a step ahead of me. He inserted it in his rear pocket. With a pat on his behind, he said he would telex all union offices to see if I had paid my dues. He knew I would have to return to recover the card. As he turned, I reflexively stretched out my hand; my brain was not involved. I extracted the card so deftly that I'm sure he later looked everywhere to find out where it dropped.

I never went to sea again.

8
Harvard to Yokohama

Senior year at college brought serious thoughts about life choices and whether graduate study was a valid means of deferring a decision. I had procrastinated in making plans since no career had yet sparked my enthusiasm.

Two of my new roommates were applying to law school. I had little interest in becoming a lawyer since I was uncertain as to what that meant. But I had even less interest in being drafted. Attending graduate school provided a deferment. I joined my roommates in taking the LSAT, which had been initiated a few years before. I applied only to Harvard Law School. I assumed I would more likely have to find a job and possibly be drafted. Even if Harvard accepted me, the tuition plus the housing seemed beyond my means. Do I now regret, in retrospect, Harvard's full scholarship that enticed me into a career that did not fit my mind?

The first year of law school passed in a flash. I appreciated the intellectual effort to determine if a killing is always murder or to distinguish a fee simple from a tail, but I wondered about its relevance to my future. As I watched and listened to my colleagues debate in class, it was clear that I did not have their passion for the law. Most knew where they hoped to go and understood what they would do when they arrived. They were at Harvard Law School to *become*. I was there because I was being subsidized.

I had not decided if I should continue with my studies when the term ended. My immediate focus was on finding a summer job. I scanned the ads in the *New York Times.* A tiny insert, no more than a quarter inch, caught me by surprise. "WANTED. A manager for an overseas Seamen's Club." No further details were provided. Applications were to be sent to the New York State Employment Office. Given the nature of the job, it seemed a bit odd for the triage to be assigned to a state agency.

I decided to head directly to the Employment Office. I showed the ad to a receptionist and was directed to an interviewer. He turned out to be a classmate working a summer job. He laughed when I explained my mission. He initially refused to submit my résumé to the prospective employer, but once I convinced him it was not a joke, he set up a meeting and provided a favorable reference. Two days later, when I was interviewed by the United Seamen's Service (USS), I understood why the State Employment Office was involved. USS was a semi-official nonprofit organization dedicated to caring for merchant seamen in foreign ports. It turned out to be a peculiar entity.

In February 1942, President Franklin D. Roosevelt, by executive order, established the War Shipping Administration to ensure the availability of vessels and personnel throughout the war. The movement of *matériel*, weapons, and troops was dependent on careful coordination requiring government control, although the men who manned the ships were civilians. The USS provided assistance, housing, and entertainment in ports around the world, comparable to facilities provided by the military for their respective forces. Given the ferocity of the submarine war that decimated cargo ships long before the US entered the conflict, housing and entertainment had to be set close to the docks so that seamen could be summoned quickly to man a departing vessel. USS reception halls and clubs were to be "a home away from home." Although by 1956, the year I sought the job, there was no longer any danger from enemy fire, five USS facilities remained in existence, a perfect example of organizational inertia. Funds came from donations, with the Community Chest serving as a major source. Most of the personnel were experienced social workers.

My first interview did not go well. Indignant that the New York State Employment Office would send a twenty-two-year-old for such an important task, I was quickly sent on my way. Since this opportunity seemed tailor-made for me, I refused to be discouraged. I composed a lengthy statement of my merits and mailed it to members of the USS board of directors. Emphasizing my time at sea and knowledge of the mixology of depth charge drinks, I told them of my firm commitment to the welfare of those in need of assistance at foreign ports. What most likely saved the day was my willingness to leave Harvard to serve the greater good. By the end of the second interview, I knew the position would be mine. Confirmation came two days later. I was to leave for Japan in one week's time to replace the manager of the Yokohama facility. I hurried to Cambridge to get a leave of absence from law school and to ensure that my scholarship would remain intact—although I was uncertain if I would ever return. The first question Harvard asked was why I wanted to take the job. Astonished by the inquiry, I responded without reflection, "Because it will be fun." The professor seemed surprised. Then he laughed and didn't ask anything more.

Orientation was brief and provided little guidance. The club was located at the base of South Pier, one of several docking stations in Yokohama, the main port for Tokyo. I was to visit all civilian ships when they arrived. After approval from the captain, I would determine if any seamen needed medical assistance or help resolving personal problems. As it turned out, those tasks were little of what I would actually be doing.

The day I departed, the USS executive director, O. J. Hicks, shook my hand and handed me a book on the history of the United Seamen's Service together with a round-trip ticket in case I had to be rapidly repatriated or was suddenly discharged. After a two-day flight, I landed at Haneda Airport, Tokyo. There was no one to greet me. I showed a card with an address to a taxi driver. As I watched the scenery flash by, I recalled the question posed by my professor when I sought a leave of absence. I wondered if I would indeed have fun.

Growing up, I had few toys. There were no stuffed animals in my bed. Railroad trains took up too much space. A dog that made a mess barely stayed a month. If I could now create an adult fantasy world, an imaginary warehouse full of pleasures that were mine alone, I would name it the Yokohama Seamen's Club—a 600-square-foot space in a one-story building just beyond a gift shop and a money exchange counter. Entering the club, I spotted an elegant bar, an open kitchen, and a large dining area seating around 100, edged by a good-sized bandstand. I dropped my bags and stood silent. A waiter approached and asked if he could help. When he learned who I was, he signaled the members of the staff, who rushed over and bowed in welcome. I imitated their movement by bending from the waist.

Jeanne, the manager I was replacing, came forward from the rear with an apology. She thought I was arriving the next day. A tall, plain woman in her late forties, she had run the club for two years. After introducing key employees, Jeanne took me on a tour. Beyond the nightclub area was a barbershop, pool tables, and a library. My bedroom was in a separate area with a rear door for access when the club was closed, which was not often because the club was open from eight in the morning until ten at night, seven days a week. As she was only staying a few more days, Jeanne wanted me to meet a former manager who had married a Japanese woman and continued to live in Yokohama since 1945, when the war ended. He could help, Jeanne said, especially with Japanese officials. Warmly received by the ex-manager, I was served the first of many teas, not yet realizing the offering was the required greeting for a guest. As my host placed the teacup on a small table, he turned it in a half-circle. I asked him why. The motif on the cup, he explained, was to face toward the guest. This was a country with customs I would come to relish.

That first night I had dinner in the club with Jeanne. The menu featured American-style food, which was quite good. Jeanne, noticing my surprise that no other tables were occupied, told me that on evenings with few ships in port, there were not many customers. But usually, seamen came in spurts throughout the day, some to change money or buy gifts. A band played five nights a week, even with the dance floor empty. Other than a few hostesses, Japanese women were not allowed in the club, not even if accompanied by seamen. There were too many whores around, Jeanne said. She did not want them on the premises. I immediately understood why the club felt dead. Why would seamen frequent a place if there were no girls?

After our dinner, the hostesses arrived, seven of them, all well dressed in Western clothes, slim and lovely, ranging in age from mid to late twenties. They walked gracefully in tiny steps as if still bound by kimono robes they had worn as youngsters. Jeanne introduced me as her replacement and slipped off to her room. As no customers were in the club, I sat with them and chatted. They all spoke English well and were willing to share their histories with me. None had been to college, which was not surprising in Japan's male-dominated society. Waseda University, considered the equivalent of Harvard and known for its elite student body, only began accepting a trickle of females in 1939.

Several of the hostesses were not Yokohama natives. They had come to the city when the war ended to find jobs that no longer existed in their small towns. Surprised to learn I had been a Harvard student, they were curious why I had agreed to manage a seaman's club and seemed eager to guide me into that role. In response to my questions, they explained why they came to the club. There were few places for single women to go in the evenings. The jazz was good. When seamen came to talk and dine, they could practice their English, although conversations were repetitive and banal. Few foreigners had seemed as interested in their lives and aspirations as I appeared to be. By the end of the evening, I knew the names of each. Toward ten that evening, Jeanne returned and advised me that I had to drive the young ladies home. That was standard practice, she said, to prevent the hostesses from commingling with the men. I later learned that Jeanme had an assistant who had been entrusted with that task, but he had left.

Given the keys to a minibus with a stick shift and reminded that cars in Japan drove on the left side of the road, I hoped I would not get lost. I carried a map that marked the streets so I could plot my route and my return. The women helped to guide me, and I dropped them off one by one. At the last address I walked the hostess to her door. As I said goodnight and turned toward the minibus, she held my arm and beckoned me to enter. It was my first time in a tatami room. I took off my shoes, relieved I had no holes in my socks. She made tea. We sipped and talked. I had no idea of what would happen or how I should take my leave. Without a word, as if it was normal, and unaware of my high anxiety, she removed her clothes. I managed to do the same. We eased onto the futon, and sex came so naturally that I wondered if I was still a novice. I found my way around her limbs, her modest breasts filling my mouth. Our every embrace was passionate and tender. Before dawn I returned to the club, marveling at my first day in Japan.

I spent the next day meeting members of the staff. They numbered around thirty. All were friendly, and almost everyone seemed relieved at the change in management. Only one, from the accounting department, was determined to scowl and make a show of resentment about my arrival. I wondered if he had been a soldier in the war or perhaps was just annoyed that he had to report to someone so young.

I began to reflect on my views of postwar Japan and its accountability for wartime conduct, especially in contrast to the emotions stirred by German crimes. The culpability for death and devastation caused by both countries ranked just about the same; so why was it that I felt no animosity when I walked the streets and said, "おはようございます"—*Ohayō Gozaimasu*, good morning—to passersby, while ten years later in Berlin, the sense of being surrounded by former Nazis filled me with dread? In part, the explanation lies with my Jewish heritage. Images of camps and the scenes detailed in the Nuremberg Trials still disturbed me. And although the Japanese herded Jews into Shanghai ghettos and sometimes imprisoned or killed them, their admiration for the Jewish people restrained them from acceding to German demands to extinguish a community with roots that reached back centuries. The Japanese also allowed refugees to transit elsewhere if the price was right. Finally, the postwar Tokyo Trials were downplayed by General Douglas MacArthur, the American in charge of postwar Japan. He had a Korean War to fight and needed Japan as an ally.

After President Truman fired MacArthur in 1951, the general spoke about the difference between the two former enemies. The Germans had pursued the war in a deliberate manner, he told the Senate, while the Japanese soldiers, acting more like twelve-year-olds, merely stumbled into the conflict. (Even the Japanese were astonished by his remarks.) While American soldiers suffered from Japanese mistreatment, Asians had endured much more. One and a half million Filipinos died, not to mention countless Chinese. Still, punishing those deemed responsible for the war and the atrocities that took place played a lesser part in the Western quest for a postwar reckoning. The desire for retribution was also mitigated by the photos of the disfigured men, women, and children who survived the atomic bombs dropped on Hiroshima and Nagasaki.

As I dined with Jeanne that second evening, she posed a question I hoped would not be raised. She wanted to know my age. As soon as I responded, her face hardened. "Why," she said, "I'm old enough to be your mo—," stopping mid-word. I understood Jeanne's offended feelings at being replaced by someone seemingly too young to direct a facility of size. Our briefing sessions had come to an end. I was on my own.

Again, I drove the hostesses home that evening. There were only six. The woman I had slept with did not appear, which was disappointing as I looked forward to another night with her. Courteously, I walked the last hostess to her door. She held it open. I removed my shoes, this time more easily, because I wore loafers, just in case. I can't say it was the same as the night before, but our embraces were still passionate. I suspected, however, that she would no longer come for the nightly jazz. Within ten days, the hostess program no longer existed.

Jeanne was gone. She left no good wishes. Entering the club from the rear bedroom on my first day in charge, I stopped to survey the premises. The pool table stood ready, breakfast odors were already in the air, a barber stood holding a straight razor pointing to a chair being readied for my morning shave. Did I dare allow the blade to scrape my neck? With ceiling fans turning slowly above, a few tables were being set with cutlery. The atmosphere felt tropical, reminiscent of a period from the distant past. Several waiters stood at attention, awaiting my command. The setting—seedy, or perhaps just well worn—suited a club the morning after. My first reaction: "This is absurd." I could issue orders or give instructions, and my untested phrases would be carried out. A few seamen wandered in and extended a welcome. They ordered lobster or steak—bedtime meals after a long night out. I waited for my bacon and eggs, not yet aware that my breakfast, prepared from hogs and chicken fed on fish meal, would soon fill the entire space with a distinctive odor.

Mountains and hills had been achieved together, as had my childhood fantasy of existing just for the day without a goal beyond nightfall. The image in my coffee cup was of Rick Blaine. I was in my imaginary Casablanca—ready to deal with anything that came my way.

After breakfast I approved the day's menu. With a list of ship arrivals in hand, I drove out to visit several piers. As I expected, there was little interest in my offered assistance. Only seamen on foreign vessels, notably the Dutch, were welcoming, and I often stayed with them for lunch and conversation. Their service on their flag vessels, unlike American ships, meant they were away from their countries for three years or more.

With the band playing to an empty floor, evenings at the club were not welcoming. The hostesses now numbered only four, then three, then two, and finally, just one. I drove that solitary young lady home, and, as with all her colleagues, I was invited to stay for tea. I asked if there was a plot to take me to all their beds. She smiled and said that in Japan there was no shame attached to having sex. Japanese men were sometimes rough; rape was not a crime. Since I seemed so sincere and made love unrushed, more interested to explore than to insert, she too wanted to have a try. "Besides," she added, "I share body, not spirit." I wondered if my newfound promiscuity was any different from the seamen at the bar? In any event, if I was destined to be a digestive or a dessert, how could I resist? I was too immature to realize that delights eaten in youth may become addictive. And that transient relations give only transient pleasure.

When the four-to-eight evening watch ended, seamen stopped in to have a drink before departing for nocturnal spots. I would often join them at the bar, although I still did not drink. Early in my tenure I met Spike and Lee, World War II veterans. They were part of the cargo armada needed during the Korean War. Over 200 commercial vessels, all manned by the Merchant Marine, were chartered to supply the fighting forces. Even after the war ended in 1953, ships continued to shuttle between Yokohama and Korean ports. Spike and Lee were in Japan so often that they had their favorite bars and sweethearts. They didn't need to dine alone at the Seamen's Club and had no interest in a home away from home. Did I know, they asked, about the bars in Chinatown? Or the brothels in the Pleasure Quarter? I had no idea. They offered to take me on a tour after we closed at ten.

In existence for a hundred years, Yokohama's Chinatown had been officially sanctioned as a special place not long before I arrived. A Goodwill Gate welcomed us to an area composed of elaborate temples, gift shops, restaurants, and bars. Spike and Lee seemed to know all the residents and their specialties. Introduced as the new manager of the Seamen's Club, I was invited to return, all drinks free. One bar owner suggested that I rent a house inside the gates so that if a drunken seaman caused a problem, I would be close by to help. I said, "Why not?" That owner happened to have a two-story house newly vacant. I became a tenant with a six-tatami room. From time to time, a nighttime shout led me to free an impoverished seaman whose pants were held hostage by an irate madam seeking payment for a visit to a hostess.

Lee slipped away to attend to his own business. Spike and I were joined by a young Japanese man who had lived in San Francisco as a child but returned when conflict was imminent. I did not ask if he fought in the war. They briefed me on the history and geography of what was called the Pleasure Quarter. As a port, Yokohama was long accustomed to foreigners who kept the quarter full at night. My new Japanese friend suggested a dealer from whom I could buy nineteenth-century prints by Utagawa Sadahide depicting life in Yokohama.

Spike and our companion led me through narrow side streets to an area not far away where young women stood and pulled at the sleeves of men passing by. The scene was immortalized in the Japanese movie *Street of Shame,* playing at local theaters at that very moment. The film followed several women struggling to break free of poverty and to prevent sons or husbands from committing suicide due to the disgrace of unpaid debts. One of the courtesans leaves the Dreamland bar and returns home for marriage. She finds her life so restricted by a husband who treats her as a servant that she quickly resumes street life and returns to the camaraderie of her friends. That film, depicting the harshness of the sex trade, was influential in the passage of legislation outlawing prostitution, enacted the month before I landed in Japan.

The brothel owners I met on my tour, however, seemed unconcerned. "Comfort stations," as they were often called, had existed in Japan for 800 years. The Yoshiwara district in Tokyo, once surrounded by a moat, had been composed of government-licensed brothels made famous in literature and woodblock prints. Girls were trained from an early age, apprenticed, and sold for life. In 1872 all indentured contracts were voided. Prostitution may have slowed, but it always reappeared in another form. Yoshiwara was a frame of mind that would never disappear.

What I did not know—and here I may be conflating bits of conversation with later readings on the subject—was that even before the war, the Japanese military trafficked women to keep its soldiers content and ready to fight. Comfort stations were created in each country invaded by Japanese forces. After the 1945 surrender, the Japanese government, with the blessing of the Allied authorities, formed a special organization, the Recreation and Amusement Association for American and British soldiers. Over 50,000 women were called to duty to keep foreign soldiers occupied, thereby reducing the number of rapes, which were already causing outrage. As John Dower noted in his book, *Embracing Defeat,* the women's reason for participating in the Recreation and Amusement Association was partly explained by an oath they took. They swore to "defend and nurture the purity of our race . . . We are not compromising our integrity or selling our souls [. . . but, rather, we are working] to fulfill one part of our obligations and to contribute to the security of our society." Licensed brothels were established with adjoining medical examination rooms to contain the rapid increase of venereal disease. GIs were given vouchers, so intercourse was virtually free. Shamed by implicit

Fig. 4. Yokohama Seamen's Club Christmas party hosted by Stanley Cohen for mixed-heritage children of American GIs and Japanese mothers. Cohen is in the second row, second from the left.

participation, MacArthur forced a change in just a year. A decade later, when I arrived, I found many mixed-race children, outcasts from society and in need of help. With this history in mind, the brothel owners we met did not believe the local police would vigorously enforce the 1956 law.

I had witnessed pre-coital conversations between seamen and the women working at the bars, had seen their side trips to an adjacent room. I could excuse these episodes as there was laughter and singing, so it did not feel like prostitution. The women were free to decline customers, as they sometimes did. Now, with Spike as my guide, I entered a real brothel for the first time. The welcome room was stark, and the mood sullen. The women's smiles were forced, their eyes unwelcoming. Unlike James Joyce's night town, the atmosphere was businesslike. The madame urged a rapid choice as she held out an English price list for by-the-hour or all-night sexual services. Noticing my unease, Spike led me out.

He told me his favorite place was the House of Many Tongues. I was puzzled by the name. He explained that intercourse was not permitted, coitus was strictly forbidden. A client received a hot bath and a vigorous rubdown with a towel. When the client spread out like a patient etherized upon a table, two women came in carrying glasses of tepid water. On their knees, they began their work. Starting with the big toe they moved in tandem, skimming their tongues smoothly upwards, pausing only to dip them in the water until a climax relieved them of their task. I declined to enter, and Spike said good night. I hailed a taxi, proud I could now say *Minami sanbashi*—South Pier—which returned me to the club.

Thanks to the tour, I understood that the Seaman's Club would never be most seamen's first choice. I even questioned its purpose in a postwar city with its own allure. While I was not in competition with the bars and brothels, I did want to make the club more welcoming. Our food and drink didn't need changing; the entertainment had to be more appealing. I enlisted nearby universities to provide demonstrations of martial arts. I added a female singer known for current songs. And I changed the rules: although single women were still not allowed on the premises, seamen could now bring their guests.

The gift shop was convenient for changing dollars into yen, but I wanted its goods to be less touristy and more engaging, featuring presents men could bring home to their families. To search for better items, I walked the shopping streets and entered a small department store with an enticing window display. As the only

Westerner in the store, I must have looked a bit hesitant. A greeter approached me. She was wearing a kimono. Her face, startlingly white, was shaped in a manner so classic that I first thought she was wearing a mask. But when she smiled, I realized it was just luminosity that contrasted with the black hair piled high above her head in the kepatsu style featured in the prints I had recently acquired. In those prints, kimonos lay open in the back to allow the nape of the neck to be admired as Japanese men sought to do. She bowed and welcomed me in English, asking, "What is your army unit?" As there were few civilian Westerners in Yokohama, it was a natural question. I assured her I was not in the military and explained my mission.

She guided me through the counters. We spent an hour talking about merchandise that might tempt foreigners. I bought a yukata—a loose-fitting robe—to wear around my newly rented house. She asked me where I lived. "In Chinatown," I explained, although I had not yet stayed there since I was uncertain about how my rooms should be used. She offered to visit and explain the customs. I knew the risk she was running, as any Japanese woman seen with a foreigner would automatically be called a whore. Her offer meant she did not care or was sufficiently liberated to tolerate the abuse.

We met that night. She wore Western garb. Her hair was no longer piled high—it hung loose, framing her face and neck and draping halfway down her back in a style called taregami. She demonstrated the proper way to slide a door, and how to keep a futon fresh. She showed me the location of the irori, the hearth buried within the floor that was used for cooking as well as for heat blankets in the dark night air. She washed my body with a cloth. After we made love, she said she had to leave. "Must you go?" I asked. She nodded and was gone.

I knew I would not see her again. She may have had a family or a lover waiting somewhere. It was like my experiences with the hostesses—a magic moment—then a puff, as if it had never happened. This scene was to be repeated some 100 times before I left Yokohama: chance encounters at a university, a passenger who sat next to me on a train, the language teacher I hired to learn Japanese who did not return when a lesson ended with an overnight stay. For those who seek precision or just like to count, I cannot specify the exact total. The ease of this practice I did not yet realize would impede my ability to forge genuine intimacy.

Years later I met an ex-GI who remained in Japan after the surrender. He made a fortune selling encyclopedias to Japanese families seeking to learn the English language and its ways. He offered a choice of either the twenty-four-volume set of the 1946 *Encyclopedia Britannica* or the smaller twelve-volume *Book of Knowledge*. I told him about my experience. "My friend," he said, "you were just a random entry to be read. The volume was then closed and returned neatly to a shelf. Only the letter E had been opened: 'exotic' and 'experiment'—that is all you were. They had no interest in seeing you a second time. You were too young and inexperienced to grasp that women, too, have their needs . . . If you had come ten years later, you would have found fewer people speaking English, and your presence would have been totally ignored. You were there toward the end of the great displacement from the war. But Japan's economy was about to explode, as would the number of tourists coming there."

The improvements I inaugurated, together with liberalization of rule, encouraged seamen to come much more often to the club. Since I reached out to the few Westerners working at consulates and banks and invited them to a Western-style meeting place, the

Fig. 5. (***Top***) Stanley Cohen presenting an entertainment act at the Yokohama Seamen's Club.

Fig. 6. (***Bottom***) Traditional Japanese dance performance at the club.

look of gloomy emptiness that had greeted my arrival was soon transformed into one of friendly noise and camaraderie.

K came at least once a week, and we often had lunch together. He was evasive about his work. He invited me to his office and introduced me to his attractive assistant, Hinoko, one of the early female graduates of Waseda University. She kindly offered to accompany me to Tokyo to attend traditional Kabuki and Noh theatre performances. In K's office, we chatted about politics and Japan's emergence as a military power. The law permitting Japan to establish a defense organization had been in existence for only two years. As much as I enjoyed talking about current events, I was uncertain why I was there. He seemed to be testing me, but why? The explanation came as a surprise: K was a CIA operative, running the agency's office in Yokohama.

The Japanese Communist Party, outlawed before the war, had been legalized in 1945. Its initial surge in popularity had been successfully countered. The party had lost all its seats in the Diet, the bicameral legislature, yet it remained a force, as evidenced by its recent May Day demonstrations against the security treaty with the United States. Part of K's function, he said, was to monitor leftist activity. Especially troubling was the communist influence among workers at the ports. K was aware that the club I managed sponsored an annual party for Japanese shipping-industry executives and the government officials who had authority over them. Without wanting to place me in an awkward position, he asked if I would mind giving him an impression of those I met.

The club hosted an annual outdoor cocktail party in a small garden adjacent to the clubhouse building. The Mitsubishi Group provided the invitation list, which included, apart from shipping executives, the minister of transport and other government bureaucrats. In the cellar of the club, I found hundreds of miniature whiskey bottles that had been sitting there for years. Evaporation had reduced the contents, and they could no longer be sold. Drawing on my Cornell bartending experience, I mixed them, added grapefruit juice and Campari, and called the result "American punch."

The gathering was the first time I had observed Japanese men at a social function. Drink was an effective leveler. *The Japan Times,* the English-language newspaper, had recently carried a story about a train accident caused by a drunken engineer. He wasn't held responsible because being drunk was considered tantamount to temporary insanity, although that rule was later changed. My American punch was very strong. I saw my guests raise their first glass, and before it even touched their lips, several of them began to sway and slur their words. The transport minister soon collapsed and was carried off. I thought we might have a scandal, but he called me personally the following morning to tell me how much he enjoyed the party. To fulfill my patriotic duty, I reported to K the amount of alcohol each minister could consume. Only later, when I attended my first Kabuki play, did I realize that I had been witnessing a ritual, a stylized rite of men who sought temporary respite from the confines of convention. Anything they did or said was erased by evening's end. The next day in the office, it was as if they had not ventured to a gathering at the club where they consumed alcohol.

The club's staff, led by Mr. Tanaka, ordered all supplies and paid the bills. My involvement with administrative matters was minimal other than to approve a monthly report to New York. At one point early on, Tanaka-san advised me that representatives of Mitsubishi, who had arranged the outdoor cocktail party, wanted to meet directly with me. Money-exchange controls were in force, but as a foreign entity, the club automatically had a dollar allocation even though all purchases were made locally. Mitsubishi had long received our allocation in exchange for providing necessities. Its executives wanted to make sure that I would never favor one of their commercial rivals.

Tanaka-san arranged a meeting. Three gentlemen arrived shortly before noon and, of course, tea was served. The scene was awkward. I appreciated the sensitivity of their having to seek the approval of a twenty-two-year-old. Still, rituals had to be followed, a bow and an exchange of cards, then talk of subjects unrelated to the business directly at hand. In Japan, arriving at a decision should be felt without the need for a formal yes or no. I tried to avoid having a long encounter and assured them our past arrangements were satisfactory. Relaxed, they wanted to know what I, personally, expected in return. Surprised that I required nothing in exchange, they insisted on taking me to lunch at what they called a very special place. I could not decline without causing embarrassment which, as a foreigner, I could not yet distinguish from a loss of face. Besides, I had not eaten in a restaurant other than the club since my arrival.

After a drive of thirty minutes, we reached a stately inn. No other guests were there. We entered a vast private room. Cushions known as zabuton lined the tatami floor in a wide circle, large enough for fifty guests to dine. A small table with chopsticks, set on a rest called *hashioki,* was placed in front of each cushion. I was told this was a famous tempura restaurant. Most foreigners were not allowed to enter. The last *gaijin,* or foreigner, who had been invited was Charlie Chaplin, a fanatic for all forms of tempura. I had never eaten in a Japanese restaurant, and I did not know what tempura was. I just hoped there was a menu in English so I could choose from lists A and B. Instead, a small door opened at the side of an inner circle of a depressed platform five feet below where we sat. A single chef emerged and cooked our lunch. I saw every move he made. I knew this was supposed to be a rare dining treat, but did my hosts know I could only compare the quality to Schrafft's? The gentle dipping into a seasoned flour batter, then the sizzle as each piece was placed in boiling oil was an initiation into sight and sound and then taste. Carrots and greens, shrimp and mushrooms came one at a time, the chef stretching over to place his art gently on my plate. There were other foods I had never seen before. I thought it best not to ask for names. We returned to the club. I thanked my hosts. Years later, when I learned of Chaplin's final visit there in 1961, I wondered if he was told that Stanley Cohen had had lunch there five years before.

9

First Love

In my first two months at the club, I worked seven days a week. I then decided to take two- or three-day trips every other week to explore the countryside. I always traveled by myself, as I felt the Japanese would be more open and accepting of a foreigner wandering alone. Besides, I had no consistent female companion to accompany me, and if I had a Japanese woman by my side, we certainly would have been shunned. I visited well-known places such as Hakone and Kyoto, staying in traditional ryokans to enjoy a quiet that contrasted with what I left behind in Yokohama. I often selected places so far off the beaten track that most of the Japanese guests were surprised to find a Westerner in their midst. Women quickly fled the mixed-gender bath when I appeared, but I was not apprehensive steaming in the nude.

Hinoko, K's assistant, renewed her offer to introduce me to a cultural side of Tokyo I had not yet had time to explore. She suggested I start with the Kabuki theatre and then move on to Noh. I often read *The Official Guide*, published by the Ministry of Transport for foreigners like me. The Kabuki-za, the main Japanese theatre, was rebuilt after the war with seats for over 2,500 attendees. Noh, it suggested, was "too aristocratic" for common folks. Kabuki was for the popular stage. "The word *kabuki* is derived from an obsolete verb meaning 'to lose one's balance' or 'to be playful.'" It may have been started by a woman, but in its early years, there was a question of "an evil effect on public morals," meaning prostitution. Thanks to a law passed in 1629, women were no longer allowed on stage. Although that decree was relaxed 250 years later, the custom still prevailed. The theatre, Hinoko explained, was considered a family place. Before the war, cooking was allowed in the stalls, and a special section had been reserved for intermediaries to sit with couples and arrange marriages.

I did not always understand the story unfolding on the stage. The performances, combining ancient drama with traditional dance, were highly stylized, with richly decorated costumes. Some actors wore elaborate *kumadori* make-up and displayed precise gestures and grimaces perfected over the centuries. Often hours long, performances allowed the audience to wander in and out of the stalls, only to hurry back en masse when a classic scene was about to begin, so they could admire a curled lip or a raised eyebrow.

Unlike with other women I had met, my relations with Hinoko were strictly platonic. We enjoyed the theater, a noodle dinner, and a small bow goodnight. I did not ask questions about her private life. Once when we were scheduled to see a theatrical performance, I arrived early in Tokyo for a walk around Shinjuku, an area known for cinema and entertainment. A sudden but intense rainstorm prompted me to enter a movie theatre. The photos outside suggested a samurai story. As I watched its opening scenes, I was certain I had seen it before, and I knew I was witnessing a masterpiece. It reminded me of *Rashomon*, one of my favorite films. Indeed, it was by the same director, Akira Kurosawa. I was attending an opening of *Kumonosu-jo*, translated as *Throne of Blood* or *Spider Web Castle* for Westerners. It was *Macbeth* transported to Japan. I immediately walked over to the Tohu offices and asked if I could distribute the film to schools back in my country. I was asked about my experience and given a cup of tea before I was politely thanked and dispatched. The film opened in New York City some four years later. Bosley Crowther, the *New York Times* film critic, was less impressed:

> If you think it would be amusing to see "Macbeth" done in Japanese, then pop around to the Fifth Avenue Cinema and see Akira Kurosawa's "Throne of Blood." [. . .] We label it amusing because lightly is the only way to take this substantially serio-comic rendering of the story of an ambitious Scot into a form that combines characteristics of the Japanese Noh theatre and the American Western film. Probably Mr. Kurosawa, who directed the classic "Rashomon," did not intend it to be amusing for his formalistic countrymen, but its odd amalgamation of cultural contrasts with the occidental funny bone.

With all due respect to the noted critic, if he had better understood and appreciated Japanese ritual, the film would have been rightly viewed with awe, as it now is by cinephiles around the world.

***

My birthday came. I was twenty-three. I closed the club and took the staff on a picnic. I still have the photo on my desk.

When I glance at it from time to time, I wonder how these employees felt reporting to someone half their age. I suspect most understood I was acting out a fantasy, engaging with each of them as a player—or a companion—in my elaborate adventure.

As the start of the school year approached, I knew that I could no longer postpone a decision about returning. I had already received my grades. Having done well, I suspect I was just feigning

Fig. 7. Staff outing, Yokohama Seamen's Club; Cohen is seen in the second row, far right.

ambivalence. I knew that if I stayed too long, I might become addicted to the many pleasures I had come to enjoy. A note from headquarters provided a convenient rationale. Gratitude was expressed for my having improved the club's finances, but a previous manager now wanted to return to Yokohama. Would I mind transferring to Okinawa to be an assistant to the long-standing manager of that club? My staff was shocked and confided that my replacement was actually a lesbian couple not well liked by seamen. They rarely visited vessels, and attendance at the club had rapidly declined under their leadership. I sympathized, but now I had a reason to resign without any qualms about not fulfilling obligations. I exchanged my return ticket, allowing a slow voyage home, with stops in Hong Kong, Thailand, Pakistan, and France.

I began my farewells. K offered to subsidize my trip if I interviewed shipping and dock personnel along my route. I declined. Hinoko invited me to Kadohei, a soba restaurant in Yokohama. She escorted me to my house in Chinatown and said she would not leave without a cup of tea. I was surprised. Until then, there had been no physical intimacy in our relationship. As I had heard that expression—an invitation to have tea—so often, I assumed she was suggesting a sexual encounter. We removed our shoes and entered the tatami room. I stretched out on the futon and expected her to do the same, following the ritual I knew so well. Instead, she filled a kettle with water and efficiently lit the charcoal in the *irori* to prepare tea, a sort of nightcap for a well-spent evening. Ashamed of misunderstanding her intent, I sat up and took my place cross-legged on a cushion next to her.

I watched as she carefully extracted small bowls and a tin of powdered green tea from her purse. Since I had once confessed that I had never managed to attend a formal tea ceremony during my fifteen-month stay in her country, I assumed she had decided to fill that lacuna in my cultural education. She prepared what she called *chakai*, an informal version of the ceremony.

As the water in the kettle warmed, Hinoko explained the reason for her choice of tea. She sprinkled water on the charcoal to maintain a certain temperature. I followed her movements to learn how to sip and savor the flavor. She offered special sweets that she had also brought. Perhaps she also spoke about the importance of ceremony, its history and how it conveyed harmony and tranquility, but I no longer remember all that she said. When the bowls were emptied, she looked at me intently. I realized this was not merely a celebration of a tradition; it was a seduction scene from a Japanese play. Without another word, she disrobed and took my hand to lead me to the futon. She stayed the night. Our lovemaking offered unexpected comfort. Our friendship had been based solely on intellectual matters and a love of culture. Now I was with a woman who sought to share both body and spirit.

Yet I assumed Hinoko thought of me as a one-night affair since she knew I would shortly be leaving Japan. In the morning, indifferent to what others might have been thinking, I accompanied her to K's office. I assumed we would say our farewells, sealed with a long final kiss. Instead, she offered to spend the last few days with me. She even invited me to her home, a modern high-rise apartment furnished with Western rugs as a substitute for a tatami room. I was introduced to her mother. I failed to grasp the reason for the visit. But on the eve of my departure, she revealed that her parents were arranging a marriage to a man of her standing, perhaps even above her social class. She did not want to accept the marriage proposal.

"I want to go with you and move to the United States," she said, looking straight into my eyes. I was shocked and stepped back, trying to get my bearings. Had I led her on by sitting next to her at a Kabuki performance as a student seeking to understand what was being staged? Or was it because I viewed her as a friend, indifferent to her sex as we talked about books and poetry? Was this a CIA plot to prepare a cover for later use? Here was a mystery I could not fathom. I explained to Hinoko that I was too young, still a student, and poor to boot. She replied that it didn't matter; she would get a job and support us both. She held my arm so tightly that I was afraid I might not be able to escape. Absorbed in my fantasy world, and accustomed to the ease of casual sexual relations, I seemed to have lost the ability to understand the intimacy and emotional depth that others experienced.

I am not sure now how I extracted myself from that awkward and embarrassing situation. I did not let her accompany me to the airport. For months afterward, her letters full of love arrived incessantly until I begged her not to continue. I was too young to grasp that her imagined life with me would be one of adventure and constant renewals, not static and subdued, the role she knew she was destined for when absorbed into the family of her new Japanese husband.

Kundera's portrait of Tomas in *The Unbearable Lightness of Being* reminded me of this farewell: "He understood he was not born to live side by side with any woman and could be fully himself only as a bachelor. [. . .] He tried to design his life in such a way that no woman could move in with a suitcase. [. . .] Tomas would tell his mistresses that he was unable to fall asleep with anyone next to him and drive them home after midnight."

My education in the "water trade"—as the Pleasure Quarter business was called—stood me in good stead on my return trip through several countries. I arrived in Nice in mid-August. It was my first trip to France, and I was unaware that it was the national vacation period with no rooms available. I asked a taxi driver to take me to the most luxurious brothel in town. I explained to the madame that I had just arrived from Asia and needed to sleep—alone. I would pay full charge. The mirrored ceiling, the double tub, and breakfast in bed were to be the last vestiges of my fantasy life in the East before my return to Cambridge.

10

After Harvard, the Army

Another chapter had closed. Acclimation to Harvard student life was eased by a part-time job as a maid I took up to supplement my savings. I remember little about the courses I took during my last two years. More interesting was my research for Professor Lewis Sohn, an expert in international law. He was retained by the State of Texas to determine the reach of its seabed when it joined the union in 1845. Under the Submerged Lands Act of 1953, state jurisdiction over offshore oil drilling rights extended for either three miles or three marine leagues (10.35 miles). The larger limit would yield hundreds of millions of dollars to the state's coffers. Texas was contesting its maritime boundary with the federal government, and the case was to be argued in the Supreme Court. I was to report directly to the Austin lawyers representing Texas. My task was to provide evidence, through the study of diaries and historical documents, that as a republic, Texas's sovereignty had already expanded to three marine leagues by the time it entered the union in 1845.

Opening old boxes and studying fading papers so engrossed me that I often missed classes merely to read an obscure memoir, even if it had no bearing on the case. The Supreme Court eventually ruled that Texas—unlike Louisiana, Mississippi, and Alabama—had provided historical evidence that its boundary was indeed three leagues when admitted to the union. Sohn encouraged me to accept a position as a lawyer in the State Department when I graduated. His reference letter, although flattering, contained a warning that I ignored: that I should be given disparate tasks as my attention span was short. I declined the offer when it came.

After graduation, I served six months in the Army undergoing required basic training. I reported to Fort Dix in New Jersey and stood in line side by side with fifty men in civilian clothes awaiting instructions. I was older than most. The barely eighteen-year-old standing next to me had a nervous tic. Every ten or fifteen seconds, he lowered his head and spit on the ground. Spitter became his name. We stood at attention while task-master sergeants strolled the field. New to my fellow inductees and to me were the names printed visibly on every breast pocket. Thus we quickly knew the national origin or cultural heritage of the soldiers as they walked past. When you have your name pinned on your shirt, you forget how prominently it is displayed. After about forty minutes, our group started to exhibit some restlessness. As the master sergeant strutted past, Spitter yelled out, "Hey, O'Brien!" The sergeant stopped and approached him, "You know me, kid?" Spitter responded, "Yeah, you're O'Brien." And then they engaged in a friendly conversation. O'Brien had been stationed in South Boston, not too far from where Spitter lived. They shared stories of the bars they had both frequented. O'Brien took his leave, telling my companion, "Look me up if you have any problems."

All eyes turned toward Spitter as if we had received a military command to turn our heads. A long pause ensued. He finally spit on the ground and said, for all to hear, "Never saw that guy before." Spitter had taught me all I needed to know in order to have a successful army career.

We next entered a reception center. I told the sergeant in command that I had a bad back but had forgotten to bring my brace.

He promptly gave me a two-day pass, and I returned home to the Bronx. When I next reported to the reception center, there was a different non-commissioned officer in charge. He saw my school record and asked me if I knew the governor, as he needed help to obtain a visa for his German mother-in-law. I agreed to help and received another two-day pass to go home for my back brace. My mother was confused.

When I finally appeared for processing, I was assigned to a unit of fresh recruits just out of high school who had signed up for a three-year hitch. I soon began acting as a foster parent to them, writing letters home when asked. I enjoyed the daily exercise, the rifle training, and the marches in the field. But halfway through basic training, one morning I woke up feeling ornery. I decided I needed a day off. Wearing my dress uniform, I went to see the sergeant of our regiment. I calmly advised him that the commanding general wanted me to spend the day working closely with him. He shrugged. What else could he do? I took the bus into New York City and stopped at the USO, the non-profit entity whose function was to help members of the service, just as I had helped civilian seamen in Japan. I was given a ticket to the Metropolitan Opera, then on 39th and Broadway. I was delighted because I had never seen an opera. I watched the *Abduction of the Seraglio* from a box all to myself.

When the performance ended, it was late, so I hurried to the Port Authority for a bus to return to the base. I reached into my pocket to buy a ticket and realized I had no money left. It was then that it struck me—I had been AWOL, and punishment was certainly in order. At that moment, I was approached by an anxious-looking Military Police. "Soldier, are you from Fort Dix?" he asked. When I said yes, he thanked God. He had to drive there and did not like to do so in the dark by himself.

I crawled unnoticed into my bunk. The regimental sergeant asked no questions, but I did pose one to myself: What was I doing? Risking so much for momentary pleasure made little sense. Yet that same impetuous streak would reemerge at unexpected moments throughout my life.

After completing basic training and being released from the Army, I remained in the Reserve for a few years. I also began looking for a job. Despite my law degree and prestigious Harvard credentials, I was uncertain whether I should seek employment with a law firm. Law-school courses do not convey what practice entails. Many of my classmates seemed to know they wanted to work in litigation or in government, help the indigent or advise the wealthy. I just wanted to earn enough to rent an apartment in Manhattan, so I could leave the Bronx apartment I still shared with my mother.

Employment opportunities for newly graduated lawyers were scarce since a recession was underway. I floated my CV to a number of firms, but I received few replies. Cravath, Swain & Moore—a leader in the field—interviewed me twice. The hiring partner, who favored me, spoke off the record and asked if I understood that it was unlikely I would ever become a partner, since that position was already filled. I was then led into a small office and introduced to the partner, whose label, as it were, was "a Jew." A few weeks later, he died in a plane crash. His obituary made no mention of his role in the firm. I wondered who was next in line? I never returned for a follow-up. I absorbed two lessons from this experience: in my naivety, I had not known there were Jewish and WASP firms; nor did I realize that I was supposed to have a goal—to become a partner. What, I wondered, did that even mean?

Another firm showed interest: Strasser, Spiegelberg, Fried & Frank. I assumed a Cohen would fit right in, and I was close to receiving an offer. My interviews went well, and the starting salary was fixed at $7,500. The final step was approval from a senior partner, Hans Frank. He stepped into the room; I expected a handshake and a simple "Welcome to the firm." Instead, he quickly read my résumé, which prominently noted my stint as a manager of a seaman's club in Yokohama, glanced at me once or twice, and said to the partner who had guided me through the interviews, "He does not belong here. He is unstable," before leaving the room. The partner merely shrugged and wished me luck.

I was so depressed that I had lunch at Schrafft's to cheer myself up. I studied my résumé to make sure I had not included the House of Many Tongues as a reference. After lunch, while loitering the streets, I bumped into Ruth and Martin Ginsburg. I knew them both from Cornell. Our relationship was cordial, but not yet intimate. I had often encountered them walking on the campus. They always seem to be together, almost a single unit, smiling and upbeat with an air of newlyweds. I explained my situation, and Ruth laughed—as a woman, she had had even more rejections than I. She was just starting as a clerk for Judge Edmund L. Palmieri of the District Court for the Southern District of New York.

Marty invited me to his office at 60 East 42nd Street, where he worked at the firm of Weil, Gotshal & Manges. I was swiftly interviewed; only the starting salary was in question. The firm had never paid more than $5,000 as a starting salary. Although I desperately need a job, I insisted on $7,500, citing Cravath and Strasser. They agreed, and a partner brought me to his office. With that starting salary, he explained, there was only one thing expected of me: "to produce."

I left his office. The hall was painted an awful green, the shade identical to the elevators in Parkchester that I was seeking to leave behind. There were no photos or artwork on the walls. The memory of the childhood hotel room with its odor and ominous wallpaper returned. "Produce? Produce what?" I was sure I had made a terrible mistake.

Starting attorneys were like stokers at the ready; our billable hours, like shovels of coal, fueled the firm's profits. Each shovelful for a client increased the margin for the partners. I was beginning to sense that this was not a profession that fit my mind.

Two superb attorneys, Gabriel Kaslow and Ira Millstein, made the most use of my time. Acting as mentors, these two partners, despite our difference in age, became companions with whom I shared dinners and who embraced me as if I were a family member. I had little sense of hierarchy. Within a short period, I was on a fast track to becoming a partner. The more obvious that outcome seemed, the greater the despondency I felt. I had always resisted the finality of "becoming" anything. A partnership meant I would be doing pretty much the same at sixty as at twenty-six. The only difference would be the amount of money I would be earning. That thought brought despair.

Millstein once asked me to write a testimony to be given to a Congressional committee by the head of the National Retail Merchants Association as to why retail stores should be exempt from the minimum wage. The night before the scheduled appointment with the client, Millstein called me into his office to ask for the draft. I told him I could not write it since I thought the minimum wage should apply. He simply said, "Fine, tell the client," and left. He knew how I would spend the night. The client arrived at 9 a.m., as did Millstein. He found handwritten yellow pages on his desk. Even though he had not looked over my text, Millstein told the client that since the testimony was verbal, it would be read out loud so the client could judge how it sounded. Millstein read it, and the client was satisfied. After the client left, Millstein threw the pages at me. While I was pleased that he had trusted me with this work, I was also unhappy that I was participating in an exercise in which I did not believe.

Kaslow was of an older generation, dignified and precise in his speech. Sometimes he would get annoyed at a client and raise his voice a few decibels. Quite early on in our relationship, I attended meetings with him and one of his clients, Congress Factors, a company lending funds to small businesses. A young son-in-law of the founder had become president. Kaslow became irate about how he had handled a transaction. He berated the young man with such rude terms that I was astonished. I later called the client and requested a meeting to explain that Kaslow was often abrupt and that he should not take offense. It never occurred to me that it was not the prerogative of a lawyer who had been at the firm only three months to take such an initiative. Kaslow never told me if he learned what I had done, but he always treated me as a son.

The attorney I most admired was Marty Ginsburg, whose expertise was taxation. Although my work at the firm rarely coincided with his, he often gave me his tax memos to read. He injected both humor and a commitment to social justice into his scholarly letters to clients. I learned that the tax code of a nation reflected its values and its goals for equality. Although he left Weil Gotshal during my second year as an associate, we remained in contact. Having tea one afternoon with Ruth and Marty, I was astonished when their daughter Jane, then about ten years old, narrated a condensed summary of a dozen operas to me and appraised the main arias. I had the same feeling as when I had tea at the Nabokovs—that of being a guest in an intellectual milieu beyond my grade.

Doubts about my chosen profession persisted, but I could not conjure up an alternative. An artist friend, Harold Jacobs, had received a Fulbright scholarship to France. Before his departure, he hosted a farewell dinner in a Greenwich Village cafe where a *Daily News* headline caught my attention. President Kennedy had been calling up reserves to counter Nikita Khruschev's sealing of Berlin, and my Army Reserve unit was being placed on full alert. Full alert meant meetings every Wednesday evening and every weekend. I had already experienced the useless monotony of those meetings. Since I had chosen to serve only six months of active duty, I was obligated to do reserve duties for five and a half years. That meant one weekend per month, eight hours per day, sitting on a bench in a school gym reading instructions about how to be a stretcher-bearer for my field-hospital unit in which every officer was a dentist.

After nine months of lost weekends, I had told the commanding officer that I could not attend because of my law firm duties. I had also complained that the meetings were a waste of time. He initially threatened me with a court-martial, but when I replied, "So be it," he realized the effort to do so would result in long, complex procedures. Instead, I was granted three months' leave, provided I attend the annual two-week summer training camp at Fort Dix. Instead of taking the required military bus, I drove my new second-hand car to report at Fort Dix. As I emerged from the car, I saw the commanding officer sprinting toward me. I thought I was about to suffer some severe punishment. "Cohen, Cohen," he yelled, "we have been ordered to spend the two weeks in the field rather than the barracks." I wondered why he was giving me this news. "We are dentists," he added, "and you are a Harvard man. You must help organize our unit for this situation." He was asking me to take charge. "Oh my God," I thought, "I'm an adult. Someone is finally taking me for a serious person."

But now, with my unit placed on full alert for the Berlin crisis, I assumed I could no longer charm my way out of attending the required meetings, now increased to twenty hours per week. That reality did not fit my mind. I decided to go and meet Harold in France. He and his guests at the cafe laughed when I revealed my plan, but I was serious. I had the same perverse feeling that had led me to take a day's leave from basic training. By going overseas, I would still be subject to military service, but only if there was a general mobilization.

On Monday morning I entered Ira Millstein's office. He did not look up. Studying a memo, he raised his arm to signal I should go away. Instead, I asked him, "Why don't I go to Paris and open an office for the firm?" He did not let me down. Waving again, he responded, "Go to Paris if you want, but get out of my office. I'm busy." I informed most partners that Ira wanted me to go to Paris to open an office for the firm. Was I a Felix Krull?

I then headed to Kaslow's office and confessed everything, including my hesitancy about my choice of the legal profession. He did not say a word; instead, he reached into his pocket and handed me a credit card. Then he went back to studying papers on his desk. That afternoon I purchased a one-way ticket to Paris for Saturday. I had five days to wait, wondering if any partners would protest.

On Thursday, the firm's partners, in disbelief, received memos allocating my work, and a meeting was convened that evening. I was never told in detail what had occurred, only that the debate was less than cordial. I later learned that Sylvan Gotshal, the senior partner and founder of the firm, had taken the matter in hand.

I had had little direct contact with him during the year I was with the firm, other than research I did for an article he published on the European Common Market. I was unaware that he was a Francophile and a recipient of the Legion of Honor. He was pleased at the prospect of having a gofer in Paris, so long as it did not cost too much. I assumed he silenced those who opposed my plan, perhaps with Kaslow's support.

On Friday, my last day in the office, a colleague came to say goodbye. He warned me, "If you go to Paris, you will never be a partner." I gave him the same look I had bestowed on the Harvard professor who approved my leave of absence to run a nightclub in Yokohama. Equating a trip to Paris with a partnership? He must be mad. No one told me I should stay; no one told me I was good to go. Yet, deep within, I understood my Paris trip as another escape—akin to leaving the Bronx when I first decided to go to sea.

11
Learning Paris

I arrived in Paris on Sunday, October 22, 1961. Harold's ship had landed a few days before. He received my cable and welcomed me before he left Paris for a painting tour. He had arranged a hotel for me on the Rue de Seine. It had no toilet. I missed the brothel room in Nice.

The Bronx was far behind, Japan just a faded memory. No office yet existed, and I did not speak French. I hoped my salary would be paid. I walked the streets, not knowing what else to do. When a period ends, it takes some time to know that it's truly dead. I was alone, uncertain what activity should fill my days, other than to sit in cafes and watch passersby.

Lives are intertwined with schedules not of our making. Secondary schools are generally nine to three. In college, we select our courses and enter the time on a pad, so we don't forget to attend. Chosen professions or occupations come with hours normal to the field. Balustrades abound, so we don't stray too far when walking on a path. In Paris, I was adrift; no schedules existed other than those within my head. Even with ample time to transform mountains into hills, I felt uneasy with the absence of any restraint on how I spent the day. My departure for Paris was no different from the childish audacity Conrad deemed a sin. Although I did not yet know the term, I had become a *flâneur*, a wandering observer without a precise goal. "To be away from home," wrote Charles Baudelaire as he described the perfect *flâneur*, is "to feel oneself everywhere at home; to see the world, to be at the center of the world, and yet to remain hidden from the world—impartial natures which the tongue can but clumsily define. The spectator is a prince who everywhere rejoices in his incognito."

I changed hotels to have a toilet in my room and to be close to the Alliance Française, so I could walk to my French language class each morning. My teacher, Nadine, pert and seemingly sweet, asked each student why they were studying French. When I responded that my goal was to open a law office in Paris, she thought I was mad. Yet, she agreed to give me private lessons and guide me into French culture, as she saw I was in an unfinished state, in need of shaping. Intimidated by her knowledge and dispassionate manner, I realized that neither my experience in Japan nor in New York was of much use in relating to this new and not-yet-comprehensible force. French women walked quickly; they were elegant, if not exactly graceful. Their movements reflected an attitude entirely foreign to Japan: each woman held strong opinions and expressed them freely, whether asked or not.

Nadine immediately took charge. Viewing films was central to my introduction to France. Art was cinema. And cinema reflected life; happy endings were not obligatory. We saw *Cleo from 5 to 7*, and she fully explained its meaning. Then, *Jules and Jim* with Jeanne Moreau, and Louis Malle's *Vie Privée* with Brigette Bardot. Little did I know that both Moreau and Malle would play a role later in my life. Nadine insisted that I buy *Pariscope* weekly and see each film a second and third time to imitate the sound of the dialogue.

As I endeavored to learn the language, I found there was so much I failed to understand in the workings of men and women on and off the screen. They seemed to be together, and then abruptly switched sides without a murmur of complaint. Sometimes the slightest gesture conveyed a truth that otherwise might be missed. One day, when Nadine and I were sitting in Le Select, a cafe halfway between the school and my hotel, she reached over and opened several buttons on my shirt. She tugged on my undershirt and said, "Never wear that again. *Jamais.*" That sudden move, simple and banal, opened an understanding of the French. I wondered, "Was I Jules? Was I Jim? And was I in a milieu beyond my capacity to handle? Would she drive me off a bridge as Moreau did to Jim?" She suggested that my passivity and aloofness made me attractive to women, but that eventually this would be difficult to sustain. This was not a New York conversation. I was surprised by her frankness, combined with an intimacy apparent in the subtitles of the French films we saw together. When I no longer had novelty to offer, or perhaps became a bore, Nadine's lessons in language and *moeurs* came to a sudden end.

With few matters to occupy my time, I explored the city, especially the Montparnasse neighborhood near my hotel. A walking pattern quickly became an ingrained habit. From Boulevard Raspail I wandered to the Luxembourg Gardens and then to Rue de la Huchette to have lunch at an inexpensive student restaurant. I returned to Montparnasse to decide whether to have a coffee at the Dôme, or Select, or the Rotonde. Select was less elegant than the others, but it was my preferred viewing place. Its squat toilets appealed to me; somehow the successful bending from the waist and my striving to avoid wetting my pants made me feel Parisian. Twenty years later, when the squats were replaced with modern toilets, I knew it was time to leave the country.

On Sundays, my customary stroll was altered. Breakfast at the Place Contrescarpe cafe, where Hemingway had sat and drank, was followed by a slow walk along rue Mouffetard, the oldest street market in Paris, to hear the shopkeepers cry and to admire the care with which the French selected fruit and vegetables. When the stalls closed, the music faded, and the crowds dispersed, it was time to stroll to Boulevard Saint-Germain to sit on the terrace of Café Flore. Was I in Paris or just in a dreamlike state, inhabiting a world I just imagined?

These early days of Parisian life were solitary, and I sometimes felt ill at ease when I should have been elated. Had I not succeeded in fulfilling my childhood dreams? The problem was that I had few people with whom I could share my day. Comfortable when introduced, I had no talent to mingle in a group or to start a conversation in a sidewalk cafe. I can't say I was lonely; my days seemed full. Besides the walks, I discovered museums and the guinguettes along the Marne. Everything was new. Oysters being opened in an outdoor stand—what were they? What was their taste? It would be years before, aided by champagne, I allowed the chill to touch my throat.

Ever since I finished school, my days had had a routine set by others. First, during my brief Army stint, then as a working lawyer—ten-hour days and weekends at the partner's home. Now with unallocated time, I had to learn what leisure meant.

12

Lawyering in France

Sylvan Gotshal came to the rescue. He sent me the first client, Frank Strawbridge, the chairman of a Philadelphia department store bearing his name, who had come to Paris to sell a building. He asked for an appointment. I discouraged him from meeting at our office, which only existed in my second-rate hotel room. Instead, the rendezvous was set at Lazard Frères, the firm hired to handle the transaction. Strawbridge wanted me to act as an interpreter. Needless to say, it was such a disaster that Strawbridge, in thanking me, asked if we had sold that building or bought another.

Gotshal also arranged the use of a temporary office on the premises of an attorney on Place Vendome. I walked there every morning, arriving sharply at nine, although there was no reason to be prompt. En route, I had a croissant and café au lait. I did not wear an undershirt to prove I was now a resident in France. Just to walk through the Place Vendome with its Napoleon column, the Hotel Ritz, and boutiques conveyed the feel of French grandeur. I felt important when I received a concierge salute. A male secretary, Stuart Bell, was available part-time. He was English and had come to France to harvest grapes in the Bordeaux region. A miner's son from County Durham, with little formal college training, Stuart took dictation rapidly in a handwriting so small I needed a magnifying glass to recall my words. Having underestimated his ability, it took me a few days to realize he was smarter and more knowledgeable than I was. "Have you registered at the American embassy as a lawyer?" he asked me. I had not. Did I know, he inquired, that unlike most countries in Europe, France allowed foreigners to practice law? I did not. I had opted to come to France simply because my friend Harold had a fellowship here. I was fortunate that he had not received a Fulbright to Poland.

Stuart told me that practicing law was divided into two parts: *avocat à la cour* or members of the bar, who required French nationality, and *conseil juridique*, who could not plead in court but gave advice. I was, Stuart explained, a *conseil juridique* since anyone, citizen or not, had the right to counsel others; even a law degree was not required. In the next few months, Stuart imparted enough information for me to function as if I knew what I was doing. And I, in turn, urged him to read for the Bar in England since a law degree was not a prerequisite. Years later, with ten books to his credit, a "Sir" added to his name, and occupying a prominent place in Parliament as a Labour MP, he invited me for lunch at the Members' Dining Room at the House of Commons.

13
Villa Seurat

With few matters to occupy my time, I continued to explore the city. I knew the 13th and 14th arrondissements so well that when I received a call from Mr. Gotshal charging me to find a tenant for a client's home in that area, I could assure him I was familiar with the quartier. As soon as I procured the key, I walked the mile to the address: 1 Villa Seurat. It was the first house on a dead-end street. I decided to move in, even though the rent was above my budget. I was indifferent to its emptiness, the cement floors painted red, the kitchen non-existent, and the coal furnace temperamental. The ground floor contained a small room for an office or a bedroom, if one did not need a toilet or a bath.

The stone stairway to the main floor, one flight up, opened into an elevated cavern, its facade composed of opaque glass plates that stretched to the ceiling some forty feet above. It was a single, uninterrupted space; no inner walls divided it into sections as most houses would. The open living room contained a stove and a tiny fridge the same age as the house, but it was otherwise devoid of furniture or fixtures—stripped, as if by a tenant anxious to depart. Another staircase led to a loggia for sleeping. The double mattress that lay idle on a platform was the only welcoming amenity. Adjacent was a bathroom in need of renovation, but adequate for my needs. From the bedroom, a small staircase led to another level with its own glass windows and a balcony. An easel in the corner and a wooden floor streaked with paint signaled its former use as an artist's studio. My uncertain wanderings in Paris were at an end; I could now devise a beginning as if I had arrived with a plan long in place.

I immediately made changes and upgrades and found nearby cafes for my morning croissant. Toward the end of my first week of residence, the telephone rang. I was quite surprised since no one knew I was there. It was a Julian Levy calling from Connecticut. He explained that he had stayed at the house a few months earlier and believed he had left some Arshile Gorky drawings there. I had no idea who Arshile Gorky was. In my elated mood, coupled with a sense of humor that often got out of hand, I responded, "You mean the children's drawings on brown paper that I used to cover closet shelves?" A brief silence ensued. "I'll be over tomorrow," he said. Before I could acknowledge that I was joking, the phone went dead. It is true I had found drawings in a closet, but had left them undisturbed. I also found numerous paintings and prints in the cellar near the furnace. These I had moved to a safer place to avoid further fading from the damp.

Julian Levy rang the bell. Before he could voice a complaint, I apologized, adding that I had not known how to reach him to retract my unfortunate remarks. Once he had the drawings in hand, he relaxed and offered to take me to tea. In the taxi he asked me if I knew Kurt Seligmann, the owner of the house. I told him no. Did I know who Arshile Gorky was? I told him no. He said, "What do you know? You are a dumb-ass lawyer from the USA. Perhaps you don't belong here."

I told him I knew how to make a depth charge. I explained Parkchester, Japan, and Harvard. When he asked me why I had come to Paris, I said the first thing that came to mind: "I'm looking for a moon-faced girl." Julian was a surrealist and understood. "Then perhaps you *do* belong here," he replied. He

Fig. 8. (*Left*) Stanley Cohen's first Paris residence, 1 Villa Seurat.

Fig. 9. (*Above*) Villa Seurat, street view.

told me that the house and the street had pedigree. Many artists lived there or stopped by to chat and drink. "Prior tenants of Kurt's house," he added, included "Dorothea Tanning, Max Ernst, Man Ray, Noguchi, and other names you would not know."

He was right.

"You are the first bourgeois resident. What do you have to say?"

I thought of Musil. "I am a man without qualities." Perhaps I might have said, "I have no goal other than to make mountains out of hills."

He suggested I walk the cobblestones of the Villa Seurat, learn who had lived there, and who lived there still. "If they ask questions, tell them I sent you to find out who you are." That was his final charge.

The taxi arrived at Rue de Rivoli. We were going to the home of Henri Cartier-Bresson. Of course, I did not know who that was. Nor did I know that Levy had arranged a groundbreaking show of Cartier-Bresson's photographic works in 1932.

Nadine's assessment had been correct: I was a blank slate. Every period in my life caused me to start from scratch. No Google or Wikipedia allowed me to pretend to have knowledge I did not possess. If I had a fast-forward button to press, I would have told Julian Levy that in 2009 I had the privilege of viewing the Gorky retrospective at the Philadelphia Museum of Art on a day that it was closed to the public. I wandered from room to room, from portraits to abstracts, hoping I might chance upon the drawings that I had given back.

By then, Levy was more than just a name to me. I knew him as a tastemaker, an "arbiter of the avant-garde." No art form was indifferent to his touch. Photography, painting, filmmaking, and performance were fashioned in his gallery and in his life. Surrealism was a point of view for him, not static but a perpetual revolution, changing with the times. He had lived in comforting circles at a time when artists and dealers were close friends, not just partners in a business venture. I would have told him that I had talked with Man Ray and had become friends with, or advisor to, Gabrièle Buffet-Picabia, Jimmy Ernst, Helmut Newton, William Klein, and Marc Riboud. Paul Strand had asked me to be his executor to aid his wife in dealing with his photographic works after his death. I still have a photo of Strand taken by Martine Franck, Cartier-Bresson's wife. I would have thanked Levy for giving Alexander Calder, whose friendship I treasured for ten years, his first New York exhibit of moving parts. Perhaps I would have cautioned him not to drink so much.

As we entered Cartier-Bresson's apartment, Levy's last remark was, "There will be others there. Just don't ask them what they do." Cartier-Bresson shook my hand. He had started with a Brownie camera, and Conrad was an influence that led him to

North Africa, as it had led me to the sea. In an interview years later, Cartier-Bresson simply said of Levy, "I owe him a great deal."

I sat by the window watching people stroll in the Tuileries, lovers holding hands. A guest sat down next to me. He asked why I was gazing so intently. I explained that I had only been in Paris for a few months. I had walked the gardens and was familiar with its parts, but this was the first time I could see the Tuileries as a whole, from the Concorde to the Louvre. I felt I had just made love to Paris and was determined not to leave. Then I found Jacques Brel, his hair patted flat, his tie askew, his *r*'s rolled, the sound so mellow. *Ne me quitte pas*. For the first time in my life, I was home.

Villa Seurat was not an ordinary dead-end street. At first glance, there seemed to be a lack of harmony as each structure was different. However, at the outset, in 1924–26, the lines were straight and clear, representing modernist design favored by André Lurçat and Auguste Perret, who built many of the Villa Seurat houses for artists of that time.

Salvador Dalí was captured by the photographer Brassaï when he lived in Villa Seurat. Ukrainian-born sculptor Chana Orloff's studio was nearby, still a place to visit. Major painters of the period—including Soutine, Modigliani, and Zadkine—were her guests. Marcel Gromaire painted at No. 3; Pierre Bertrand worked next door. Opposite was Jean Lurçat, sketching for his contemporary tapestries. The last house on the street was the residence of the sculptor Diego Giacometti, who often posed for his brother, Alberto. No. 1 was built for Frank Townsend Hutchens, an artist who died in 1937. It was then purchased by my landlord, Kurt Seligmann. Invited into the surrealist camaraderie by André Breton, Seligmann was also well known for his prints and study of magic and the occult.

Fig. 10. Kurt Seligmann painting formerly left in Stanley Cohen's residence and later returned to the artist. Works by Seligmann are held in the Museum of Modern Art. Kurt Seligmann, *Un dimanche (Jubivillad)*, 1938. Courtesy of the Seligmann Center at Vision Hudson Valley. © 2026 Vision Hudson Valley / Artists Rights Society (ARS), New York.

Attending an exhibition of his work in New York in 1939, Seligmann avoided capture by the Nazis. He never returned to Paris. He taught at Brooklyn College, wrote articles with Meyer Schapiro, and gave painting lessons to Robert Motherwell. After a long illness, he died by putting a bullet in his head, not long after I moved into Villa Seurat. Arlette, his widow, whom I visited some years later, told me that Kurt advised her never to sell the house. It had always been rented to artists and their friends. I had, as Levy had said, broken the narrative.

I settled in and hardly left the premises during my first few months. I installed a shower, and to mask the kitchen equipment, I designed an upright dining table that could be unfolded when needed for meals. Other than a built-in sitting couch attached to a wall, no other furniture disturbed the 700 square feet of open space.

My first Paris spring arrived. When spring unfolds in Paris, it overwhelms all the senses; it is more than smell or sight. It arrives so suddenly that color replaces gray, and the transformation of the city is as swift as Dorothy's arrival in Oz. There is a hint of sex, a chance encounter behind a chestnut tree. This uniqueness would cause Henry Miller to sigh: "God knows, when spring comes to Paris the humblest mortal alive must feel that he dwells in paradise." Spring in Paris signals a special regularity governing life, not unlike the reflexive pull guiding migratory birds, a pattern so consistent that it too seemed to have been ordained by God. It is the season for asperges, the season for fraises de bois, the season for the cure at Vichy, and the season for planning the sejour in the South of France, Deauville, or Biarritz.

I also had my routine. Villa Seurat Street is where I walked every day—all 150 yards of it. I had hoped to meet my neighbors, or at least to observe their studios at work. As I walked past No. 18, I thought of Henry Miller. He came to live there just as his novel, *The Tropic of Cancer*, was published in 1934. I was not familiar with the book, so I hurried to buy a copy. George Whitman, the owner of Mistral, soon to become Shakespeare & Company, a bookstore I already knew and where many expatriates hung out, remarked, teasingly, that I was a year too late. The book had been removed from the obscene censorship list. Whitman told me I should not read Miller without George Orwell's essay "Inside the Whale" at my side. He added that I should know Miller's influence on Anaïs Nin and Lawrence Durrell and their influence on him. They attempted to create a literary movement, sometimes dubbed the Villa Seurat Group. All three had collaborated to have their books published about the same time by Jack Kahane and the Obelisk Press. They likewise appropriated *The Booster*, a country club newsletter that they converted into a short-lived avant-garde publication with contributions from Dylan Thomas and William Saroyan, as well as excerpts to promote their own work.

As I still had only a modest amount of legal work to occupy my day, I carried the *Tropic* and a small stool to sit in front of No. 18, Miller's ex-home, to read random excerpts from the book and feel the atmosphere in Paris the year that I was born. It now seems a childish gesture. What was I trying to prove? That I was worthy of being a resident of the *rue*? My usual time was late morning after a coffee at the Cafe Zeyer, where Miller had done the same. I chose that time as New York City had not yet opened for business, and I would not miss a call that rarely came.

The foreword of *Tropic* was written by Anaïs Nin. She was Miller's lover, muse, editor, and financial backer when he was broke. It was unlikely the book would ever have appeared without her cutting excess words, financing its publication, and smoothing relations with Maurice Girodias. Nin sought to escape the comfort of a bourgeois life. "I want an adventure so much," she wrote in her diary at age seventeen, "something grand, something sublime!" And Miller filled the void. He became a lens screwed into her head. She saw scenes of Paris that had escaped her view:

> I walked through the streets which Henry taught me to love. Water is being thrown on the sidewalks and swept by an old man with a broom. Dirt is floating down the gutter, windows are being opened, meat hung on hooks, vegetables poured in baskets for display, wheels are rolling, bread is baking, children are skipping rope, dogs are carrying the weight of downtrodden tails, cats are licking off bistro sawdust, wine bottles are being carried up from the cellar. I love the streets.

Miller lacked a filter to screen thought, tongue, and type. Words came rushing out like a faucet left open. Charismatic and energetic, he charmed most who gave him shelter and seemed unconcerned as to the conditions in which he lived. Freed from restraints imposed by culture, Miller encouraged Durrell and other writers to roam in a world whose language they might not otherwise have adopted as their own.

Miller did not mention Villa Seurat by name. He left that to Nin's diaries published over the years. "I began to explore Villa Seurat," she wrote.

> It is a charming street. The houses are all small, and in various colors of stucco. Most of them have studio windows. The street is cobblestone and as the sidewalk is so narrow, one often walks in the middle . . . I found a studio there for Henry. As I walk down the Villa Seurat with my red Russian dress, I feel in love with the world again, in love with the whole world.

That whole world would soon collapse into war. What troubled Orwell as he weighed Miller's talents was his egotism and his disinterest in the world, as if he were immune to coming events. He was a Jonah, passively accepting evil. "When *Tropic of Cancer* was published," Orwell was to write, "the Italians were marching into Abyssinia, and Hitler's concentration camps were already bulging. Of course, a novelist is not obliged to write directly about contemporary history, but a novelist who simply disregards the major public events of the moment is generally either a footler or a plain idiot."

As the war approached, Miller fled to safer zones. Nin's admiration began to fade. Certain elements of his writing she considered burlesque, and she balked at his single-minded view that reduced "all women to an aperture." She noted his fear of events that would trouble his private way of life: "I saw Henry trembling and groaning, although he was the only one who left Paris and had no one to worry about except himself. Cabling right and left for money to sail back to America." With Miller gone, the energy that held Nin captive waned. Even Villa Seurat seemed sad to her as she took a farewell look before leaving for the States. "Tragedy seeped into the houses, from outside. It could not be shut out any longer. Villa Seurat and other places once so illumined with life began to die under my eyes. Houses turn to corpses overnight when we cease to live and love in them."

During one of my sporadic sessions on the street with *Tropic* in my hands, I saw a female figure approaching, but the woman was not wearing a red Russian dress. She had a determined walk, neither aggressive nor indifferent, just resolute. Speaking French, she asked whether she could be of help. I told her I was a resident of the Villa Seurat and was merely reading in front of No. 18. She, too, lived on that street, just adjacent to where I sat. Switching to English with a perfect accent, she invited me to the lunch she was making for her son, as he would soon be home from school.

Her name was Riva Boren, and she was a painter. She showed me her studio and works in progress. Born in Paris, she had lived for a period in New York after the end of the war to study art, but returned to attend Académie de la Grande Chaudière, one of the more famous art schools in Paris. She offered to give me French lessons a few mornings each week for a modest sum. I began to progress, although I could never outgrow my Bronx accent. After a few weeks, she asked if I would leave my door open some evenings as she needed the warmth of a body to quiet her active nature. I was surprised, as there had never been a signal of any sort. Riva, eight years my elder, struck me as handsome rather than beautiful in a classic way. Her face was slightly sunken, giving her cheekbones an impressive prominence. Her gaze was steady and sometimes difficult to absorb. There was a touch of olive in the color of her skin.

She arrived at No. 1 a few nights later. Finding me in bed, she slipped in without a word. As I expected, there was not an ounce of excess fat, just a firmness to her body. A mole on her lower right jaw brushed my chin when she sought my mouth. When our lovemaking was complete, the sigh Riva emitted disturbed the silence of the night; it sounded like a cry for expiation or a signal of distress that I did not comprehend—at least not until I knew her story. She was not Riva Boren. Instead, she was a Borensztejn, a wearer of the yellow star, a piece of cloth that was the difference between life and death. When she no longer wore the star, she stored it in her mind and eternized it on canvas.

She had been raised in Paris by parents who had fled pogroms in the Ukraine—first to Warsaw, then Vilnius, and on to France—their lives paired with episodes of history alien to a mind like Miller's. Becoming French citizens, the Borensztejns felt safe with the birth of two children—first, a son, Bernard, and then Riva, sometimes called Rosette. The Vichy government had little sympathy for Jews, whether citizens or not, and no direct orders from

Nazis were needed for roundups day or night. Riva's father and brother were arrested in June 1942. Transported to Auschwitz, their deaths were recorded the following month. Dissatisfied with killing only males, they put females next in line. Zofia, Riva's mother, age forty-three, was seized in July 1944 as the Allies were about 100 miles from Paris. Imprisoned first in the notorious Drancy transit camp, she was one of 1,310 prisoners transported as Convoy 77, the last major death train to Auschwitz. Of them, 836 were quickly gassed, including Zofia. Such numbers conceal the anguish that arises from the loss of any one individual, the disbelief that remains when we seek to understand what happened to a lover or a father.

Fig. 11. Painting by Riva Boren, who later taught Stanley Cohen French and lived in hiding during the Nazi occupation of Paris.

Avoiding capture at age fourteen, Riva tiptoed through Paris and hid in attics and toilets until the end of the war. What were the memories that sometimes surfaced in the middle of the night? After the liberation of Paris, did she wait all day at the transit center of the Gare d'Orsay, like Marguerite Duras, checking lists of deportees? Nothing, Duras noted in her diary each day, nothing. Those waiting learned of camps that had just been freed, bodies found still warm. Then the arrival of those barely conscious who were asked: "Did you know . . . ? Were you in Belsen when 2,000 were shot as the Germans fled? Were you at Buchenwald during the last massacre?" But why ask questions of those who could hardly talk? "You couldn't say he's thin," Duras wrote, "It's something else—there's so little of him left you wonder if he's really alive."

After visiting distant relations in New York, Riva returned to Paris to study art. Jacques Lanzmann found her in the cafes of Montparnasse. "Riva, my first wife, was a beauty that all the Montparnos fought over in vain," he wrote. She was said to be inaccessible. "With her majestic demeanor, she floated her sensuality from terrace to workshop, a book or an easel under her arm. A woman she was, ample, dark with golden flecked eyes."

Jacques Lanzmann and his brother, Claude, had been part of a resistance group and were still active with the politics of the left. Jacques wrote novels and lyrics, worked in mines, walked deserts, and was well known when he fell in love with Riva. Their initial interaction was like a conversation between Bogart and Bacall, direct and no-nonsense, straight to the point. Following a dinner early in their courtship, he accompanied her to her home and did not leave for two years. To get married, he sought the approval of Jean-Paul Sartre and Simone de Beauvoir. De Beauvoir was having a long-term affair with his brother, although "affair" is not a proper description for the love that Simone felt at the age of thirty-nine. When Claude first asked her to join him to watch a film, she burst into tears. "Something, I had no doubt of it, was beginning." And when their bodies connected, "We began to build our future by telling each other the past." "I am a Jew," Claude said, "I still harbor bitterness toward the *Goyim.*" When he later made the film *Shoah*, a documentary about all those responsible for the Holocaust, she understood.

After their child was born, Riva and Jacques separated, for reasons I do not know. Their rupture was bitter since Lanzmann would later complain he rarely saw his son.

About that time, Clancy Sigal arrived in France. Self-described as a leftist charmed by violence, Sigal boasted that he went AWOL from the Army in an effort to shoot Hermann Göring at the Nuremberg Trials. Communist-leaning and blacklisted, he left the United States one step ahead of the McCarthy hearings. His autobiographical account of his drive across the country, which ended with his departure, was a well-received portrait of the Fifties. Walking the Paris streets, lonely, troubled, and ill at ease, Sigal fell in love with Riva. He claimed he was encouraged by de Beauvoir who, according to Sigal, considered Riva as her "unofficial daughter." That, however, seemed inconsistent with Jean-Paul Sartre's opinion, as he urged Sigal to abandon the affair. Riva continued on and off with Lanzmann. Sometimes Sigal would see them walking arm in arm. He could not decide whether to harbor guilt for undermining their marriage or to simply enjoy the bliss of traveling with Riva through Italy. He was fascinated by her interest in other women. As a couple, they danced in lesbian bars in which he took an almost orgiastic pleasure.

On a snowy day, he trudged through Paris with Riva as she sought documents to confirm her parents' deportation in order to obtain a governmental stipend. Thwarted by French indifference, "She burst into tears, the only time I saw her cry," wrote Sigal. The relationship faltered because he preferred demonstrations in the street, but these revived her bruised memories of the war. Sigal claimed he had to leave Paris when his visa expired, but most likely he just wanted to escape from having to decide whether he was Jules or Jim. He moved to London and became the longtime lover of the Nobel Prize winner Doris Lessing. Tormenting her with his manifold affairs and stories of Riva, who came to London for a visit, he noted in his diary, "Periods of my life every dame I meet wants to lay hands on me." Sigal contacted Riva once again when I was still in Paris. He came to the city to aid deserters fleeing the war in Vietnam. In his memoir, describing how her brown hair was now streaked with gray, he concluded: "Still the most beautiful woman in France."

I gave Riva comfort when neither Lanzmann nor Sigal could. At the beginning of our relationship, I did not know the circumstances that brought her to my bed. I was oblivious to the meaning of either the pockmarks from stray bullets on stone walls or the pockmarks that remain hidden in the minds of those who had fought or fled during the war, what Sigal termed France's black years. But as Riva slept in my bed, I thought of other women who often lay there and wondered with shame if I was growing into another Henry Miller, seeking a convenient aperture that would open and close at my command. I had as yet absorbed little about the emotions and events that formed the lives of those I was meeting.

Riva eventually went off to India and Nepal, seemingly to find refuge from memories of the past.

Assimilation, Jean Piaget claimed in his study of infants, is just the first step to accommodation, that is, the change of conduct that full understanding brings. I had not yet reached that stage. Two young women whom I had known in New York City offered to visit me in Paris, hoping for a permanent relationship. They each left, saddened as if I had misled them—and perhaps I had, not comprehending the impact of my ambivalence toward marriage and adult life and of my indifference as to who was lying next to me.

At some point during that time, a memory intruded. I recalled the phone call during my first year at Cornell when I learned that my father had died from pneumonia developed after a prostate operation. On the trip home, I was unable to recall any moments of intimacy with him, and no feelings of despair or distress washed over me as I joined my family gathered to mourn the dead. Uncles and aunts tiptoed on the shiva floor offering condolences I was forced to accept, and I realized how estranged I was from a family I felt I hardly knew. My mother was inconsolable, but I never knew if my father's death was a burden or offered her relief. I pressed her to get a job—her first—and she thrived. My only inheritance was a six-month subscription to the *Daily Worker.*

14

Making Friends with Artists and Writers

In those early years in Paris, I often hung out in cafes. I became adept at pinball machines known in France as *flippers.* Many of my new acquaintances just scraped by successfully avoiding full-time employment. Surprised to find a companion with a law degree who shared their excitement for pinball, they took to me quickly. I became popular as an easy touch, advancing funds to my growing circle of struggling friends.

One day, when I had racked up a record score, I was met with applause and an invitation to have a drink at the Rosebud. I knew I would have to pay. "What is the Rosebud?" I inquired. My newly adopted convives feigned alarm that I had not yet walked Rue Delambre just off the Boulevard du Montparnasse. The Rosebud was a bar and eating place known for its long list of cocktails, chile con carne, and the jazz records that played until 2 a.m., an unusually late closing time for a Paris eating spot. Perhaps, I was told, I might even see Jean-Paul Sartre and other notable writers. When I confessed I knew little about jazz, their incredulity knew no limit. Black jazz artists were celebrated in France, and there were more jazz boites in Paris than in all of the United States, they claimed. My companions felt obligated to further my education, first with a nightcap in the Caveau de la Huchette and then off to the Blue Note, their favorite place. If lucky, Bud Powell might play. I was silent not knowing who Bud Powell was. My escorts were welcomed as habitual customers, and I was introduced to Altevia Edwards, otherwise known as Buttercup.

Bud Powell, I learned, had a troubled life. Drugs, drink, depression, police beatings, and electroconvulsive treatments had all impacted him, but he was still a genius, as Miles Davis and other peers attested. Buttercup had become his keeper when Powell was just thirty and in danger of being certified as incompetent and of an unsound mind. The two of them moved to Paris in 1959. I soon found the Blue Note a comfortable place to spend an evening. I enjoyed watching and listening to Bud as he curled over the piano, communing with his instrument. Why Buttercup, presumably his wife, engaged me in conversation each time I came, I do not know. Perhaps I have an open face, or perhaps she knew I paid the bill for the table. Bud rarely talked; he could only speak to piano keys. Buttercup would grab his hand if he reached for an alcoholic drink.

Buttercup called me one day and asked if she could stop by Villa Seurat. She arrived carrying a cardboard box. Powell had left for New York without any notice. She wanted me to advance funds so she could fly there and bring him back; he needed her care to keep him straight. The box contained a dozen tapes of his unpublished music which she offered to leave with me as security. I advanced the funds; she repaid me months later, returning without Bud or any explanation. Until years later, when I saw the film *Round Midnight* and had dinner with the director, Bertrand Tavernier, I had no idea of what had happened. Befriended by a young jazz aficionado, Powell was led by him to New York to play final concerts in Birdland. With drink and drugs back as companions, Bud could not retain that gig. He died two years later. I never knew for sure if Buttercup was a harmful influence on Powell or had kept him alive during his Paris years.

Although there were other American lawyers with offices in Paris, I preferred to socialize with my friends from the artistic community. None would be more dear than Marc Riboud and his then-wife, Barbara Chase-Riboud. Marc was a Magnum photographer whom I met at Cartier-Bresson's apartment when I accompanied Levy there for tea. A mixture of courage and modesty, Marc traveled the world with a camera in hand. Among the events he documented were the arrival of Ayatollah Ruhollah Khomeini in Iran; the Solidarity movement in Poland; the end of apartheid in South Africa; and the mood in the United States before the election of President Obama. Not long after we met, he returned from Cuba with photographs of Fidel Castro. He had been in Havana with the French journalist Jean Daniel, who was carrying an offer to Castro from President Kennedy to begin talks to normalize relations. Kennedy was killed while Daniel was meeting with Castro. The headline of Marc's 2016 obituary in the *New York Times* read "photojournalist who found grace in the turbulent."

Barbara's talent with both pen and trowel was enough for three. She excels in writing novels and poetry, and in crafting sculpture. The first African American to have an MFA from Yale, she has been exhibited at the Whitney Museum and MoMA. She received the Carl Sandburg Award for Poetry and wrote the groundbreaking novels, *Amistad* and *Sally Hemmings*. The latter was harshly criticized for its revelations of Jefferson's relations with a slave.

Marc and Barbara were among the first to welcome me to Paris. They were, to my mind, the ideal artistic couple, a Stieglitz and O'Keeffe, each superb in non-competing forms of creativity, unlike Pollock and Krasner. With two handsome children, they seemed to embody a most charming family life. Marc claimed he was the black sheep of his distinguished Protestant family: one brother was president of Schlumberger, the offshore drilling company, and the other was president of Danone, the French multinational food company. Barbara was more astute, predicting that she and Marc would become more famous than the successful members of the Riboud family. I had underestimated the ambition, drive, and focus that artists need to excel. Their work ethic was such that Marc was hardly home; museum shows, wars, and upheavals all irresistibly summoned him. For Barbara, her Black identity posed obstacles to the success she was determined to attain.

Aware that their success and notoriety left little time for domestic life, I was nevertheless sad when asked to mediate property arrangements before their impending divorce. This was not a legal matter. As a friend I had to divide the silverware and other items. I managed to retain the friendship of both Marc and Barbara, although I later spent more time with Marc. After his death in 2016, his second wife, Catherine, asked me to join the board of the foundation to preserve Marc's works. I remain on it.

As my professional obligations slowly began to develop, a stroll along Villa Seurat no longer began my day. Although I had handled sporadic matters for clients of Weil, Gotshal & Manges, my one-man office had no commercial client that required continuous legal attention. My first such client, sent by the firm, was Associated Manufacturing Corporation (AMC), the buying office for its member department stores, and notably, for the Federated Department Stores, including Bloomingdale's. AMC had branch offices in most European countries to purchase merchandise for drop shipment to its member stores. The executive vice president, Norman Tarnoff, decided to open an office in Paris to coordinate operations.

Norman and I got along well. Indeed, as with most clients who were foreigners in Paris, we developed a close personal relationship. I often dined with him and his wife, Dorothy. Tarnoff asked me to ensure that the various AMC offices complied with local laws. In particular, I was to visit Florence, Munich, and Vienna on a rotating basis. This was a law practice I could really enjoy. This client, together with other matters, although limited in scope, generated enough income that I obtained permission to open a small office near the Champs-Élysées. I even had a part-time secretary.

A second matter sent by the firm turned out to be even more meaningful. The sculptor, Jo Davidson, had been a client. He died in 1952, leaving most of his estate in trust to his wife, Florence, who passed away ten years later. I was asked to obtain the signatures of their two sons to allow them to receive distribution of the assets. Both were living in Saché, a village in the Loire Valley halfway between Tours and Azay-le-Rideau, a three-hour drive from Paris. I called Jacques Davidson, one of the sons, to make an appointment. Extremely friendly, he gave me driving directions to the Manoir de Becheron, a house and studio bought by Jo in 1926. As it was run as a B&B, he invited me to stay the night.

A few days before I left, I had dinner with Joseph A. Barry, a foreign correspondent for the *New York Post*, married at that time to Naomi Barry, the food columnist for the *New York Herald Tribune*. I was fond of them and was often invited to their home for dinner. I welcomed our conversations because I had a lot to learn. Barry had given me his first book, *Left Bank, Right Bank: Paris and Parisians*, which proved an invaluable guide as I found my footing in the city. When I casually mentioned the planned trip to Saché, I was astonished to find that Joe knew the Manoir de Becheron quite well. It turned out that during his last year in the military, he was stationed near Paris and had become quite friendly, as did other GIs, with Gertrude Stein. Stein had spent the entire war in a nearby French village, returning to her home at 27 Rue de Fleurus when Paris was liberated in 1944. Joe not only brought her food and other items from the Army canteen but also mailed her letters and ran errands for her. Stein even introduced him to Pablo Picasso as an adopted nephew. Joe drove Stein, from time to time, to Saché to visit Jo Davidson, who had made the iconic bust of Stein as a Buddha figure. In July 1946, he was behind the wheel when pain from stomach cancer struck Stein. Joe quickly drove her to the American Hospital in Paris where she died a week later.

"Come," Joe Barry said, "I still have the key to her place." He led me to Stein's apartment where the ghosts of Picasso, Hemingway, and Fitzgerald still convened, though the walls were bare of the paintings she had collected. The atmosphere, even in the dimness of twilight, captured the aura of the great writers and artists who gathered to toast their respective triumphs with Stein as host. Years later, the image of that visit reappeared when I watched Woody Allen's *Midnight in Paris*. I was played by Owen Wilson; he was as naive and dazzled as I had been.

If I was introduced to art and surrealism through the Gorky drawings accidentally left behind in my Villa Seurat apartment, my education in the world of sculpture was furthered by the need for a signature on a legal document. When I arrived at the Manoir de Becheron, Jacques Davidson gave me a tour of the house and Jo's studio. I was greeted by Roosevelt and Eisenhower, George Bernard Shaw and D. H. Lawrence, John D. Rockefeller and Woodrow Wilson, and a hundred other masks in clay and figures carved out of stone. Even Joseph Conrad and Rudyard Kipling were there. Of course, a terracotta of Stein also resided in that

Fig. 12. Gertrude Stein (*right*) and Alice B. Toklas (*left*) in the salon of their apartment at 27 Rue de Fleurus, Paris, 1922. Photograph by Man Ray © Man Ray 2015 Trust / Artists Rights Society (ARS), NY / ADAGP, Paris 2026.

room. "That's Gertrude Stein," the writer had said when Jo Davidson had finished, "that's all of Gertrude Stein, that's all of Gertrude Stein there is." She exchanged with him a portrait she crafted into words:

> What does he say to me? He says that it is finished. And now I know that I smile. No, not if it is you who are speaking to me. [. . .] That is what I mean when I say that there are no hippodromes, no oil and clothes, no fountains, no soldiers and no swings. He has so often been seated. You know and I know.

Did I know then, did I know that Stein cast into bronze would remain permanently affixed in Bryant Park due, in part, to my effort to place her statue there?

The weekend at Becheron was charming. The welcome of Jacques and his wife Zabeth was impeccable. There was something comforting about being a guest at the dinner table, followed by walks along the river banks. I was invited back, but first I had to obtain the signature of his brother Jean, who lived in a mill on the River Indre less than a mile away.

The setting was exceptionally lovely—a tiny private island accessed by an old stone bridge. There was little land other than a mill and a miller's house. The interior of the latter was primitive compared with the furnishings and style of Becheron. The biggest contrast, however, was the greeting. It was icy. I felt like an uninvited guest. Sitting at a simple wooden table in the kitchen with Jean and his wife Sandra, together with an older couple introduced as Louisa and Sandy Calder, conversation was limited to the matter at hand. I left as soon as the document was signed, and only then did I realize I had just met the artist whose works hung

Fig. 13. Sculpture of Gertrude Stein by Jo Davidson installed behind the Stephen A. Schwarzman Building (42nd Street Library), Bryant Park, New York; installation facilitated in part by Stanley Cohen. Image courtesy of Bryant Park.

Fig. 14. William Klein, Paris, 2016; from left: Klein, restaurant owner, Cohen.

on the walls or were installed on the walkway adjacent to the bridge. I had no plan to return, believing my next visit would be limited to Jacques and his cordial reception. Little did I know that I was destined to be the owner of that tiny island known as the Moulin Vert.

I returned to Becheron several times, always welcomed and treated as a family member. The Davidsons were very social, often hosting dinner parties and gatherings in their garden. Sitting next to an attractive Belgian model, Jeanine Klein, we talked about politics, race relations in my country, and the withdrawal of French troops from Vietnam while Americans inched into the war. I accepted an invitation to visit the Paris studio of her husband, William Klein, a well-respected photographer who was working on his first film, *Qui êtes-vous, Polly Maggoo?* I attended the film's screening and accompanied Klein to its fiftieth-anniversary showing in New York City. He died in 2022.

Klein, like Barry, served in the Army and was likewise stationed in France before his discharge. The substantial GI allowance, greater than the salary of the average French worker, encouraged him to register at the Sorbonne and study painting under Fernand Léger. Although perhaps less known in the United States, Klein is considered in Europe as one of the most important photographers of the twentieth century. His images of movement and violence influenced a generation of contemporaries. The same was true of his films, most of which I watched as he edited them.

Klein's reputation as irascible and difficult was well deserved, but that may have been because he was a perfectionist when it came to showing his photographs and films. This created tensions that museum directors often asked me to unwind. As he aged, walking became difficult, but that did not deter him from flirting with the waitresses. Once in New York, I helped him from a taxi; he leaned on my shoulder to walk a few steps to the entrance of his hotel. At that moment, an attractive young woman emerged to smoke a cigarette. Bill pushed me away and straightened up to talk to her. I left without a goodnight.

Klein introduced me to Helmut Newton. Although I was not as close to him as I was with Klein, he became a friend with whom I enjoyed dinner-table talk. His wife, Alice Springs, was quiet, but her photographic work was as distinctive as his. Sometimes, Helmut would call me from a distant time zone. In the middle of an Australian shoot for *Vogue*, he wanted my advice on how to avoid paying a foreign tax on his fees. His aversion to the tax was less a response to financial distress than a result of still being a Neustadter, still in flight, though his name now was Newton. As with the GIs who sought calm in Paris or a Boren with a past,

Fig. 15. *Rue Aubriot* (*YSL + Nude*), Paris, 1975, by Helmut Newton. Print from the collection of the author. © The Helmut Newton Foundation / Trunk Archive.

a Neustadter became a Newton but could not be free of the inheritance that came with his former name. The refugee was in his heart. Days in a concentration camp after Kristallnacht, separation from his parents, an escape, first to Marseille, then to Australia to be placed in an internment camp, before becoming an army driver—these are events that were not lightly shed. If I cooked dinner when he returned, he placed an envelope rather than wine on my table.

Somehow, I had succeeded in having a lifestyle appropriate for someone who had little ambition other than to make mountains into hills. No plan, no blueprint had brought me to Paris. All that occurred seemed to be based on chance; and yet here I was, with few professional burdens, and expanding friendships with talented artists and writers whom I would never have met if I had remained in New York. Those were the days, my friend, I thought they'd never end. We'd sing and dance forever and a day. We'd live the life we choose.

15

The French

Americans, most of them untouched by war, came as tourists to enjoy Pigalle and Le Moulin Rouge, unaware of the political divisions in French culture. When I landed in Paris, socialists, communists, and Gaullists were on the street; police with guns checked identities; and rioters protested Algerian independence from France while the Fifth Republic was still in an experimental stage. I had paid little attention to this turmoil, more concerned as I was with my own tenuous existence, uncertain of how long I could remain in Paris. The very month of my arrival, hundreds of Algerians were killed by the French police; many drowned in the Seine after being thrown off bridges. This massacre, I assumed, was a one-off event, since I viewed a demonstration or a crisis in my country as a simple occurrence unrelated to any historical trend. This meant I did not think like a French person. The French are endowed with a historical memory and with a logic that groups seemingly disparate episodes into a pattern, a systemic whole.

The French may have a reputation for being unwelcoming to foreigners, but during my initial years in Paris, I was warmly received even by those to whom I was casually introduced. I was open; the Harvard pedigree helped; and it was still a period of gratitude toward Americans, despite the rhetoric of the country's president, Charles de Gaulle. A Frenchman about my age, Jean-Luc de Carbuccia, kindly invited me for dinner at his apartment on Avenue Foch in the fashionable section of Paris. That was followed by an offer of a weekend at his parents' home in Sainte-Maxime on the French Côte d'Azur. I had never been there, so I was delighted to accept.

The house was on the water, its architecture was Moroccan, and each guest room opened directly onto a fair-sized pool. The luxury of the setting contradicted the weary feel the house conveyed. It was run down, the furniture pre-war, the carpets heavily worn. Jean-Luc's father, Horace, in a wheelchair, barely nodded when I arrived. His mother, Adry, was robust and often swam in the pool; to her I did not exist. Jean-Luc seemed to disappear. Saint-Tropez was nearby, so I went out to visit the town. It was August, and the cafes were seasonably full. Although I knew only a few French people at that time, it seemed as if they were all there. Each greeted me and asked me where I was staying. When I mentioned the home of de Carbuccia, some expressed surprise. I was led to the Café Le Sénéquier for an espresso and a chat.

Horace, I was told, had been the owner of *Le Gringoire*, one of the highest-circulation newspapers before the war. Although it published both political and literary material, it became known for its antisemitic articles. Its pro-Nazi stance only hardened as the Germans began to lose the war, and it remained so until the German defeat. After years of hiding in Switzerland and Italy, Horace was tried by a military tribunal in 1955 for collaborating with the enemy. Yet, after only a few months of incarceration, he was freed under an amnesty program, his record wiped clean.

I was about to receive a French education. As an author, publisher, and intellectual, Jean-Luc's father had hosted a salon frequented by the greatest poets and writers of pre-war France. And although his stance on the war was abhorrent, his offense lay in the words he spoke and published. Intellectuals in France are generally immune from prosecution or censorship unless their conduct harms others. True, a writer, Robert Brasillach, was executed for his extreme language against the Jews; but he was regarded as just too pro-German, and his execution later caused regret.

"Have you visited Sacré-Coeur?" I was asked. "Of course." "What do you see from the church's steps?" And before I responded, the lecture continued. "You see a French contradiction if you gaze thoughtfully. You stand on Catholic orthodoxy and are confronted with modernity—a secular monument, the Eiffel Tower—challenging the *eglise* as to which will reach heaven first. The Tower, the Metro, and the 1889 World's Fair—all arrived at the same time, leading some to say it was a Jewish plot to undo France." My companion continued, "This nation is fighting the same divide that caused the French Revolution, the Dreyfus trial, and the Algerian War. We have not yet confronted, nor adequately explained, France's role in World War II and the widespread acceptance of the Vichy regime."

Jean-Luc, I was told, believed the armistice with the Germans ending French fighting in 1940 was the correct course for the nation. He excused the excesses of the Vichy government that followed, and truly believed, as many did, that the armistice saved lives even as thousands of Jews were deported to the camps by the French police. My head spun with names and conflicts I did not recognize. I had been in France for over a year, yet knew little about the country except for its oysters and wine. Despite my relationship with Riva, I was not conversant with the history of the Vichy government, and I had erroneously concluded that Jews had suffered only when France was under Nazi control. It was not until I read Robert Paxton's 1972 book, *Vichy France: Old Guard and New Order*, did I understand the full extent of French conduct under Nazi occupation.

I wondered if Jean-Luc thought it amusing to have a young Jew as his parents' guest. I returned to the de Carbuccia house, packed, and slipped out without seeing Jean-Luc to say goodbye.

16

Alexander and Louisa Calder

Jean Davidson telephoned me. Confessing he knew no other lawyer in Paris, he requested my help in arranging a demonstration against US involvement in Vietnam. The war was about to escalate. Small protests, especially among students, had touched a few campuses; draft cards had been burnt, but no major demonstrations had yet emerged in Paris. This was to be the first. Sandy and Louisa Calder were to be the main sponsors.

As with most requests for help at this early stage of my Paris life, I did not consider these inquiries to be legal matters; rather, they were stepping stones to friendships and relationships I hoped to forge. I reached out to a French lawyer, who helped me obtain a permit allowing a group to stand at the fringe of the Place de la Concorde so long as traffic was not impeded. The American Embassy, at my request, agreed to accept a petition. Writers and artists would meet the night before the demonstration to write a letter of protest. The gathering was to be held at the home of Gloria and James Jones on Île Saint-Louis. Looking forward to meeting the author of *From Here to Eternity*, I entered a smoke-filled room crowded with the expatriate community of Paris. I knew no one there apart from the Calders and the Davidsons. Gloria was in charge; Jim, a bit reticent. Maria Jolas, wearing a Calder brooch, pulled me aside to talk about a committee to stop the war. Jolas, Jean explained, was a well-known translator and publisher, responsible for bringing out James Joyce's *Finnegans*

Wake. Her pre-war literary review, *Transitions,* had provided a platform for many of the great experimental writers of that period, including Ernest Hemingway.

A debate continued for some time about the wording of the document explaining the folly of American intervention in Vietnam. Draft after draft was written, then pushed aside. A merry atmosphere was beginning to emerge, even as time was running out. While everyone else drank, I wrote the petition in longhand, and Gloria neatly typed it. As it circulated for signatures, I kept watch to ensure there were no whiskey stains.

The demonstration itself was solemn and went without a hitch. Gloria and I were delegated to knock on the embassy door and hand-deliver the petition. I thought we would be welcomed by the ambassador, Chip Bohlen. Instead, I later learned, the CIA station chief in Paris was the one to receive our document.

I thought no more about the incident until a few weeks later. Norman Tarnoff called me to his office. He wanted to know why I had led a demonstration in Paris against American policy in Vietnam. I was stunned by the question. Norman's son, Peter, was special assistant to Henry Cabot Lodge, the then ambassador to South Vietnam. A report of the petition had arrived on Peter's desk. No writer, no artist, nor Jones nor Calder, nor any of the recognized names were mentioned in the CIA report. Only Stanley Cohen, a lawyer in Paris, was cited as the leader of the protest.

I was so pleased to have my name, at last, in print, that I immediately boasted to Davidson and Calder about the outcome of our event. Because they had long dossiers with the FBI, they were quite amused. Jean then suggested I rent the islet I had briefly visited. He had just moved into a farmhouse on a hill nearby to escape the flowing water around the mill, which he and Sandra believed was a hazard for their children. I accepted without a moment's reflection, even though I had little knowledge of what the property was like. I had only spent ten hurried minutes in the kitchen of the main house.

It was 1965. And so began my relationship with Jean and Sandy, until Sandy's death in 1976 and Jean's in 1980.

The stone house, with two stories and an attic, was simple and sparsely furnished. It was filled with tiny objects—evidence of a Calder stay. The toilet seat, off balance, was held in place by his wire curl. If I failed to finish a bottle of wine, I could use a special cork to save it. Adjacent to the house was a separate stone building with remnants of a milling wheel. The only furniture was a billiard table for Jean and Sandy's daily game.

Fig. 16. Alexander Calder, wine-cork object. © 2026 Calder Foundation, New York / Artists Rights Society (ARS), New York.

I have often been introduced as Alexander Calder's lawyer. It is a label I do not like since it implies a formal and professional relationship. Our relation, instead, was one of neighbors whose friendship broadened and expanded as the years went by. I sometimes intervened for him on small matters—canceling wine subscriptions that he had been tricked into accepting, or serving as a buffer so he could avoid an interview he had too rapidly agreed to. But my role resembled that of a younger member of the family rather than that of an attorney on retainer. When he died, I was officially engaged by his family to help with matters of the estate. I then dealt with museums to house his works and created a French foundation along with a Calder Prize, so that his home and studio could remain available to artists—quietly absorbing his talent as they slept.

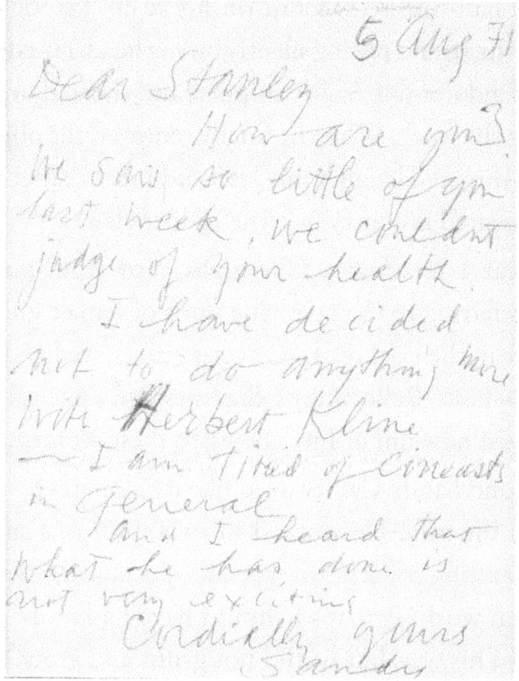

5 Aug 71

Dear Stanley

How are you?

We saw so little of you last week, we couldn't judge of your health.

I have decided not to do anything more with Herbert Kline — I am tired of cineasts in general

And I heard that what he has done is not very exciting

Cordially yours

Sandy

Fig. 17. Alexander Calder, handwritten note to Stanley Cohen. © 2026 Calder Foundation, New York / Artists Rights Society (ARS), New York.

As soon as I rented the Moulin Vert, I began spending most weekends there. I assumed, in my excitement, that tenancy meant becoming part of the Davidson/Calder families. I was fortunate they did not rebuff my walking into their homes uninvited to sit down and chat. What eased my way was a story I told Sandy about my army career. I explained that I had a very small head that tapered to a point. Only a child's hat would fit me, and that was difficult to find at Fort Dix. Whenever we were on parade, the officers assumed I was mocking them, as my hat slipped down to my ears, shielding my eyes from their gaze. I was rewarded with kitchen-police duty. Calder found that story to be his kind of humor. He led me to his small studio to test my pointy head by balancing a half-finished mobile on my scalp. I stood as still as possible, a wire strand resting silently on my head. I used one hand to ensure it did not fall. Sandy snipped and sheared other pieces to complete the work. When he finally removed the object, he let out his full-throated laugh. Only later did I realize that this small ritual had assured my entry into the Calder clan.

One year I received a Christmas card from Calder and Davidson referring to the revolving door of female guests at the mill. This year, the card read, "Of your guests, we liked numbers 6, 12, and 14 best." Reflecting on that message, I felt ashamed and wondered just how unfair I was being to these women.

Louisa and Sandy Calder lived like troglodytes in a cave just adjacent to the mill. He worked in two studios, a small stone house for painting gouache on special paper, and a modest atelier for his metal work. Perhaps I should have had more sense and stayed out of his way, but he did not grunt and growl as was his habit when displeased. A work of art lay complete in a crevice of his mind. No gesture was wasted as he fashioned a mobile that fit that vision. With a surgeon's precision, he cut metal into perfect shapes, leaving no waste to discard. He sensed the weight needed for each piece to achieve a balance required for the mobile to come alive at the slightest touch of a gentle breeze.

Just beyond the bridge that led to the Moulin Vert was the separate house that Sandy called the *Gouacherie*. In the mornings he walked over to that studio to begin work in the ground-floor atelier that seemed no larger than a king-sized bed. Sometimes I would follow him, squeezing in by the table where his paints were spread out, to watch him work. We rarely spoke. His hand would slightly shake as it moved toward the paper with his brush. After the initial stroke, all excess movement disappeared. So steady was the effort that a quickly drawn triangle or circle appeared perfect, as if it were machine-made. He didn't seem to mind when I asked that a face he painted in black and white be given a line of red. A few years later, when our intimacy was strong, he signed a notarial document granting me preference in acquiring that studio when no longer used by him.

I did not know, as I watched Calder work, that he had already been diagnosed with Parkinson's disease, according to his grandson. His mastery of the gouache brush and the billiard cue that he held steady each day when playing with Jean belied that diagnosis. His hand did not shake when he extended his cue to change the score by sliding corks placed on a wire he had strung between two posts.

Fig. 18. Alexander Calder, gouache watercolor, modified and dedicated to Stanley Cohen. Photograph by Lisa Vollmer. © 2026 Calder Foundation, New York / Artists Rights Society (ARS), New York.

Once the Calders moved into their new house, high on a nearby hill, I dined with them more often. The large windows offered an unobstructed view of the Indre Valley—simplicity confronting the Renaissance. Simplicity was an appropriate description for the way the Calders lived: the house was spare, devoid of any excess furniture other than a farm table for dining and a couch by the fireplace. The main room was a single, uncluttered space, the decor sparse—pots and pans lining the wall just above a stove, adjacent to a Miró painting, and a wooden shelf for spices.

Louisa was a wonderful winter companion. We shared a whiskey with water in front of a fire. Sandy would draw a design on the canvas backing for each of us. He specified the colors,

Fig. 19. Rug based on an Alexander Calder drawing, knitted by Louisa Calder and Stanley Cohen. Photograph by Lisa Vollmer. © 2026 Calder Foundation, New York / Artists Rights Society (ARS), New York.

and we bought Moroccan wool to hook into the proper place. Recalling these evenings that gave me so much contentment, I now realize that I adopted Sandy and Louisa as the parents I wished for but never had. With them there was intimacy: talk of the Vietnam War, of deserters hidden nearby, and so much more. If silence fell, it was a pause that harbored comfort, not the isolation I had known in my youth.

I accompanied the Calders and one of their friends, the Spanish-born painter and sculptor Joan Miró, to Saint Paul de Vence for a retrospective exhibition at Fondation Maeght. Although by this time I was familiar with Calder's current works, primarily large stabiles, I had not yet been to an exhibit that showed his range. The Maeght show grouped objects from the 1920s to the present: forms in wood, the Cirque Calder, and works that seemed utterly fragile yet that moved with determination and strength, all in colors that felt Calder-made. Indeed, had I viewed this series before I met him, I might well have been so awed by the majesty of the work that I would have been more hesitant in our relationship. When the Maeght exhibit went on to the Louisiana Museum of Modern Art in Copenhagen, I did too. The presentation there, amid walls bathed in white, was even more impactful and left me with an even greater admiration for a neighbor who had welcomed me as a friend. Perhaps it was my innocence that allowed our intimacy to develop—I had approached him as someone who delivered bread, not as a renowned artist.

Saché, an isolated Loire Valley hamlet, might seem an odd choice for someone with a restless soul, but whether with guests or by myself over a weekend, I never felt bored. Days passed with simple tasks or a five-mile bike ride to Azay-le-Rideau with a stop halfway where wild dill grew. A fresh *ficelle* awaited me, and the butcher knew my name. Neighboring farmers planted corn from

Fig. 20. Alexander Calder delivering bread to Stanley Cohen's home, Saché, France. © 2026 Calder Foundation, New York / Artists Rights Society (ARS), New York.

seeds I carried from New York. When the corn ripened, I offered samples, but the locals shunned the ears, insisting corn was only for their pigs.

There is a letter in Julien Levy's file dated 1932 that suggests that the first show of Cartier-Bresson's photographs should take place in two of his gallery spaces—side by side, graphic and anti-graphic—in order to properly compare his work with that of his contemporaries, Alfred Steiglitz and Paul Strand. A 2012 joint exposition of Strand and Cartier-Bresson reprised that idea, featuring the two as "static and fluid," as the catalog put it. That was the way I thought of Jo Davidson and Calder. The former's portraits symbolized stillness, while Calder's works embodied movement.

Jacques and Jean illustrated graphic and anti-graphic too, by the manner in which they lived. I rarely saw Jacques after moving to the mill, although our relationship remained cordial. When he was forced to sell Becheron for financial reasons, he asked me to house all of Jo's masks and busts on the top floor of the mill. I often sat there late at night as moonlight slipped through the sky, illuminating each face in turn. Gandhi sat there, still. Marshal Tito and Mussolini confronted Marshal Foch and General Pershing.

Among the bronzes were also several unsmiling Russians whom Jo Davidson had cajoled into posing when he traveled to Moscow in the 1930s. All had since died, erased from history on Stalin's orders. Now they lived only on the third floor of the mill. I wondered what they discussed when no human was there to eavesdrop. I later convinced Dr. Maury Liebowitz, vice president of the Knoedler's Gallery and a partner of the industrialist and art collector Armand Hammer, to buy the Davidson collection, which he then donated to the National Portrait Gallery, while Gertrude Stein's statue went to Bryant Park, adjacent to the New York Public Library.

17

The Hunt

One of Sylvan Gotshal's French friends invited me several times to dinner at his Paris home. Somehow, I always felt out of place among the haute bourgeoisie and the formality of drinks, dinner, and cigars. Perhaps my unease was due to uncertainty as to which fork I should use. It was clear that the invitation was to thank Gotshal for his help in shielding the owner's assets during the war.

My host also had a large property not far from the Moulin Vert and insisted that I join him and his guests for a Sunday autumn ritual: the hunt. I accepted since it was on my way home from Saché. I assumed this meant a casual walk through the woods, but I had the sense to wear a jacket and a tie. The gathering was composed of generals and well-known businessmen. A few guests came with uniformed gunbearers. Talk was of Africa and the lions, India and the tigers they had killed. Given a shotgun and a number, I was instructed to follow the procession in my car. Each guest would stand behind a post that corresponded to their number. Beaters would flush the game, and we would just aim overhead and soon hear a plop-plop-plop as the birds fell from the sky. When we returned to the château courtyard, the birds were laid out in pairs for us to take home, but the custom was to decline so that the beaters could retain the game for a well-earned dinner.

I thanked my host and tried to leave, but an after-hunt dinner was customary. I was obligated to stay. I sat at the end of the table;

no one spoke to me. After the meal, the women and men went into separate rooms—the women to gossip, the men to smoke cigars and drink cognac. I was the last one to join the men. As I entered the room, I heard someone say in French, "Voilà l'Americain. He must know how to shoot a pistol." Unknown to me, a candle had been placed at the bottom of the fireplace, and each guest was taking turns to extinguish the flame with a bullet from a pistol. The revolver was thrust into my hand, cocked and ready to fire. It exploded as my arm snapped back in a reflex motion, my finger on the trigger. The bullet entered a wingback armchair. There was silence in the room. My hand was shaking, and I thanked God no one had been sitting there. In my uncertain French, I suggested that I take the armchair home as a trophy for my wall. No one laughed. Instead, they urged me to continue shooting at the candle, which made no sense since I could not steady my hand.

Needless to say, I was not invited back. I have never touched a gun since that moment. Even now, when I think about that evening, my hand shakes at the memory. What would my life have become if a guest had been seated in that chair?

18

Michael Harrington

In 1961 an acquaintance asked me to handle the legal requirements for the wedding of Michael Harrington, the socialist author of *The Other America*, to Stephanie Gervis, a journalist for the *Village Voice*. It was respect at first sight. Seán O'Casey had taught me the joy of Irish rhythm on paper when I read his *Inishfallen, Fare Thee Well*. I heard that same Gaelic lilt in Harrington's voice. Although not pronounced, the lilt signaled an inheritance of which he was proud, conveying a passion and a sincerity. A marriage certificate was easily produced for the town-hall wedding. Michael arrived in Paris several months before Stephanie. I dined with him several times. He had not yet received the notoriety that was about to descend with the publication of *The Other America* in 1962, after his stay in France. Although some critics complained that the book did not reveal anything about the US that we did not already know, Harrington's clear writing made readers *feel* the misery of poverty in their affluent nation, forcing them to acknowledge the existence of the poor whom they had otherwise refused to see. Being poor was not a matter of choice; it had become "a separate culture, another nation, with its own way of life." Harington's analysis spurred the effort by Presidents Kennedy and Johnson to ease the pain of the poorest Americans.

In our talks, I learned of Harrington's hesitancy to study law after his first year at Yale and of his relationship with the pioneering social activist Dorothy Day, co-founder and leader of the Catholic Worker Movement. Harrington and I shared our respective army experiences—his some eight years earlier than mine, but with a pronounced difference. True to his beliefs, Harrington had refused to tote a gun, claiming "conscientious objector" status. He was "terrified at [his] own audacity in challenging a gigantic system of authority," while I, Spitter-made, felt I could bend it to my will. I admired Harrington for what he was, and I admired him for all that I wasn't.

Harrington could hold a crowd firmly in his grasp. I once accompanied him to London to hear him speak in favor of a Labor Party candidate for the House of Commons. It was a Saturday morning at a crowded shopping center. The shoppers were engaged in their weekly chores, darting in and out of the supermarket. When the Labor Party candidate spoke, the pedestrian scene did not change at all. Then Harrington took the stage. He had no notes. Armed only with outrage, he began to speak. It was as if a pause button had been pressed. The traffic seemed to stop. Baskets were no longer pushed. Everyone seemed charmed by the cadence of his talk as words emerged from somewhere deep within. Genuine and passionate, he conveyed an image of what life was and what life could be. Unable to depart until his soliloquy ended, the crowd then signaled their release with an explosion of applause. The world, Harrington made me feel, was broadly divided into two types—people who were concerned with poverty and all its ills, devoting their lives to fostering solutions, and people who remained in their private universe, satisfied with making mountains into hills.

After their marriage, I offered the house in Saché to Stephanie and Michael. They stayed for several weeks. I came on Friday nights and returned to Paris on Sundays. Stephanie usually slept late, but Michael woke up at five to study Greek or to work on a book. I had my coffee at seven and talked with him until nine,

Fig. 21. Cohen residence in Saché, France.

when he returned to bed. I continued to see them each year during my sporadic trips to New York, usually for dinner at their home in Greenwich Village before they moved to Larchmont.

19

Jewelry, and the Fall of France in World War II

My visit to the de Carbuccia home in Saint-Tropez illustrated how little I knew about World War II in France despite observing the turmoil in Riva's life. That was about to change. I was invited in March 1965 to the home just outside of Paris of the artist Niki de Saint Phalle, which she shared with Jean Tinguely. During dinner, I was chatting with a pleasant, middle-aged woman seated next to me. She said, "I understand you are an American lawyer with an office here?" When I replied yes, she asked if I could help her.

In 1940, she explained, her mother had sent her and her brother Hervé, aged seven and nine respectively, to the United States in the care of a governess. They left on the last liner before the French government dropped out of the war. Soon after their arrival in New York City, they learned that their mother had died in an automobile accident in southern France. A box of jewelry, their only possession, had been turned over to the American federal authorities. After decades of repeated attempts, they had been unable to recoup the jewelry without paying substantial customs duties, penalties, and estate taxes—sums far beyond their means.

The story, which she told in a calm and measured tone, seemed rather peculiar. I asked her to send all of the details to my office. She thanked me, and as she departed, she said her name was Anne de Vogüé. Her mother, she added, had been Countess Hélène de Portes, who had been in a relationship with Paul Reynaud, the French premier. These names meant nothing to me. A few days later, I received a large file with affidavits, court filings, news clippings about the war, as well as letters—some personal, others directly related to the effort to recover the jewelry. The matter seemed less a question of American estate taxes and customs duties than I had been led to believe. It was more of a family drama suitable for a novel.

At the outset of the war, Anne's mother had deposited jewelry and other items in a bank's safe-deposit box in Arcachon, near Bordeaux, where the family had a home. Alice Mayer, her children's governess, was instructed to remove the jewelry from that box upon receipt of a coded message should the war turn against the French. In mid-May 1940, when the German Army was poised to enter Paris, the message was transmitted, and passage to the United States was arranged for Mayer and the children. Material in the file contained details about the jewelry I was being charged to recover. Mayer had been hesitant to personally transport the wrapped leather case to the United States, fearful of losing it or being charged with theft. Hélène de Portes therefore entrusted the package to a friend, Princess Guy de Polignac, who was sailing on the same vessel. Upon their arrival in New York, the jewelry was handed over to Mayer before anyone learned of de Portes's death. The governess was perplexed as to how she and the children would survive, as their only assets were that box of jewelry and a small sum of cash.

For a short period, Mayer and the children lived in Southampton, Long Island, with the Sloane family of furniture fame, an acquaintance of de Portes. The box of jewelry rested in a bank safe-deposit box. It was odd, I thought as I read the letters in the file, that the children were refugee wanderers, sent to America with few resources and no place to reside. Shortly before the accident that killed de Portes, Reynaud had written to Edna and George Doriot asking them to welcome the children into their home in Boston. Doriot was the first French-born graduate of the Harvard Business School and was teaching there at the time. He was soon to become a US brigadier general. He and Reynaud had become acquainted years before.

The jewelry was inventoried and turned over to a prominent law firm, and an administrator was appointed for the estate. France, New York, and Massachusetts were queried as to their respective interests. Count Henri de Portes, although separated, was still legally married to Hélène at the time of her death. He insisted that his children return to German-occupied France in the summer of 1941. In a novel, Henri would be described as a ne'er-do-well. Reputed to be involved in the black market, he may have been more interested in the return of the jewelry than in the care of the children. When I read the letters and sworn statements, I tried to imagine the emotional impact of this turmoil on two young children living in a new country with surrogate parents, a mother deceased, and an absentee father forcing repatriation to a Nazi-dominated city. The children did return to France, without the jewelry, and were soon ousted by Henri. They refused, he claimed, to obey him; they were unruly, just "wanting to do as they please."

After the war ended, Henri persistently sought ownership of the jewelry, while the children diligently resisted their father's attempts. Henri died a pauper in 1971. Van Cleef & Arpels, the French luxury jeweler, sought a final payment for a valuable platinum necklace sold in the 1930s, which was likewise claimed by a Jane Engelhard in an interpleader filed in the United States

District Court in Massachusetts. A man's watch was returned to Reynaud, and three baby teeth were released.

The jewelry, imported in the name of Hélène de Portes, apparently violated customs regulations then in force; federal estate taxes and interest thereon were also being asserted by the US Treasury, which had taken possession of the jewelry. All discussions of settlement among various claimants seemed to have come to a halt when I was approached by Anne.

I was surprised that estate taxes were in question until I realized that the present US–France treaty on double taxation only came into effect in 1949. The provisions of that treaty would have spared the estate from American taxation. However, a 1940 law imposed taxes on all personal property located in the United States that was owned by a deceased French citizen. The appropriate term in the applicable law was *situs* of the property, that is, its proper place of rest in relationship to the taxing jurisdiction.

I had an idea—and here is where my ignorance of historical matters proved a benefit for the de Portes's heirs.

European history had not been a hallmark of my American education. I had only limited knowledge of the events leading to the French collapse in 1940, so I quickly skimmed several articles. There were few detailed histories published in English at that time, other than Reynaud's and Winston Churchill's memoirs. War began on September 1, 1939, when Germany invaded Poland. France was not attacked until May 10, 1940. German forces quickly advanced, threatening Paris. The government fled first to Tours and then to Bordeaux. After 86 days in power, Reynaud resigned as premier when the Nazis approached Bordeaux. He claimed he wanted to continue the war from a base in the French colonies in North Africa, but he was not supported by the majority of the cabinet, resulting in his resignation. With

Reynaud replaced by Marshal Philippe Pétain, an armistice agreement with the Germans quickly followed. Reynaud, with de Portes at his side, fled Bordeaux by automobile, only to drive off the road, resulting in her death.

Their destination seemed to be an open question. If Reynaud was indeed heading to North Africa, as one journalist suggested, his mistress would surely have accompanied him. She, I imagined, as a dutiful mother, would have insisted that her children join them. If so, the children and, therefore, the jewelry, were only in transit and never fell within the American tax jurisdiction because America was not their intended place of rest, which is what the legal definition of "situs" required. If Anne could find a witness confirming that North Africa was indeed her mother's destination at the time of the accident, I could test my theory with the appropriate American authorities.

Henri Pagezy, an industrialist whose home in Montpelier was to have been Reynaud and de Portes's overnight stop when the crash occurred, signed an affidavit confirming that the couple's ultimate destination was Algiers. He referred to conversations he had with de Portes in which she confided that she "expected her children to rejoin her."

I flew to Washington in October 1965 and had a lengthy discussion with a representative of the United States Customs Service. I obtained his agreement to have the duties and penalties waived if I succeeded in convincing the Internal Revenue Service to renounce estate taxes on the basis of my situs argument. The Treasury agent was a young man about my age who had inherited the de Portes case when he joined the IRS. He knew as little about the war as I did. I presented my argument. After he met with some unnamed supervisor, I was advised that my theory was accepted. I never knew if he was truly swayed by my analysis or if the department was simply exhausted with the matter. Nevertheless, the jewelry was to be released.

When I inquired about the formalities for delivery, I learned of a problem about which Anne had failed to alert me. Over a lengthy period, several law firms had represented her and her brother. Failure did not deter these firms from filing liens to ensure payment of their fees. I was also informed that Jane Engelhard, then married to Charles Engelhard Jr., an extremely wealthy industrialist, claimed one of the necklaces. In order to obtain this piece of jewelry, I first had to get a release from her attorney, Robert Meyner, the former governor of New Jersey and son-in-law of the politician and diplomat Adlai Stevenson. He exhibited some surprise at my success when I contacted him. He invited me to lunch and explained that his client's first husband, Fritz Mannheimer, loaned a valuable necklace to Mme. de Portes for a 1939 ball in Paris. Engelhard now wanted it back. It was the kind of story that occasionally made the practice of law engaging.

Jane Engelhard was born as Marie Annette Jane Reiss in Shanghai in 1917 to a Jewish businessman who was also the Brazilian consul in that city. She eventually found her way to Paris, and married Fritz Mannheimer in June 1939 after working for him as a nurse. Jane was then just twenty-one; Fritz, forty-eight. Paul Reynaud was the witness at the ceremony. Mannheimer, a leading currency trader, was considered one of the richest men in the world at the time. Described in his obituaries as "Europe's de facto central banker," he died two months after the wedding under what some claimed were mysterious circumstances. His Dutch bank was found to be insolvent. A daughter, Annette, was born after his death in December 1939; she later married Oscar de la Renta. Mannheimer's massive art collection was seized and eventually attracted the attention of both Adolf Hitler and Hermann

Göring. As ownership was unclear due to the claims of non-Jewish creditors, Hitler purchased the collection at a rigged auction for an amount significantly lower than the actual value. Recovered at war's end by the Monuments Men, most of his collection can be viewed today at the Rijksmuseum and at the Metropolitan Museum of Art. Jane had successfully pursued the return of some of the paintings. In short, she was very rich.

I explained to Meyner that Anne and her artist husband Guy de Vogüé had only modest means compared with Engelhard, but my urging was to no avail. Meyner made it clear that while Engelhard had maintained warm relations with Reynaud until his death, she detested Hélène and insisted on obtaining the necklace. It was my first indication of the controversy surrounding the countess's character. Before becoming premier, Reynaud had been the French minister of finance. With an impending economic crisis, he engaged Mannheimer, rather than a traditional bank, to syndicate the refinancing of the French governmental debt. Scattered hints in the files led me to surmise that Mannheimer most likely "gifted" the necklace to de Portes. Practicality ruled. If the return of the necklace was a personal matter for Meyner's client, I proposed that she pay all of the past legal fees and costs. After an amicable settlement, the necklace was released to Mrs. Engelhard, and I obtained the remaining jewelry. Placing them in a shoebox tucked under my arm, I returned to Paris. Anne and her brother were delighted, as was the Sotheby's auction house a few years later.

Doris Lessing explains a phenomenon everyone experiences. When a new subject or name comes to your attention, "Then suddenly it is everywhere, on the television, in the newspaper, on the radio, [. . .] and a book falls open at just the relevant place." And so it was with Hélène de Portes, a name which, six months

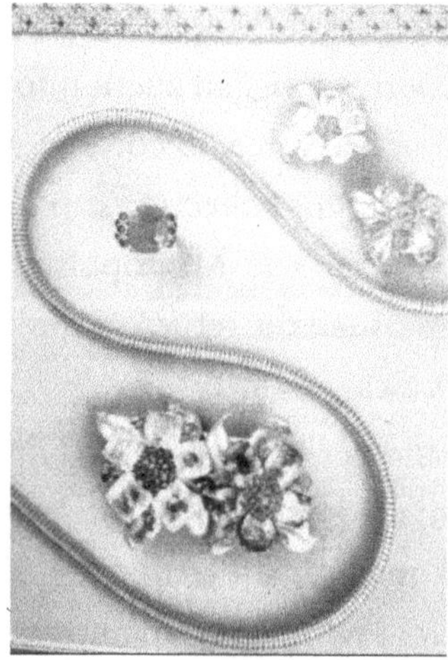

Fig. 22. Jewelry seized by the US government and later restituted.

before my trip to Washington, would have been utterly meaningless to me. Over the next few years, with the appearance of new historical accounts of the period, de Portes's name became inescapable, often coupled with negative comments. In William L. Shirer's *The Collapse of the Third Republic* (1969), she is introduced in the very first chapter as someone who exhausted Reynaud and led him to abandon the struggle against the Nazis.

Shirer placed the blame on the countess for France's decision to drop out of the war and abandon its ally Britain, noting: "It was only the presence, conduct and influence of Hélène de Portes which can truly explain the attitude of Paul Reynaud, his significant mistakes, his indecisiveness, his hesitation at crucial moments, his loss of time, and failure to act and take command [. . .]. In short, there is no other explanation [. . .] for the last-minute resignation of Paul Reynaud in favor of Pétain [. . .]." Reynaud's departure from office had important consequences. With the armistice in force, France began its slide into the Vichy collaboration with Nazi Germany and the systematic deportation of Jews to concentration camps. No other explanation? I find that to be a powerful statement about a decision that would cause a nation to reflect on its shortcomings for decades after the war. Why was the sin—if it was one—of seeking an armistice to end France's involvement in the war ascribed to a woman rather than to the person holding office? Why had Reynaud repeatedly insisted that he had no choice?

I had dealt with the problem of recuperating the jewelry in a narrow, lawyerly way, without any thought to the historical context that caused Anne's mother to have her and her brother sent to the United States in the care of their governess. I had not initially focused on material in the file that seemed unrelated to my mission to recoup the jewelry, nor did I grasp that several letters were of historical significance. The more I studied the period and reviewed the material in the file Anne had left with me, the clearer it became that Reynaud and de Portes were not headed for North Africa. If I wanted to be melodramatic, I might claim that I was the last person to be seduced by the countess, having advanced that very claim to secure the release of the jewelry. I even became a footnote when a historian requested a copy of the Pagezy affidavit to support his ill-conceived theory that Reynaud had planned to go to North Africa. That footnote now fills me with shame.

And that was not the end of the story. Anne passionately wanted to confront and challenge those who had accused her mother of having had close relations with Nazi leaders. Several memoirs and magazine articles, including those in the United States, advanced conspiracy theories concerning the relationship between de Portes and Hitler's entourage, especially Hermann Göring. Although the Doriots, whom Anne considered her surrogate aunt and uncle, warned her not to delve into her mother's conduct, Anne could not resist.

Fig. 23. Hélène de Portes.

"I never tried to have any opinion on the matter," she admitted, "perhaps I feared discovering the truth." Aunt Edna added that reliving scandals of the past could only lead to "much unhappiness."

Determined to defend a mother whom she hardly knew, Anne fired off letters of complaint to newspapers and authors whenever an article or a book included a hint of Hélène's pro-German inclination. She believed the male leaders who had governed France during the war were seeking a scapegoat for their failure. "They all try to purify themselves by putting all the responsibilities on my mother," she wrote in one of her letters to the Doriots, "describing her with a strange and snarling hatred."

Harold Nicolson, who had been a member of the British Parliament, as well as a journalist, a diplomat, and the husband of Vita Sackville-West, said in an entry in his diaries published in 1967 that de Portes surrounded Reynaud "with fifth-columnists and spies." Anne protested. Nicholson's son, Nigel, who had edited his father's diaries, suggested that she should have someone write a book to clear Hélène's name. And if so, he agreed to add a footnote in later editions of his father's diaries, but he refused to remove that entry.

Not long after the fall of France in 1940, Nicolson hosted a London dinner party. His guests included a former Reynaud aide, Maurice Dejean, as well as General Edward Spears, Churchill's liaison to Reynaud. The conversation turned to the collapse of France. "[Spears] told the [unbelievable] and [impossible] story of Hélène de Portes [. . .]. We discussed how it came about that this frowsy soiled woman with the dirty fur tippet managed to sway the destiny of a great nation." According to Spears, her influence was due to Reynaud's inferiority complex because of "his small stature and that she made him feel tall and grand and powerful. 'Had Reynaud been three inches taller, the history of the world might have been changed.'"

Anne was engaged in an impossible task which could not be won. Her mother had become a means to rationalize the defeat of a nation. Failed nations are tempted to seek a causal link between catastrophe and the unforeseen, wrote Professor E. H. Carr in his classic study, *What Is History*. "In a group or a nation which is riding in the trough, not on the crest of historical events," Carr adds, "theories that stress the role of chance or accident in history will be found to prevail." Justifications based on Cleopatra's nose, Napoleon's cold, or the charms of a woman are used to obscure the deeper faults that cause a country's decline.

Intrigued by the stories surrounding de Portes, I arranged interviews with those who had known the couple. Most interviewees were forthcoming. Hélène's sister, however, rejected my overtures and spoke disparagingly about her sibling. A particular delight was spending an afternoon with Mireille Hartuch, the widow of Emmanuel Berl, a writer, journalist, and historian. Berl had known de Portes and Reynaud. In his book about the Third Republic and its collapse, he described meeting the countess in Bordeaux. I believed his wife accompanied him, and I hoped she might be able to describe the atmosphere during the week of Reynaud's resignation. I was not aware that Mireille was a superstar. Not only was she a famous French composer and singer, but she had also been a presence on the London and New York stage and a Hollywood co-star of Douglas Fairbanks Jr. and Buster Keaton. When I entered her apartment, I saw a doorway with a traffic light attached. She noted my surprise and explained that her husband could only enter if the light was green. I explained the reason for my visit, but she no longer had any memory of the events that had brought me to her apartment. She apologized, stood up, and said, "This I remember." She gracefully moved to a grand piano and proceeded to play and sing her songs for a good thirty minutes.

I would have liked to continue with my research and interviews and was even tempted to write an article based on de Portes's unpublished letters, which I realized provided new insights into the French defeat and Reynaud's decision to resign. But I still had obligations to build the Paris law office. As my work began to increase, further efforts to pursue this study were placed on hold—but not abandoned.

20
Max's Kansas City

I usually returned to New York for an annual Christmas trip, in part to remind the firm that I still existed, and in part to see family and friends. In New York, the law-firm world had changed and continued to evolve. Separate Jewish or WASP firms were soon to be a concept of the past. The number of attorneys in each office was growing astonishingly fast. Weil, Gotshal & Manges was no exception. When I was hired, I was lawyer No. 23. While I was in Paris, the number of lawyers had risen to more than 100 and was on its way to 1,000. Most associates whom I had known were no longer there, replaced by recent graduates. The Lincoln Building offices could no longer house the growing staff. A move to the more prestigious General Motors Building was planned. After all these years, my Paris office was of little concern to the new partners. I was told I could be useful by entertaining clients who wished to expand their activities to Europe. I willingly agreed.

In 1965 my friend Mickey Ruskin opened Max's Kansas City, a bar and restaurant on Park Avenue South that soon became a haven for artists and writers, the place to be and be seen. Whenever Mickey needed a break from New York, he would stay with me in Paris for a week or two. Max's opening coincided with one of my return trips to Paris, so Mickey decided to throw a farewell party for me. The invitation read "Goodbye Stanley, Hello Max." Here was a chance for me to debut entertaining clients and their wives. I asked Mickey for a prime table. To prepare them for dinner, Mickey suggested I borrow his van to take my guests to a screening of an Allen Ginsberg film.

The film, I believe, was about Ginsberg's partner, Peter Orlovsky, riding a bike. He never seemed to stop and might have masturbated en route to who knows where. The executives were not impressed. When we arrived for dinner in Max's backroom, few were in a good mood. To reach our table we had to push through the crowded bar and fully packed tables lining the wall. The noise was cacophonous, and the walls were covered with paintings not yet recognized as important works of art. One of the wives objected to wading through the throng. I insisted that the steaks were exceptional. When we were at the table, she said, "I'm sure there are cockroaches here." As I was responding with "Nonsense," a roach walked across the table. I was never asked to entertain clients again.

21

Turning Thirty—Now What?

Three had replaced two as the first number of my age. That transition stimulated a flurry of introspection as to what my goal in life should be. I was leading a sybaritic existence, fortunate to have a stress-free career, unlike the pressures that attorneys endured in New York. I had no direct supervision, and timesheets were doodles on a pad. Surely, this was a lifestyle for someone who had little ambition other than to make mountains into hills. Each return from New York made me realize that Paris was indeed my home and would remain so unless some catastrophe arose or a decision from the law firm signaled its end. I did not believe the latter would occur, provided I earned enough to avoid needing subsidies. The Paris office generally had income sufficient to cover expenses, and my salary had risen to $25,000.

But apart from the retainer from AMC, there was no steady source of income. Days passed without a client knocking. Many French lawyers seemed to prefer dealing with me as a lone practitioner rather than consulting with established Wall Street firms. For the most part, I handled estate and other matters of a personal nature. When an American resident in France dies, administration is required in both countries to gather and distribute assets and to pay debts and taxes. Sometimes the French heirs continued to seek my advice.

One young man inherited a fortune from his American father. Enamored of horse racing, he entered into a partnership with the son of a wealthy Greek shipowner to create a breeding stable. Both were addicted to attending the Longchamp Racecourse and betting almost every day during the racing season. The amounts bet by Costa, the Greek partner, were so substantial that they could not be placed at the normal gaming window without impacting the odds. Instead, he invited a representative from Ladbrokes, a hundred-year-old London sports gambling concern, to sit in his box and record the wager. To reduce costs, Costa next decided to telephone his wagers to London rather than have someone fly over every day. Alas, he initiated the call only after the horses had already left the gate. I flew to London to stop a lawsuit by Ladbrokes and to prevent a scandal.

Costa could not resist the urge to bet big. On Sundays in Paris, the cafes brimmed with people playing the tierce, the selection of three horses in a particular race. The odds were so high that a fortune could be made if the horses finished in the order of the bet. One Sunday, toward midnight, I received a call from Costa asking me to come to his apartment in the Hôtel Plaza Athénée. His living room was filled with smoke and the sound of clacking beads. I thought it was a wake. Costa explained that he had just won the equivalent of three million dollars from his tierce bet, but the French organization that ran the betting had refused to pay. There was a limit to the amount each person was permitted to bet, and Costa had far exceeded the ceiling by sending his chauffeur each Sunday morning to some twenty cafes. He had been doing that for over a year but had never won.

I suggested we contact *Le Monde*, since the newspaper was publishing articles criticizing the running of Pari Mutuel Urbain (PMU), France's state-authorized horse-racing betting operator. It was clear that his excess betting was well known; fair play would be our message. The bead clicking stopped, and we toasted his winnings with a glass of ouzo. At 6 a.m. Costa called me once again; he could not tolerate the publicity since he had promised his family that he would not gamble. His allowance would be stopped. I said three million is a lot to forfeit. How did that compare with his allowance? "300,000 dollars," he replied. I expressed surprise, as his annual expenses clearly exceeded that amount. After a brief silence, he said, "Each month."

The Champagne Trade Association, a long-standing client of the New York office, requested that I accompany the CBS journalist Charles Collingswood to Reims. I was delighted. Collingswood had covered the signing of the unconditional surrender of Nazi Germany on May 7, 1945, which took place at a schoolhouse in Reims. He was returning to that French city to broadcast one of the first Early Bird satellite programs: a conversation with former president Dwight Eisenhower and the British general Bernard Montgomery from the same schoolhouse. The broadcast was to occur on the twentieth anniversary of that historic moment. The Trade Association asked me to urge Collingswood to utter the word "champagne" while he spoke to millions of viewers. Thinking it unethical, I refused. But Charles, a professional, opened the program by announcing that he was in the heart of Champagne country. Both Collingswood and I received a case of superb bubbly.

22

A Law Office of My Own

These legal matters, although interesting to handle, did not ensure enough income to allow expansion or the development of a real office. I was uncertain if I even wanted to change my way of life, which was satisfying and allowed ample time for travel, for stays in Saché, and for playing pinball machines in cafes. I lived alone and enjoyed the freedom. Unless I am introduced, I'm not adept at initiating small talk. I rarely frequent bars in search of companionship. At a cocktail party, I'm timid. If I see a woman across the room with whom I'd like to chat, I stand immobile by the canapes in the hope she will ask me to hold her glass while she is inserting a chip into a dip. Today, reflecting on my hesitation to initiate conversation with women I do not know, I'm surprised that I nonetheless had such an active sexual life. I did not understand until later that I was part of the 60s generation. In a bookstore in Copenhagen, a young woman wanted to talk about books. We talked for the entire weekend. In Iceland at the Fisher–Spassky chess match, a woman interrupted my fixation on the chessboard to give me other lessons. The process of changing air tickets in Athens earned me a friend who afterwards visited me in Paris several times a year.

My downstairs room became a haven for those seeking a place to hang out and relax. An artist, Martin Sharp, came from London for a while after designing album covers for Jimi Hendrix, Eric Clapton, and Marianne Faithfull, and a poster for Bob Dylan. I gave him a key when I left for my Christmas trip in New York. I returned to find every inch of floor and wall covered in his style. It was a bit overwhelming. I could no longer hang the paintings I had collected. So I thanked him, and he returned to Sydney to become a New Age star. He is well remembered for his psychedelic art and his film *Street of Dreams* in honor of the frequent late-night-show guest and falsetto singer, Tiny Tim.

Clearly, my one-man office could never develop into anything other than a welcome mat for Americans on vacation. I had a checklist of things to do. Some were obligations; others enhanced my life—such as when Ruth Bader Ginsburg passed through before a lecture tour to have dinner and offer an insight into her career. Really, from the start, a law office in Paris had only been a figment of my imagination. Was it now time to close this section of my journey, to see what life still had in store? Should I return to New York and an existence that I had so far successfully done my best to avoid?

I began to think how law firms in France were organized. An inner voice tried to intervene. "Don't go there," it said, "you will no longer have time to turn mountains into hills." I ignored the warning. The American firms long established in Paris were permitted to employ French lawyers who were not members of the prestigious French bar. These lawyers had the same status as me, *conseil juridique*, which allowed them to give advice and draft agreements but not to appear in court. And although that describes most legal work, there was a certain reputational standing of members of the bar, the *avocat à la cour*, especially when dealing with government officials. At that time, all meaningful foreign investments in the country required French governmental authorization. I wondered if there was a way to overcome the prohibition imposed by rules of the profession, so that French and

American lawyers—members of the respective bars—could work together as a single firm.

I had developed a relationship with Emile-Jean Bomsel, an *avocat à la cour.* Perfectly at ease in English, he was one of those lawyers who exude both competence and culture. Most members of the French bar were single practitioners whose offices were at their homes. Bar rules for home offices were strict. The entrance had to be separate from the exit, to provide discretion for clients. Couches were not permitted, to avoid unprofessional coercive payments from female clients. Bomsel was already beyond the home-office stage, though. He had a firm of some six lawyers, which was a decent size at that time. I began to explore the possibility of sharing office space with him. Although uncertain as to whether I could produce enough legal work to sustain my part of it, I felt that with the growth of Weil, Gotshal & Manges in New York, the clientele for the Paris office would certainly expand, provided we had the capacity to handle complex commercial matters. "If you build it, they will come"—that was my belief.

Over time, Bomsel and I began to feel comfortable working together. I proposed acquiring office space with two distinct floors—the members of the French bar on one, the *conseil juridique* on another. We would operate as a single firm, sharing revenue. I prepared a budget and returned to New York, believing that Weil would agree, since the investment was modest in relation to the firm's current size. I was wrong. They wished me luck and told me that I would be better off on my own. The firm would continue to send me clients as it had been doing.

Why did I have to alter the lifestyle to which I was well suited? I was not unhappy; the income was slight, but I had no need of more. Did I truly want to test my skills against other American attorneys in Paris whose offices were expanding and had assured futures? Or was the very difficulty of setting up a firm the incentive for change, since I could no longer live in Paris for a fifth year without a pivot to a different adventure? As the planning with Maître (his title) Bomsel was far along, I decided to proceed, using my savings for the rent. In 1966, we opened our offices at 44 Avenue des Champs-Élysées. The worst that could happen, I believed, was that I would end up barricaded in Villa Seurat, preparing marriage certificates, reading Henry Miller, and making mountains into hills until the sheriff came to evict me.

The space was gracious and included a kitchen and dining room. I furnished my own office with walls in fabric and paintings. I spent the first day admiring the view of the Avenue des Champs-Élysées. And yet this adult world engendered unease. I thought of placing my desk chair high up on the wall with a rope ladder for access and a client's seat adjacent so we could look down on the world below. I can't explain the trajectory that followed, nor do I want to tick off all the legal matters that I handled. I will not pretend that I disliked the routine called law. The practice in France was substantially different from that in New York. The latter was generally divided into separate specialties and expertise, while French clients entrusted their legal representative with a wide range of problems.

For an American client, it was necessary to translate customs and mores. There were many *faux amis* to explain. A French company's president was not the same as an American CEO. The pace of negotiations in Paris was anathema to an American businessman who had to return home at a precise time. When a large American company wanted to purchase a small French family entity, I was asked to arrange lunch with the owner. I explained to the American CEO that this was only to be a chat, and that no offer should be made. I translated the lunchtime conversation.

Dessert came, and my client insisted that I make an offer of one million dollars since he had a plane to catch. That was more money than this small-town French entrepreneur had made during his forty years in business. I argued with the American client until he issued a terse "do it." Shocked by the sum, the Frenchman was speechless for a few moments, and then asked me, in French, if the American was a Mafia member who sought to buy the company for some illegal reason. Nine months of meetings and luncheons ensued before an agreement was reached.

A French company that manufactured and had installed monorail transportation systems in several cities in France decided Atlantic City, New Jersey, needed one as well. When gambling was introduced and casinos were built, the hotels were required to spend a certain amount of their income on improvements to the city. In addition, hotel-casinos were compelled to design and construct their reception areas as potential Metro stations. The initial urban plan called for parking all cars on the outskirts of town and for the parking areas to be linked to hotels by rail or other transportation. The French firm was quick to respond, and its executives asked me to accompany them—not to translate, since most spoke perfect English, but as a just-in-case. Presentations were made to the mayor, the city council, and the casino managers. Everyone was enthusiastic, but I discerned skepticism and disinterest in the faces of the casino executives. After the presentation, I was pulled aside. "Tell your friends that no one is going to build something that will take clients to another casino." He put a friendly arm on my shoulder, and, with a gentle squeeze, explained, "You know what we call improvements? We use laundries to clean our sheets and towels. That's enough improvement." I had a hard time explaining the conversation to the French executives.

I learned much from Bomsel. We once went to the French Treasury department to seek approval for an investment. We met with Jacques Chirac, its director, who was shortly to become the president of France. Just the three of us sat there, as if for tea. Bomsel mentioned a museum exhibit he had just seen. Chirac reported having been to the theatre and that the play was well received. After ten minutes of such cultural exchange, Bomsel stood up to take his leave. I was about to shout, "What about the file?" when I remembered the professional poker player who threw a hand just to discover someone's tell. I kept silent, knowing that Bomsel was a master of his craft. As soon as we left, I looked at him. He merely said, "It's approved."

If it were not for Michael Harrington, I'm uncertain whether my law office would have succeeded, or at least have progressed as rapidly as it did. I had gone to New York to see if I could encourage various law firms to send cases to our new office. Before I returned to Paris from one of my trips to New York, I had dinner at Michael's home, during which a phone call came. It was a Bernie Cornfeld calling from Geneva. The conversation was heated. I heard Michael say, "Bernie, I'm a socialist. If I wrote anything, it would not be favorable." Michael hung up and explained that he and Cornfeld had worked together in Brooklyn on social causes and union organizing. Bernie had then gone overseas to sell mutual funds to American soldiers in Asia and Europe. Cornfeld had become, Michael thought, quite successful in creating a company, Investors Overseas Services (IOS), and now he wanted Harrington to come to Geneva and write articles to combat recent problems that IOS was having with the Securities and Exchange Commission. Michael suggested that if I were ever in Geneva, I should call Cornfeld to explain why his appeal was denied. When

I left, I told Michael that it was unlikely I would ever meet Cornfeld.

Although I was separating from Weil, Gotshal & Manges, our relations were still cordial. A few weeks later, I was asked to attend the Geneva funeral of one of the firm's important clients. The ceremony and house visit took longer than expected, and I had to stay in Geneva overnight. Not knowing what to do, I recalled the conversation with Michael and telephoned Bernie Cornfeld, who quickly invited me for dinner. "Be at the Griffin Club at midnight." He arrived with several women and quizzed me on my career. He insisted that I postpone my departure and come to his office the next morning. Since I was curious and had no appointments, I stayed two days. Cornfeld was optimistically expanding IOS to become a major force, not only for the sale of mutual funds but also for underwriting securities in conjunction with major European banks. FDR's son, James Roosevelt, had been hired, as well as prominent lawyers from New York and California. I met them all. Few spoke French or had any experience in Europe. My impression of this good-natured lot was of college students having a fraternity party that could well end in disaster.

At the end of the two days, Cornfeld asked me to join IOS as his sort of assistant. He offered a sum that was beyond my comprehension, but as I had given my word to Me. Bomsel, I declined and left Geneva, believing I had missed a significant opportunity. The following week, I received a call from Barry Sterling, one of the new IOS recruits. A wealthy attorney and successful businessman, Sterling had convinced Cornfeld that he should be based in Paris and wanted space on our office floor. Moreover, a joint venture was being proposed to the Banque Rothschild in Paris, and I was asked to assist. I met with Nathaniel de Rothschild and

François Mayer, a principal executive of the bank; it was the beginning of a long relationship, although it would take fifteen years before I became an advisor to members of the family. Thanks to Sterling, other matters from IOS followed, and our office expenses were easily met. I later joked with Harrington that everything that happened thereafter I owed to the Socialist Party.

IOS collapsed in 1970. The company had issued shares to the public, and its executives felt rich. Homes were built in London, toilets shaped as thrones. Then a downturn in the stock market precipitated a run on the IOS shares and its underlying mutual funds. What IOS needed was an institutional partner whose reputation would calm holders of its funds. In the end, high-flying financier Robert Vesco had been selected to clean up the morass. Vesco, a fraud obvious to all except the IOS board, did unwind the assets—by diverting them into his pocket—before fleeing to Costa Rica and then to Cuba. Cornfeld spent months in a Geneva jail cell.

23

Skipping Out on Someone in Israel

For my birthday in 1967, I decided to visit Israel. It was to be my first vacation since I moved to France. The Syrians celebrated too, with a major air and artillery battle. The Six-Day War was over before I left Paris.

An acquaintance, whom I hardly knew, asked me to take a small package to a cousin in Tel Aviv. I called the recipient as soon as I arrived. I was told it was for a different cousin who lived in Jerusalem. I thought that was a bit odd, but as I was headed to Jerusalem, I agreed to deliver it. Jerusalem was under military occupation as its eastern section had only recently been annexed. When I telephoned cousin number two, he insisted I come to his home as soon as possible and added that his street was well known since the mayor, Teddy Kollek, lived next door. As soon as I knocked, a smallish man rushed out. There was no greeting, other than a "Shh, my daughter does not know why you are here." And neither did I. He sat me in a vestibule and listed all of his assets: movie theatres, a construction company, and many more businesses. At the end of his hurried recital, he said, "Now I'll introduce you to my daughter." I wondered what this was all about. She entered the room and seemed most pleasant and attractive. We chatted about the usual—what I wanted to see, how long I was staying, and other topics one would raise with a first-time visitor. I thanked her for her suggestions, and just as I was about to leave, she added that she would be glad to help me explore the town.

She was an extraordinary guide, shepherding me to sites I would not have seen if I had wandered by myself. Assiduous in the completion of her duty, she did not leave my side for the three days and nights of my stay. I expressed my gratitude and said goodbye just as if I were in Japan. I was off to Herzilia and the beach. She insisted on meeting me there. As soon as I checked into the hotel, the phone rang. It was cousin number one. He wanted to meet me right away to discuss certain matters and was coming to the hotel. He did not wait for my response. I knew my weakness and was fearful that I would say yes to whatever was being planned. I suspected that many Israeli families were desirous of having their children emigrate to the United States. My passport status was perhaps more important than my personality.

Fearful of a confrontation, I checked out of the hotel and drove north. At dusk I arrived at Metula. There was no hotel, but I found a pleasant room in a private home. Footsteps outside the sliding door of the bedroom disturbed me during the night, so I opened it to complain. A military unit greeted me. Lebanon was just a hundred yards away.

Why was I fearful of meeting with and responding frankly to cousin number one? Perhaps I naively believed he would make me feel guilty about the short-lived romance and suggest I had assumed an obligation. I felt, not for the first time, that there was a defect in my personality that inhibited openness in intimate matters.

24

The Disco Queen

I don't recall how it started, but Régine Zylberberg, the Disco Queen, suddenly appeared in my life. Neither Régine nor her clubs had been part of my vision of things to do in Paris. I am not a late-night man. I prefer a book in bed with a cup of chamomile or vervain tea to ease me into sleep.

Régine asked for a meeting at her home, just above New Jimmy's, a place I knew from the noise but that I never had an urge to enter. Most likely I would not have been allowed past the door. Régine and her husband, Roger Choukroune, welcomed me. We talked while Régine got dressed, and a doctor gave her shots of vitamin B. Régine explained that she had invented the discotheque. She wanted to expand and sought my advice as to the best model to use. I was surprised how quickly she seemed to accept and trust me as an advisor after a mere half-hour of conversation. First, she concluded, I had to have dinner at her club at Rue de Ponthieu to see how she operated. She wanted me to be there at ten. "That is my bedtime," I explained, but saying no to such a dynamo was impossible.

Over the next few weeks, I dined at Régine's club several times. The food was excellent as she had an arrangement with Michel Guérard, a three-Michelin-star chef. The noise was deafening; I could not understand why anyone allowed themselves to be exposed to the pollution she called sound. Régine explained that the decibel level increased each hour to encourage the customers to dance. Evidently there were many who enjoyed the atmosphere. Movie stars, an English princess, and Arab royalty were anxious to be seen there. A throng gathered at the entrance each evening, pleading for admission, wondering why a Bronx Jew was waved through with a bow. I usually left before dessert. That became a joke. One evening Régine sat me next to the actress Catherine Deneuve, one of the world's most beautiful women. At the end of the dinner, Régine proposed a toast to me since it was the first time I had stayed until the end. By then my friendship with Régine and Roger was very close. I received more than one call a day, and she often wanted me to stop by to chat as I went home from my office.

I proposed that she consider franchising, as her name had international recognition. Hotels might want to install a Régine discotheque to attract more guests. I prepared a form agreement. Régine reached out to Le Meridien, a chain of hotels then owned by Air France. I accompanied her twice to Rio de Janeiro and Bahia for Mardi Gras and to the darkened rooms that had opened under her name. Travelling by plane from Paris with Régine by my side, I certainly received an education about her drive and her need to succeed. Like Riva, she had a Polish heritage and hid from the Nazis during the war. Starting out as a hat-check girl and singer, she pushed her way upward.

Listening to her tales, I was once again struck by how wartime hardships had shaped someone who was my friend, yet whose experiences I could not comprehend. Determined to achieve more, she wanted to expand. But discos were not her aim; instead, she wanted hotels and resorts branded with her name. I, she said, should be her partner in this effort. I was noncommittal, but I saw that her force was her personal magnetism. On nights when she was elsewhere, or if she no longer hosted the club in Rio, the crowds diminished.

Fig. 24. Régine opening her nightclub in London.

Régine and I had a disagreement regarding a London partner who approached her for a franchise. Régine wanted the aristocratic crowd and movie stars to frequent the club so that others would come and stare. The setting was ideal, the roof garden of a Biba store in Kensington. I thought that a Malaysian immigrant, although successful in selling jewelry, might not be the best financial partner for Régine. The spectacular opening welcomed Princess Caroline of Monaco, actors Sylvester Stallone and Jack Nicholson, a few Rothschilds, assorted lords and some Guinnesses. I sat at an end table, as there was no one else there from the Bronx. I felt concern for the financier who was quoted in the *New York Times*: "I went to Régine's in Paris and couldn't get in," Mr. Ram explained. "Meanwhile, I had my eye on this spot for a long time, and I just got the idea to put the two together." I don't know how much money he lost when it closed. I had had enough of glitterati for a while, so I gave the contract forms to Régine's husband, Roger. He was both smart and competent, and I urged him to replace me in later negotiations. I retained my friendship with Régine and my table at Reginette's in New York. That is where I first met Jeanne Moreau.

25

Jeanne Moreau

Jeanne, Régine, and I had lunch in Régine's apartment just above her restaurant. Moreau had not changed physically since her landmark 1962 film, *Jules et Jim*. Charmed by her presence and her conversation, I thought of my first language teacher, Nadine, and of my first year in Paris, when everything was new. In the summer of 1979, I encountered Moreau a second time. She had aged. A brief marriage to William Friedkin had ended with him filing for a divorce in California. I was asked to assist her in those proceedings. For reasons that remain unknown, Friedkin just locked the door and did not even give back her clothes. Moreau was short of money, and I was glad to help. I assumed that she was too proud to request assistance from Pierre Cardin or Louis Malle, with whom she had been previously linked.

Hoping for a negotiated settlement, I engaged Mickey Rudin, whom I had known from his representation of Frank Sinatra and his relationship to Steve Ross. That was a major error. I should have realized that Mickey preferred to maintain his reputation as a tough guy leaning on women for his male movie-star clients. My office arranged an air ticket for Jeanne to attend the scheduled court hearing. She was surprised that I did not plan to fly with her. I explained that I was not a member of the California bar, so there was little I could do there. When I had no news about the results of the court hearing or settlement discussions, I called her to find out what had happened. I was shocked to hear that she had decided not to go. Friedkin had his divorce, and Jeanne did not even have her clothes returned. Ashamed that I had not responded adequately to someone at the low point of their life, I questioned once again my devotion to working in the law. Had I not gone to Los Angeles because I thought I might not get paid? I was not proud that I had thought of her as a client rather than as a person with a storied history who had turned to me for help.

Sometime later, Jeanne and I met for lunch, and I apologized. She assured me that the divorce had been for the best. In order to start over, she had decided to leave that whole period of life behind. She did not want to face Friedkin in court or try to resuscitate a relationship that was already dead. After the divorce, her career blossomed once again; fifty films were yet to come. An interview that she gave to the *New York Times Magazine* in 1989 summed it up:

> "I work more now," says Miss Moreau in her gravelly voice, "because at this time of my life I am not disturbed from my aim by outside pressures such as family, passionate relationships, dealing with who am I—those complications when one is searching for one's self." She pauses. "I have no doubt who I am."

I wished I could have said the same about myself.

26
Hollywood

In 1969, I received a phone call from Doug Netter, a film producer I had once helped resolve a contractual matter so minor that I had not even requested a fee. "Don't ask any questions," he said. "Just fly at once to Los Angeles. You have a reservation at the Beverly Wilshire Hotel." I had never been to California. My workload was light at that moment, so off I went. Indeed, I did have a suite held in my name. A note awaited me. "Don't unpack. Come immediately to the offices of MGM."

Shown into a conference room where Netter presided, I was introduced as an expert in the international financing and distribution of films. The general counsel, Frank Rosenfelt, looked at me askance. I wanted to respond with a shrug to suggest that Netter must have been smoking pot. The subject being discussed was whether to distribute Michelangelo Antonioni's film *Zabriskie Point*, whose quality was apparently in doubt.

At the end of the meeting, Netter pulled me aside. He explained that the financier Kirk Kerkorian had just taken control of the company and had named Jim Aubrey as president and he, Netter, as number two. They had much to do to turn the company around and did not trust the team they had inherited. For that reason, he reached out to me. I had never drafted a contract in that field; my experience was limited to *watching* films. Doug wanted to show the staff that he was now in charge, and I was just a prop. Before I could protest, he told me to take a plane to Rome to meet with Antonioni and screen the film. He then left for a meeting.

When I returned to my Hollywood hotel, there were abundant messages in my box from many leading actors requesting cocktails or dinner. Sophia Loren was most persistent. I thought I could ask her for suggestions for a good restaurant in Rome. Then I looked closely at the messages. They were for Nat Cohen, the president of EMI Films. I laughed out loud because I had really thought they might be for me; after all, this was Hollywood.

I don't know how many hours I was on a plane or how long I sat in a minuscule screening room with the renowned director. Antonioni did not know why I was there. Had I been clever, I would have told him the entire story, and I'm sure we would have shared a laugh. Instead, he viewed five copies of the film to make sure there were no defects. And I sat there the entire time, having to endure the desert that was the setting of a film that was not the master's best. It was the second time I used the word "surreal." Morning came, and we discussed other subjects as we drank caffé doppio.

I called Netter to say that I did not understand the film. It was paid for; only prints and marketing costs were needed. And it was too late to cancel, even if the film didn't have the grandeur of Antonioni's earlier masterpieces.

I was next invited to a London screening to view *Ryan's Daughter,* a romantic epic directed by David Lean. Aubrey, Netter, and I were left alone to watch the final cut. I had no idea why I was there. Both complained, in private, that the film was a dud. I suppose they were surprised when it received four Academy Awards nominations, winning two. The Aubrey–Netter team lasted about three years; Rosenfelt was named president in 1972.

I had very little legal work for MGM other than these meetings, which made little sense at the time. Aubrey called me once with a mysterious message. I would, he said, receive a visitor who would come with his approval. He could not say more. Not long thereafter, I was invited to a suite at the Prince de Galle Hotel. Two gentlemen were waiting for me. I was shown CIA credentials, and they suggested I consider the talk confidential. As they explained, agents were often housed in offices of film companies throughout the world, but when international distribution of films declined, they sought out another base. Would I make space for an African American lawyer who was to investigate student riots in France? I could not believe the absurdity of the request. I politely explained how rapidly his cover would be blown in a new firm with a very small staff.

Preston Robert Tisch, president of the Loew's Corporation, invited me to a cocktail party to celebrate the opening of the Churchill Hotel in London. Tisch had just hired my firm to negotiate the rights to construct a hotel in Monaco. Bomsel was to meet with Prince Rainier. I had a nice chat with a guest whose openness, charisma, and charm were evident. Although I don't usually ask, I wondered what he did. He responded that he worked for Warner Bros. With some hesitation, he told me he had just become the chairman of the board. His name was Steve Ross. He was about to leave for Cannes to attend his first festival for the showing of *Woodstock*. Of course I went along.

At the dinner following the screening of *Woodstock*, I saw Ross look around to study the glamorous women in the hall. An injudicious comment slipped from me. "Steve," I said, "your life is about to change. You will be divorced within the next few years." He was surprised, telling me he had been happily married for some twenty years. It was due to his wife that he had begun his career by owning funeral homes and parking lots. Years later, he was not pleased when I reminded him of that conversation.

The film world is clannish and gossipy, and for me, it was just make-believe. My involvement was slight, and yet to be seen dining with MGM executives or with Steve Ross attracted some film work, even though I had little experience in that field. After I handled a matter for Vincent Malle, he introduced me to his brother, the director Louis Malle, whose presence, dress, and movement exemplified elegance. Charged with helping on a possible censorship problem for his film *Murmur of the Heart*, I flew to New York to meet with the distributor. The film dealt with incest and starred Lea Massari, whom I wished had been my mother.

Saul Cooper, a publicist for United Artists, whom I knew socially, was elevated to head the studio's Paris office. Filmmaking in France for US companies was more of a side pocket rather than a major activity. Co-productions with French producers took place in order to obtain generous French government subsidies. Saul asked me to be the company's local lawyer. I thought it wise to first call Bill Bernstein, the United Artists general counsel, who was well known in the industry. I outlined my Hollywood career. He was amused by my recitation and appreciated my frankness, but advised me not to be concerned. He would send me forms and monitor my work.

Saul, a lovely man, had trouble saying no to projects that came his way. Unknown to me or to United Artists management, he agreed to a multi-film deal with a well-known French producer, a transaction that was beyond his authority. Erik Pleskow, the studio head, came to Paris to fire Saul. He asked me to contact the French producer and advise him that the arrangement was canceled. Although the agreement with the French producer might have made sense for the studio, Pleskow wanted the company's rules to prevail. He was a person whose dignity and authority were clear as soon as he entered the room. His family had made the last train out of Vienna before the Nazis entered. Lacking knowledge of English and starting as the "coffee boy" after serving in World War II, he went on to revive the United Artists with *One Flew Over the Cuckoo's Nest* and the films of Woody Allen.

Our exchange with the French producer was brutal, but Pleskow and I held firm. The producer left, vowing revenge against America. Pleskow was pleased with the result and invited me to a screening room to view a film whose editing had just been completed. We were alone as we considered the merits of Bernardo Bertolucci's *Last Tango in Paris*, a highly erotic film. "How French it was," I thought. I had never heard of the young actress, Maria Schneider, but I was familiar with her walk, her hat, her casual ease regarding sex, her lack of concern about ending a relationship. The problematic nature of the scene that caused a stir, Brando's use of a stick of butter in what was later revealed as a nonconsensual act of anal sex, escaped me until the reviews came out. Schneider, just nineteen, was unaware of what had been devised. She was later quoted: "I felt humiliated and, to be honest, I felt a little raped, both by Marlon and by Bertolucci. After the scene, Marlon didn't console me or apologize. Thankfully, there was just one take."

Pleskow arranged a perk—a room for me at the Cannes Film Festival, which I attended for several years. The festival seemed designed to allow those roaming the halls to find a sympathetic ear into which to pitch a project. When I opened my door for the breakfast tray, a pile of scripts awaited me, with handwritten notes affixed. "I saw you last night with X or Y. Please read this and pass it on."

Although our law firm was progressing as I had hoped it would, and my work was interesting, I remained restless and uneasy about engaging in an office regimen. Perhaps Professor Sohn and Hans Frank had been right. Deep within me there was a degree of anxiety because I had not yet found the vocation that fit my mind. I recalled a question on the aptitude test that I had once taken. "If you read the Sunday *New York Times*, what section do you open first?" I responded: "The Book Review." That answer still remained valid, as did my subscription to the Sunday paper, which arrived in Paris on the following Wednesday. As though reading should only be a Sunday-morning activity, I placed the paper on my doorstep on Saturday night. Reading it a week after its date of issue did not impede taking delight in this well-established habit. I once told that story to Roger Cohen, the Paris columnist for the *New York Times,* and he spun it into an article. As Roger wrote, "It's a reminder of how to control rather than be a slave to time, of the need to be imaginative and humble in our thankfulness, and of the fact that news can wait a week."

27

Turkey, the Perfect Escape

In July 1969, Neil Armstrong and Buzz Aldrin walked on the Moon. The December issue of *National Geographic* contained an excellent article on their mission. The issue also included a story that seemed lost in the excitement of examining photos of the human penetration of space. It was about the *Yankee*, a fifty-foot ketch, owned by Irving and Exy Johnson, a couple who spent their lives filming and writing books about their sailing adventures. They had just traveled along the southern coast of Turkey, an area relatively unknown and certainly not yet ready for tourists. Using Strabo's *Geographica* as a guide, they followed Strabo's itinerary as if the book had been recently written rather than in the 1st century CE. Nothing seemed to have changed.

I purchased an English translation of Strabo's book describing his travels along the Turkish coast. Although my law firm was still in its infancy, I could not resist the chance to take to the water and follow the *Yankee* lead. Perhaps I already regretted the decision to have an office on the Champs-Élysées; perhaps I remembered Conrad's view that the sea was a calming influence. I chartered a crewed sailboat with room for six, two guest couples for each leg of the route. We would start in Bodrum. The first guests would disembark in Antalya, where new friends would join for the return to the starting point. No one could complain that the trip was boring or too long.

In 1970, this part of Turkey was an area rarely visited. The coast and coves were ours alone to enjoy, as no other boat was in sight. There were few usable roads to the temples or graves carved into the mountainside of the ancient villages that Strabo encouraged readers to explore. Each night we would read an excerpt from Book VI in anticipation of the next day's harbor. We traversed Lycia, whose history was intertwined with the conquests of Alexander the Great. Although this area was once controlled by slave-holding pirates, it evolved into one of the earliest democracies. Strabo notes: "There from each city to a general congress, after choosing whatever city they approve of. The largest of the cities control three votes each, the medium-sized two, and the rest one."

Fig. 25. Architectural ruins, Turkey.

Fig. 26. Architectural ruins with carved tomb, Turkey.

In the mornings we swam in secluded coves, gathering amphorae that had lain idle and undisturbed for 1,000 years. In the afternoons we were explorers, following Strabo's movements from mountains to ravines, finding amphitheaters, tombs, and remnants of Saint Nicholas. The latter, known for his generosity, had been transformed into the Santa Claus myth. This trip made clear to me how much I preferred striking out for places unknown rather than residing in a lawyer's office.

One of my guests, Bob Towbin, became addicted to steering the sailboat through narrow shoals. Following our voyage, he purchased the ninety-foot *Sumurun*, a classic built in 1914 and once owned by the British novelist Vita Sackville-West. I was a guest on an early cruise when Towbin berthed in Cannes for the film festival. Inviting director Bob Fosse and actor Roy Scheider to join us for lunch and to show off his boat, Towbin sailed a bit too far from shore on the very day that Fosse's autobiographical film *All That Jazz*, starring Scheider, was featured at the Palais de Festival. When at last we berthed, Fosse and Scheider hardly said goodbye before they raced to change into tuxedos just in time to take a bow.

28

Albert Speer

The existential crisis beginning to take hold of me was temporarily resolved by a telephone call from David Puttnam. He and his partner, Sandy Lieberson, had created a company, Visual Programme Systems, to make and distribute documentary films for the then-new media format of video disks. Sandy had recently produced the film *Performance* with Mick Jagger. Puttnam had not yet received the prestige that would later come with his work on *Chariots of Fire, The Killing Fields,* and *The Mission,* among others. I was interested in the documentary films they were producing about the rise of Nazism and agreed to represent them on a pro bono basis.

Some months later, Puttnam called to suggest we fly to Germany and purchase an option for the film rights to Albert Speer's recently published memoir, *Inside the Third Reich*, already an international bestseller. Speer, a young architect charmed by Hitler in 1931, rose to become his Minister of Armaments and Munitions. Highly competent, Speer enabled Nazi Germany to prolong the war. At the Nuremberg trials, he disarmed the judges by assuming responsibility while denying knowledge of what others were doing. He accepted a degree of guilt for Nazi acts because, he claimed, he did not know, but should have known, if only he had made the effort to do so. By this stratagem, Speer avoided the death penalty and was sentenced to twenty years at

Spandau prison. He published *Inside the Third Reich* not long after his release.

I read Speer's book in 1971 when it became available in English. The *New York Times* review by John Toland, a noted military historian, surprised me. Speer, he wrote, was "decent and intelligent [. . .] fully admitting his guilt." Toland concluded that the book was "an earnest attempt [. . .] to atone for mistakes . . . ." I disagreed. Speer's memoir did not pass the smell test. His recall of incidents was inconsistent with what was actually taking place in the factories, in the camps, and in the minds of Hitler, Himmler, and Goebbels, with whom Speer was intimate. On finishing the book, my immediate reaction was that Speer was seeking to deflect charges of direct personal accountability for the horrors perpetrated by the regime he supported. Instead of introducing a defense of "just following orders," the one adopted by his co-defendants, Speer acknowledged fault because he failed to ascertain what was happening. That was a clever side step, I believed, not an admission of guilt for helping Hitler.

Speer's memoir was published at the height of America's involvement in the Vietnam War. The Pentagon Papers had been published by the *New York Times* in June 1971, chronicling past failures of the US government to be transparent in regard to the war. Four students had been killed at Kent State University in Ohio while protesting. Cambodia and Laos were being subjected to intensive carpet bombing. Years later I had lunch with Henry Kissinger, who insisted that our intervention in Vietnam would have ended differently if the bombing of Laos had been allowed to continue. Deaths from that ordinance continue to this day. And although Lt. William Calley was convicted for his role in the My Lai massacre of Vietnamese villagers, his sentence of life imprisonment was commuted by President Nixon. He served only three years—under house arrest. Where was accountability for violations of the rules of war?

Disparate as they might initially appear, all these incidents touched directly or indirectly on the responsibility of individuals for illegal or immoral acts they witnessed or were committed on behalf of their respective governments. As I had already been thinking about such matters, I was receptive to Puttnam's suggestion about acquiring the film rights to Speer's book, although I thought it unlikely that Speer would grant an option to two relatively young prospects.

We flew to Berlin to meet the German publisher, Wolf Jobst Siedler of Ullstein Verlag. Puttnam charmed. I signed the check. My account was emptied. I was surprised by how rapidly the negotiations were concluded. Only later did I grasp that Speer may have preferred to entrust the film adaptation of his book to those with limited historical knowledge of the period, men who would probably adhere to his version of events.

I had a specific idea of how to make the film. I thought of *Rashomon* as a model—a retelling of the same events in several ways that would reflect, but also slowly undermine, the ambivalence that Speer sought to evoke in his memoir. Each episode would unveil Speer's conduct differently. In so doing, the film would peel away the facade he had constructed. The final episode would be newsreels that contrasted Speer's conduct with actuality. I set about finding a writer for each section. My view of his conduct, compared with that of Toland and other reviewers, was not mainstream. Indeed, I may have been among the first to question Speer's veracity, his battle with the truth, which was the subtitle of a 1995 book by the journalist Gitta Sereny. She seemed to come perilously close to excusing Speer's conduct, which gave rise to the noted historian Richard J. Evans's conclusion that she "was unable to penetrate the mask."

For the historian Lord Acton, responsibility is not susceptible to division; participation is participation. "Historic responsibility," he noted, "has to make up for the want of legal responsibility." Historians have both the obligation and "the power to inflict a moral judgment." That applies equally to the person who authorizes the act, the person who commits the act, and those who rationalize the act. Of course, Speer was clearly answerable for his conduct as Hitler's Armaments Minister. But I wanted the film also to illustrate Speer's inaction during the early years of the Nazi regime. The film, in my view, was to ensure his responsibility.

Fantasizing that I was a part-time producer, I had tea with the economist and former USs ambassador to India, John Kenneth Galbraith, at the Ritz Hotel in Paris. Galbraith had been in charge of analyzing the impact of the Allied bombing campaign on German industry and was the first person to interview Speer at the end of the war. His notes from that meeting with Speer confirmed my instinctive reaction to the latter's memoir. Galbraith believed Speer was seeking to ingratiate himself with the occupation force, hoping to be viewed as a technocrat who could both help the Allies oppose the Soviet Union in the early days of the Cold War and revitalize a devastated Germany. I wanted to start the film with Galbraith's conversation with Speer. He agreed to write that segment.

A few days later, I had lunch with playwright Arthur Miller at Brasserie Lipp. I had recently met him when he came to Saché to visit Sandy Calder, who was his neighbor in Roxbury, Connecticut. I am sometimes astonished by my impertinence. Miller was perhaps the greatest American playwright of the twentieth century, as well as a successful screenwriter. He had endured a hostile reception from the House Un-American Activities Committee and was ultimately found guilty of contempt because he refused to reveal the names of friends and colleagues who had communist affiliations. Blacklisted by Hollywood for a period, Miller avoided prison only when sanity was restored and his conviction overturned. He had also had to deal with the emotional toll of his divorce from Marilyn Monroe and her subsequent death. Now, between the herrings and the choucroute, he was being asked to write a segment of a screenplay by someone he hardly knew.

Miller was hesitant to be involved with what he initially termed a Holocaust project. Unveiling Speer and his misconduct, I suggested, was a subject considerably different from a film about concentration camps. Since he had already written the play *Incident at Vichy*, I reminded him that Speer's story was about complicity and about good and evil—themes central to Miller's dramas.

He agreed to reconsider.

I had not yet grasped that Puttnam just viewed me as a guy with $25,000 of seed money for the project. He rarely discussed production plans with me, and I was unaware that he was already in talks with Paramount Pictures to sell the script and rights to the option I had acquired. I later learned that the idea to approach Speer originated with Andrew Birkin, then a twenty-six-year-old, who had been writing scripts for Puttnam and had previously worked for Stanley Kubrick. That explained why Birkin was engaged to work with Speer. I had been surprised by the choice, irrespective of Birkin's talent, since I believed the subject matter required someone with greater knowledge of the historical context in which Speer operated.

Pressed by Puttnam to place my own efforts on hold, I was embarrassed that I had been presumptuous in my solicitation of two well-known figures to write drafts for a film that had existed only in my mind. I nevertheless decided to make several trips to meet with Speer at his home in Heidelberg while Birkin was debriefing him. Speer welcomed me cordially. Tall, with broad shoulders, he had a pleasant face and the same sincere demeanor that may have disarmed the judges at Nuremberg. Years later when I visited Alger Hiss at the request of Paul Strand, I was struck by his physical resemblance to Speer. File cabinets filled with archival records lined the periphery of his office. His collection of documents was a defensive weapon to unleash if accusations about his conduct were revived. There were no family photos in this room, evidence perhaps that his relationship with his six children lacked warmth, although they had visited him while he was in Spandau prison. His desk, bare of any papers or mementos of his life, served as a barrier, an impediment to intimacy.

Speer was guarded and wary during our talks. I wondered if he was uneasy with a Jew—although he had already met with several Jewish groups after his release. At our initial meeting, I inquired mainly about his time in prison. I asked what had the most emotional impact on him during his twenty years in Spandau. He thought for a moment. With a sly smile he spat out "tooth powder" as if he were still brushing his teeth. He then explained. He detested the taste of tooth powder, the standard prison issue. Friends slipped tubes of toothpaste to him. That was convenient, he said, because he used the empty tubes to smuggle drafts of his memoir out of Spandau for editing. As he was reminiscing, Speer's face softened when he recalled the taste of mint or other flavors. The images in my mind were of camp survivors, filthy and emaciated, liberated by American troops.

A significant and lingering controversy involving Speer turned on whether he had been present at a 1943 meeting in Poznan when the SS leader Heinrich Himmler gave a speech encouraging the Gauleiters to accelerate the Final Solution. Speer abruptly interrupted one of our conversations when he learned that an article placing him at that meeting had just been published. He needed a respite to prepare a response consistent with his claim of ignorance. In our next meeting, I assured Speer that I did not want to talk about the Poznan "incident." Nor was I going to raise the subject of his precise knowledge of what was occurring in the death camps or his use of slave labor. It was not that I thought those matters were unimportant; rather, I believed the answers would be obvious. I wanted to concentrate on the "smaller" events that he had specifically mentioned and clearly acknowledged in his autobiography. I would gradually extend the questioning as if I were conducting a *Caine Mutiny*–style court-martial. I decided not to hold a placard with the number six million in bold print.

"Today, I'd like to talk about Werner Finck." Finck had been one of the stars of the Berlin cabaret scene in the 1930s. Cabaret comedians provided the social and political satire of the period. Imagine Mort Sahl, Lenny Bruce, or Jon Stewart. In 1931 Finck told a joke about Nazi parades. If they were "hindered by rain, hail, or snow, all Jews in the vicinity would be shot." A few years later, such jokes became more perilous. When Speer, with Hitler's approval, published grandiose plans for a vast urban renewal of Berlin, he became a cabaret target. I read Speer what he had written: "Werner Fink [sic] made fun of these projects [and] was sent off to a concentration camp [. . .]. His arrest took place, incidentally, just the day before I meant to attend his show as proof I was not offended."

That statement, I said to Speer, was no different from claiming you had a Jewish friend as proof you were not antisemitic. "Why were you 'not offended' by the fact that he was thrown into a camp?" I questioned. He was ill at ease, as if thinking, "I had covered my tracks so well, only to be tripped up by a young Jew and a Berlin comedian." He sensed that I had a list of similar inquiries about why he was not offended by the cascade of events he had witnessed, all of which were described in his book. He was right. But I never had a chance to raise these matters because Speer walked out of his neat and paperless office without a word.

I wanted to know if Speer was offended when Goebbels closed cabarets and independent media. I wanted to know if he was offended by Goebbels's habit of blackmailing actresses into having sex with him. I wanted to know if he was offended as he strolled around the streets and saw the broken glass and broken lives after Kristallnacht. Was he offended when he accompanied Hitler on his victory lap in Paris and encountered worn-looking refugees transporting their worldly goods in baby carriages on the side of the road while "the self-assured German troops" marched in the center of the city? When Hitler impulsively confided that he had contemplated the destruction of Paris to better ensure the reputation of Berlin, was Speer remorseful that his immediate reaction had been exaltation "for the prospects of soon resuming work on my building projects"? Did he still believe that "Hitler scarcely ever said anything about the Jews, about his domestic opponents, let alone the necessity of setting up concentration camps"? If Hitler had been so silent—how could Speer know what was happening?

So ended my last conversation with Albert Speer.

Even if I had failed to extract a verbal response from him and my questions remained unanswered, Speer did provide a devastating description of the Nazi inner circle. He depicted their craven interactions with Hitler, their constant flattery in order to secure their hold on power, and their attempts to discern Hitler's desires from his long and repetitive dinner-table monologues—all to better carry out his wishes, spoken or implied. From Speer's depiction emerges a portrait of complicit enablers that has universal implications and remains repugnant to this day.

When I traveled to Heidelberg, I usually flew there just for the day and did not substantially interact with Birkin, who left me alone to converse with Speer. Birkin had been meeting Speer daily to record details of his conversations with other Nazi leaders to insert into the script. Perhaps I sensed Birkin and Puttnam were seeking to do a movie I would find very ordinary and unchallenging, based mostly on the limited confessions contained in Speer's book. I thought more about those who had suffered at Speer's hands and wanted to question the truthfulness of his claims to limited knowledge of that suffering. Speer became fearful that the script would include incidents that my questions raised. He urged Birkin to refrain from being as precise as I had been. I had not seen a copy of Birkin's draft when Puttnam arranged a sale of the option and the script to Paramount.

The film was never made. Paramount may have bought the rights to kill a project that might have conflicted with its planned production of *Hitler: The Last Ten Days*, starring Alec Guinness. The Holocaust hardly figured in the script. Neither Birkin nor Puttnam seemed to understand that a film studio run by Jewish executives would have little interest in a script that failed to convey outrage about events that defy explanation. The Birkin script, although critical of Speer by placing him at the Poznan meeting, nevertheless followed the thesis Speer had laid out in his memoir, which normalized his conduct during the war. Hitler himself was treated in the script as a conventional person. Birkin has Hitler musing, "I want myself—just to hang up this old grey jacket on its nail and go back home [. . .] and leave all these problems to my successor." This aside to Speer supposedly took place just when the two men were accelerating the deployment of destructive V-2 rockets against the civilians of London.

I have long wondered how differently things would have turned out if Arthur Miller had signed on to the project. His imprimatur, coupled with his skilled recreation of Speer's descent from an ambitious architect to a perpetrator whose crimes rivaled those of the other Nazi leaders, might have been a masterpiece.

Puttnam wanted to make a film. I wanted to record a lesson for future generations. It may have been difficult to make a meaningful film about Speer in 1971. Few books had been written dissecting him and the myth he was trying to construct. Most journalists and biographers viewed Speer as a non-political technocrat. Indeed, a 1982 TV film based on Speer's memoir follows the Birkin–Puttnam error of viewing Speer's "personal struggle" and "gradual realization," rather than unearthing his deep and significant contribution to the horrors of the Nazi regime. Over the years, as new archival material became available, historians rendered moral judgment on Speer's direct involvement in death and destruction. Among the books that best dismantle the obstacles that Speer created is Adam Tooze's *The Wages of Destruction* (2006). The Speer myth that he was a nonpolitical technician could be revealed as a fantasy if you made the effort, as Tooze did, to compare what Speer claimed with what was actually happening in the camps and the factories under his control.

In his 2015 biography, *Speer: Hitler's Architect,* Martin Kitchen writes: "It was the Speers that made the regime possible."

And he adds, "This hollow man, resolutely bourgeois, highly intelligent, totally lacking in moral vision, unable to question the consequences of his actions, and without scruples, was far from being an outsider. He was of the type that made National Socialism possible." That accurate insight was absent from Birkin's script, but I believed it summarized all that needed to be said. I did not envision I would ever again be engaged in a film project about Speer, who died in 1981. I was wrong.

In 2015, the same year the Kitchen book appeared, I was invited to a private screening in New York City of a documentary film, *The Decent One*, produced and directed by Vanessa Lapa, an Israeli filmmaker. That film followed the career of Heinrich Himmler who, as head of the SS, the Nazi paramilitary organization, was largely responsible for constructing the extermination camps and implementing the Holocaust. Somehow, a cache of Himmler documents had been removed from Germany by GIs and ended up a half-century later under the bed of an Israeli diplomat who had died in Tel Aviv. Vanessa's father bought the collection, and she used extracts from the Himmler letters and diaries as the voiceover soundtrack.

I was impressed with Vanessa's film and invited her and Tomas Eliav, her capable sound designer, to meet with me. Relating my earlier experience with the Speer project and its failure, I suggested they consider making a film about Speer comparable to their Himmler documentary. They agreed, and I advanced $25,000 to get them started, the same amount that I had originally paid for the Speer option. I put them in contact with Sandy Lieberson, with whom I had remained in close contact. Sandy arranged a meeting between Lapa and Birkin, who had retained his notes and audio tapes of his conversations with Speer.

"I flew into Manchester this morning," Lapa wrote to me in February 2016, "and spent the whole day with Andrew in Wales. It has been an amazing day. Overwhelming, fascinating and extremely challenging. I thank you for 'pushing' me in the direction of Speer and the film Paramount never released. I told you when we first met, after the screening of *The Decent One*, that your Speer story will find closure. Today I can confirm this to you with great enthusiasm. Thank you again and again." I was promised a seat at the Academy Awards ceremony. Although I had recognized Lapa as one who engages in her work enthusiastically, I had underestimated her emotional needs, which soon became evident.

In a surprising move, Lapa had invited Errol Morris to participate in the making of the documentary as a co-director. She later claimed that it was Morris who asked to be involved. Morris's *The Thin Blue Line* is one of the most esteemed documentaries ever made; equally brilliant was his interrogation of Robert McNamara for *The Fog of War*, which won the 2003 Academy Award for best documentary. Morris was a superstar. But I had mixed feelings when I learned that he might be co-director. With him on board, I knew the film would be largely based on interviews of Birkin, for that was Morris's usual method. My concept of using archival material to document Speer's conduct might well be viewed as secondary, as would any role for me.

I was not told that the funds I advanced had been used by Morris and Lapa to fly to London and do a day's shooting with Birkin, who had already made his Speer audio tapes and the original script available to Vanessa. Had agreements been signed? Had they already allocated the tasks? Would I still be involved? I had made that a condition when I first met with Lapa. Before I could raise these questions, Morris advised Birkin that he wanted full control as the sole director. Lapa and Tomar would be producers.

I received emotional phone calls from the Israelis, fearful that Birkin might side with Morris. After apologizing for not keeping me informed, they asked me to protect their interests. They were concerned that Birkin might well prefer to continue the project with Morris. I read the transcript of Morris's interview with Birkin. I quickly realized that my ideas about how the film should be made were both less interesting and less impactful than Morris's. He had already extracted from Birkin's account of his sessions with Speer the material that would serve as the film's scaffolding. Morris's main thesis would be that Speer continued, successfully, to revise history. I suspected that Birkin and Puttnam would appear as Speer's unwitting co-conspirators.

In the Morris interview, Birkin acknowledged that he rationalized Speer's ambitious embrace of Hitler. The Nazis were a nasty bunch, commented Birkin, "[b]ut Speer seemed to be a man not unlike ourselves at the time he got his break with Hitler . . . I identified with him very strongly because I had had a very strong relationship with Stanley Kubrick." At another moment, Birkin reveals, "I was trying to write him [Speer] as the main character for a movie with whom I wish the audience to identify [. . .] to come out [. . . of the theatre] saying there but for the grace of God go most of us."

Good and evil inhabited all of us—that was Birkin's view. Striving for success, who among us could withstand the temptation of a relationship with someone whose power could advance that goal? It was challenging, thought Birkin, for anyone to turn down the possibility of becoming a famous architect even if it meant supporting Hitler. Kubrick? Good and evil? Birkin was not suggesting Speer's innocence, but he was allowing him to elude historical responsibility for the singular enormity of attempting to extinguish Jews, gypsies, and gays. In the transcript, Birkin readily admitted that if he had been Jewish, perhaps there might have been greater emphasis on the Holocaust. He conceded that if he had had the same experience as Stanley Cohen's first wife (who will eventually make her appearance in this memoir), who had been abused by the Nazis, perhaps the script would have been more critical of Speer.

I thought that if I could resolve the question of co-directorship that now prevented Lapa and Morris from working together, the resulting film might be a masterpiece. I assumed—whether by arrogance, naivety, or a failure to appreciate the force of the artistic ego—that I could reconcile the differences between Lapa and Morris. I then began a series of telephone calls and text exchanges with Morris. Disparaging my initial concept, which he deemed no different from other films, he wrote to me: "How many experts are needed to say that Speer was aware of the Holocaust? Yes, it should be said, but there is a deeper story to be told." Morris wanted to do this film very badly. He suggested that I try to convince the Israelis to embrace the idea of a film by Vanessa Lapa and Errol Morris—that is, produced by Vanessa Lapa and directed by Errol Morris.

Lapa refused to consider any arrangement other than being co-director, and she began to feel I was supporting Morris, which I was not. I just wanted to have the film made. I also failed to persuade Morris to accept Lapa as co-director, even if he retained control of the final cut. Lapa believed there was a conspiracy to oust her from the project. She thought Morris and I were seeking to influence Birkin, but neither of us had been in touch with him. Nevertheless, she rushed Andrew to Tel Aviv for a three-day shoot so as not to lose momentum. Although Lapa was an excellent documentarian, she had little experience in conducting a dialogue, a skill of which Morris was a master. I continued discussions with

Morris. He wondered if he should send the tape of the interview to Birkin. I encouraged him to do so. I also alerted Andrew that he would become the focus of the film, much like McNamara had been in *The Fog of War.* Also, he, as well as Puttnam, might be criticized for their failure to see through Speer's self-serving revisionism. I was still under the impression that I could resolve all outstanding conflicts.

When Birkin returned to England from Tel Aviv, he requested an edited version of the interview Lapa had filmed. After several weeks without a response, Birkin became uneasy, suggesting that he might not go forward with the Israeli team. Vanessa, emotional and still fearful of losing control, reacted strongly in a telephone call with Andrew, and that triggered a response from him: "I cannot work with you. I've experienced meltdowns from actresses in my career, but never from a director." Birkin wanted an idea of "what sort of film" she had in mind. Vanessa was furious that Birkin had received the Morris cut. She believed it was evidence of a stratagem to supplant her. She did not understand that I had approved sending the cut and that Morris was not trying to replace her. Indeed, he had no interest in proceeding unless all parties agreed. She then insisted Birkin sign a contract before she would reveal any aspect of her plans. My relationship with her was in complete decline. Morris still tried to work out an arrangement with Birkin, even on a non-exclusive basis, allowing both him and Lapa to do separate films. The absurdity was that Lapa had no rights. Morris and Birkin could have decided to do the documentary, but everyone dealing with Lapa tried to be fair, while recognizing her emotional state.

In January 2019, some three years after I first floated the idea, Morris sent me a note: "I most certainly have not given up my interest in making a film about Speer. [. . .] I need your help." He added, "I know you were hopeful that there was a way that I could work together with them. I would not rule out that possibility." I tried to intervene, unaware that Lapa had already completed her own film, *Speer Goes to Hollywood,* which was on its way to the Berlin International Film Festival. The film, consisting of actors reading extracts from the tapes and archival material, presented an appropriately critical portrait of Speer. What caused vociferous debate, however, was the use of material, altered from the original, which portrayed Birkin as an apologist for Speer and, to some, as antisemitic, which was certainly not true.

I only learned of the film's existence when I received an email from a friend alerting me that I had been listed in the credits as an executive producer. In Lapa's initial interviews with the press, I was cited as the original impetus for the project. This was upsetting. I had not been in contact with her for a long time, and she had not had the courtesy to send me a copy of the film. Harshly criticized by Morris and the documentary-film community for using actors and for misleading the public who believed the soundtrack captured Birkin and Speer's actual conversations, Lapa was also faulted—according to Birkin—for adding material not in the original tapes or for presenting it out of context. Whether or not because of this controversy, Vanessa and Tomar decided to distribute the film themselves. Other than a brief showing at the Film Forum in New York City and in the absence of a streaming venue, the film never found an audience.

29
James Baldwin

Not long after my first involvement with the Speer project, I received a telephone call from a French accountant seeking advice on an American tax matter. At the end of our conversation, he told me that his client was James Baldwin, who was then living in Saint-Paul-de-Vence in the south of France. He added that he was representing Baldwin without charge as he admired his work. When I responded that I did too and would be glad to help, he suggested that I join him for lunch when his client was next in Paris. Over the next few months, I had several meals with Jimmy (as I now called him) in Paris, usually with his companion, a gifted photographer, J. R. Scott, Jr., who gave me a photographic portrait of Jimmy for his birthday.

Right before one of my work trips to New York, Jimmy asked me to meet with Richard Marek, his editor at Dial Press, and seek, on his behalf, an additional monetary advance and more time to finish a book. I was surprised at the request since he did not seem short of funds and could have spoken directly to Marek, with whom he had a close relationship. He also must have had an agent or an intellectual rights lawyer who could have done this over the phone. Baldwin was sometimes mysterious. I complied, not as an attorney but as a friend. I met with Marek in Manhattan. He seemed surprised, and his response was vague, but he agreed to do something to satisfy the request. When I returned to France, Jimmy was pleased and invited me to spend a weekend at his home in Saint-Paul-de-Vence.

Fig. 27. James Baldwin; photograph by A. Scott, a gift to Stanley Cohen on his fortieth birthday.

We dined at the Colombe d'Or, the Michelin-star restaurant near his home. I probably wanted to impress him, so I related in detail my attempt to make a film about Albert Speer. I added that one of the themes I wanted to explore was complicity, that is, responsibility for inaction, the standing by while millions of people were herded into camps. Baldwin neither scowled nor smiled, probably thinking I had not understood his writings from decades earlier in which he had condemned the white race for their refusal to recognize the systematic oppression and destruction of Black lives. "It is the innocence," he wrote, "which constitutes the crime." "In your education," he said to me, "whether in the Bronx or at Harvard, the subject of slavery or the treatment of the Blacks was just covered in a sentence or two, not even worthy of an entire chapter." This was one of the motifs he explored in his dramatic 1965 debate with William F. Buckley, Jr., at the Cambridge Union Society in England. Africa was all but unknown to white Americans until they fought in World War II and found a continent first populated by Blacks—some good, some bad, just like them.

We were no longer having a conversation. A conversation was an exchange in which Jimmy spoke with a throaty, raspy voice. Now the ideas he was developing were expressed in a soliloquy, voiced in a softer, silky manner with the last syllable of certain words stretched out to leave an echo in the mind. He continued with his lesson. While the Holocaust is rightly condemned, with memorials erected and reparations made to atone for the murder of the Jews, the Nazi perpetrators came from a particular moment in time, not spread out over centuries, as was the case with those who committed crimes against Blacks. The number of those involved with the slave trade was so vast and the timeline so extensive that accountability lay not solely with one nation gone mad but with the entire white race. That made amends vastly more elusive for Blacks than for Jews. These may not have been his exact words, but my account conveys his response to my feeble attempt to impress a writer and intellectual of his stature.

We returned to his house. It was early, so I retired to read in bed. It was a bunk-type berth in a tiny library. Sometime later the door opened, and Jimmy entered. Without a word, he pulled down the blanket and crawled into the bed next to me. I did not move or say a word but continued reading. I felt the gaze of his large, liquid eyes just a few inches away. It was a small bed. Over the years, when I think of that night, the bed gets smaller and smaller. After a decent interval, I turned my head and simply said, "Jimmy, I'm not interested in men." He immediately got up and walked to the door. Turning toward me, he said, "Stanley"—then a pause—and he was the master of the pause—"you are missing the best night of your life."

During Baldwin's pause, which seemed to last without end, I looked up at him from the low bunk bed. He was no longer limited by his modest height; indeed, he appeared to expand into a black marble statue of enormous proportions. He had chosen me as a lover. And I knew from the experience of a friend, the filmmaker Michael Raeburn, who had worked with Baldwin on the screenplay for *Giovanni's Room,* that love and creative work were often combined. Did his interest in me signal an opportunity to spend working time together, perhaps allowing me to realize a fantasy of writing a novel? Should I have accepted the implicit invitation of a creative life which had so far eluded me? And was his request to meet with his editor merely one step to lead to the seduction now unfurling? . . . All of this went through my mind during that interminable pause.

On the plane back to Paris, I wondered: Was Baldwin more interested in my body than my mind? Then I thought, would my epitaph read: "Here lies a person who never made love with James Baldwin"?

I mean this as a metaphor, of course, never having been deeply involved in the creative process.

30

Travels with Toby Molenaar

I developed a close personal relationship with Puttnam's partner, Sandy Lieberson. He had started his career as an agent for major stars, including Mick Jagger, the Rolling Stones, Richard Harris, Peter Sellers, and Sergio Leone, before becoming a producer. Eventually, he was named head of production, first for MGM and then for Twentieth Century Fox. He helped reanimate the prestigious Cuban International Film and Television School and still gives lectures on the making of the original *Blade Runner*. No one in the professional film industry has a better reputation for honesty and straightforwardness than Sandy.

Whenever I traveled to London, I stayed with Sandy and his then-wife, Marit Allen, a film costume designer. A visit when I was turning thirty-eight changed my way of life. When I entered the Lieberson apartment on Mount Street, I realized he had another guest, Jacoba Molenaar, familiarly known as Toby. Lithe, attractive, with short auburn hair, she had a quiet demeanor that radiated warmth and encouraged conversation as we unpacked. Born in Holland and subjected to Nazi abuse as a child, Toby had moved to Zurich after the war, and then to the Mallorcan village of Deià. She was twice divorced. The second time was not long before I met her. Her husband had run off with a younger woman. In short, she was fragile when we met. At the same time, her career as a photojournalist was blooming. Included in her resume were shoots in British Columbia, India, the Rann of Kutch, Afghanistan, and

Nuristan. Time-Life books on the Amazon and the Arctic featured her photos, as did London Sunday newspapers. When I first saw her, she was in London to meet with the editor of the *Observer* to discuss a story about Mondragon in the Basque Country of Spain. Of course, I invited myself to meet her there.

Mondragon, a mountain town an hour's drive from Bilbao, was known for its forward-thinking worker participation in industry. The Mondragon Corporation, one of the largest in Spain, is the umbrella for a series of co-ops and factories that are worker-owned and often studied as a model for industrial societies. While Toby interviewed its leaders and took photos, I walked through the town, fascinated by a culture of which I had been ignorant. After a few days, she returned to Deià, and I to Paris. I offered to visit her.

I knew nothing of Mallorca, and even less of Deià, long a haven for writers and artists. Toby explained that the patriarch of the village was the poet and novelist Robert Graves, who had settled there in 1929 at the suggestion of Gertrude Stein. Graves insisted on our meeting to extend a blessing or a blast as he weighed my right to consort with Toby. Her relationship with Graves and his wife, Beryl, was extremely close. They traveled and vacationed together. Graves sometimes edited her journalistic copy. If she wasn't one of his white goddesses, she certainly was under his protection. Indeed, prior to our meeting, I reread his most famous works, *The White Goddess* and *Goodbye to All That,* his memoir about fighting in the battles of Loos and the Somme during World War I. I also studied a few of his early poems. I wondered if I dared to ask: What was the trumpet sound that beckoned poets to go to war? Not yet mature, and with names so pure—Siegfried, Wilfred, Rupert, Edmund, and Ivor—they all rushed with Robert to fill trenches with odes describing their fall.

But the boys who were killed in the battle
Who fought with no rage and no rant
Are peacefully sleeping on pallets of mud
Low down with the worm and the ant.

Graves had been badly wounded in the war, and false reports of his death devastated admirers. With a shell wound to an upper thigh, a finger turned septic, and shrapnel in his lungs, it was not surprising that his death was pronounced prematurely.

I shared with Graves a love for a certain part of female anatomy, the nape of the neck. Graves's poem evoked a faded memory of my Yokohama ladies.

To speak of the hollow nape where the close chaplet
Of thought is bound, the loose ends lying neat
In two strands downward, where the shoulders open
Casual and strong beneath, waiting their burden,
And the long spine begins its easy journey:
The hair curtains this postern silkily,
This secret stairway by which thought will come
More personally, with a closer welcome
Than through the latticed eyes or portalled ears.

Graves's writing was so intertwined with his own life that private emotions and public lines became indistinguishable. I was uncertain what thoughts were his, and which had come from the American-born poet Laura Riding, whose complicated relationship with Graves and his family made the love triangle in *Jules et Jim* seem like a child's fairy tale. Instead of driving off a bridge, Riding plunged from a window after an argument. Graves followed suit, albeit from a lower floor, landing unharmed.

Toby warned me that Graves was a prima donna, often wandering through the village, followed by an entourage absorbed by his verbal genius and accepting his claims that he was never wrong. As I walked the stone paths through the olive trees chatting with Graves, who at seventy-five was still a lively and elegant man, dementia, which would soon envelop him, was not yet discernible. Wisps of white, unkempt hair lifted by the wind gave him the air of a deity. "My hair," he once said, was "fed on the best brains in England." His nose, off-center, a heritage of school rugby, suggested an ex-boxer rather than a romantic seeking love. But why attempt to describe a face already immortalized by Graves's own pen?

> Grey haunted eyes, absent-mindedly glaring
> From wide, uneven orbits; one brow drooping
> Somewhat over the eye.

The word *égérie*—a muse—had been added to my French vocabulary as a result of my involvement in the recovery of the de Portes jewelry. Every writer delving into the collapse of France in 1940 applied that label to the countess. She was depicted as a successor to Mme. Roland of the Girondins, compared to Thérésa Tallien of the Directoire, and to Mme. de Maintenon, King Louis XIV's second wife. *Webster's New International Dictionary* offers "woman advisor" as a definition, but I thought the French *égérie* held a deeper implication. In *The White Goddess*, Graves alludes to Egeria as a nymph whom he associated with midsummer promiscuous love-making, but he does not mine the concept or its meaning in any detail. I was sufficiently immodest to explain its origin to him. I told Graves that I had heard that term so often that I had become fascinated by its origin. I had traced its use to Numa Pompilius, the legendary second king of ancient Rome, who had succeeded Romulus and ruled for forty years. Numa, desirous of imposing religious order on an unruly population, retired at night to a sacred grove and returned at dawn with instructions and legislation allegedly imparted to him by the nymph Egeria. Visible only to Numa, the commands of Egeria could hardly be contested by the populace.

In the mid-nineteenth century, Balzac and his contemporaries popularized the literary use of *égérie*, with meanings ranging from muse and fortune-teller to source of inspiration and influence. After a citation by Marcel Proust in *The Guermantes Way*, the word was accepted by the Académie Française in its 1932 dictionary. *Égérie* became known to every French schoolchild as denoting an influence, perhaps hidden, on a political or artistic person. *Égérie*—or its English equivalent, egeria—has never been incorporated into everyday English conversation. It is uncomfortable to say, even if true, that Nancy was the egeria of the Reagan administration or that Hilary also played that role for Bill. Besides, the sound is harsh in English. In French, *égérie* (like *chérie*)—pronounced *ejereee*—rolls gracefully and sensually off the tongue.

For Graves, a muse was a source of inspiration for love and creativity. While egeria could be defined in that way, the French had broadened its connotation so that it was a descriptive term for a determined woman who seeks to impose her will rather than remain a passive observer of a man's success. After my lengthy discourse on egeria, I asked Graves if he thought that word, well worn in France, was illustrative of how women were perceived in that country—not passive, but strong-willed and manipulative, like Lady Macbeth, ready to instill strength into a faltering male. I sensed a smile emerging on his rugged face. He liked the image and suggested that I write a book. I promised to do so when restlessness no longer possessed me.

Toby later told me that although I had talked too much, I had passed the test. Graves introduced me to Beryl, who was neither a muse nor an egeria, but an anchor, who, in Toby's words, kept him "attached to earthly life." At his age, sexual obsession no longer dominated his days, nor did one still hear gossip that half the infants in Deià bore his genes.

After my walk with Graves, I entered a cafe to have a cortado, a habit formed in Spain. A walrus-mustached customer sat at a corner table with a chessboard beside his cup. Without a word he motioned me to join him. He was Jakov Lind, a writer whose life had unfolded along "a makeshift path," not the one he had originally intended. As with anyone who escaped the Holocaust, whether by luck or chance or by burrowing deep within the earth until the evil winds had passed, Lind, like Riva, carried a survival ribbon on his sleeve, invisible except to those who were also on the wrong path at the wrong time.

Lind was eleven in 1938 when the Nazis marched into Vienna. "God lost his chance to be recognized by me," he would later write. He left by train for Rotterdam and The Hague. Living under an assumed identity, he first hid in an attic warren and later found a hiding place on a farm. Then, having obtained a false passport, he worked on a barge on the Rhine, hoping his shipmates would not divine his Jewish birth. "I have to survive to see the capitulation," he wrote, "because my existence has a purpose . . . I must live to see the end." Later, after passing skeletal human remains on the road from Bergen-Belsen, he reached a tent camp on the outskirts of Marseilles. From there, he snagged a boat to Palestine and ended up in another internment camp. When he finally came into his own as a writer, his preoccupation with survival permeated his books. I embraced his friendship, enjoyed our many talks, and paid for his funeral when he died in 2007.

Toby was invited to Brazil by the government tourist office to photograph remote areas for its travel brochures. A small plane and a guide were provided. I went along. We first spent a week on a ranch in Marajo, an island as large as Switzerland, located in the mouth of the Amazon, not far from where it meets the Atlantic Ocean. The fluvial-maritime archipelago of which it is a part is the largest in the world. Archaeological sites there revealed pottery and other clues of advanced settlements stretching back to pre-Columbian times.

Raising cattle and water buffalo were the main activities on the island. At night Toby and I hunted yacare caimans with our host. With the assistance of skilled Marajoara escorts in small boats, we illuminated with flashlights the reptiles' red eyes just above the river's surface. We carefully draped a lasso around their mouths and pulled the small ones into the boats. I declined to share in the BBQ that followed.

Astride a water buffalo, I followed Toby through both the savanna and the swamps as she photographed the varied landscapes and chatted with the local women. Riding the buffalos through tall grass somehow resulted in an allergic reaction that made me have to urinate every few minutes. I was therefore uncomfortable when we flew on a tiny plane to Manaus, our next destination. In 1971, Manaus had not yet become the eco-tourist attraction it is today. Other than its great opera house, built in the 1880s–90s by the rubber barons who got rich there, Manaus was then a drab outpost. I was still suffering from my urinary issues when we next set forth by plane to fly deep into the jungle, where we bunked with a construction crew that was building a portion of the vast trans-Amazonian highway. I should have carried an empty bottle as a precaution, but I was told it was only a twenty-minute flight. I peed right before we left.

Flying over the pristine jungle offers a remarkable sight. The uninterrupted green carpet below spreads out in every direction.

"Infinite" is too modest a description for what we saw. Our plane had few instruments. The pilot was trying to find the highway, since that is where we were to land, but after more than the promised twenty minutes, the pilot announced he was lost and could not find the road. He said he had no choice but to return to Manaus. By this point I was in agony. Then the pilot at last spotted the camp, and we finally landed on a dirt road, little more than a thin pathway with the jungle encroaching on either side. Like a shot I was out the plane door and dashed into a thicket to relieve myself. With eyes closed I remained immobile until the pressure in my groin subsided. I must have set a new record for duration.

Surprised at the eerie quiet, I finally opened my eyes. I was shocked to find myself surrounded by natives in loincloths carrying bows and arrows. Several were children; all were barefoot and short in stature. I had not heard their approach. They must have been observing me all along. Although initially apprehensive and uncertain of my welcome, I assumed they were friendly since the camp for the construction workers had been established in their area for several months. Massacres of settlers invading native land had taken place elsewhere. Raising my hand in greeting, I thought to say, "I'm a friend of Nicholas Guppy." Guppy was the first white explorer of the Northern Amazon. He wrote about his year-long stay with the Wai-Wai tribe. He, too, had been encircled by half-naked natives with immense bows and arrows when he arrived in their territory. I had met Nicholas, a noted botanist whose father had discovered several species that bear his name, when he came to Saché to visit Sandy Calder. He later stayed with me for a few days at the mill to view the *Ephemeropterae*, known non-poetically in English as mayflies. Once a year, millions of these aquatic insects emerged from the river to seek the nearest light, to mate, and then to die before dawn.

The natives that surrounded me did not smile in welcome as they did for Guppy; their countenance seemed grim. I was hesitant to even say hello, but they stepped aside to let me pass. I wondered how their lives would be transformed by the influx of foreigners sure to come when the road was complete. Fifty feet away from where they and I stood in silence was the plane, an indication of change, a tiny distance but a century of time. I eased my way toward Toby in the camp. The plane departed, the newly opened dirt road its runway. Jungle vines were already stretching from one side of that road in a slow creep that made me question if the pathway, an intruder in a land of green, could long exist, or if it might infect pristine nature with an affliction not yet understood.

We were scheduled to remain in the camp for the next two days. A huge tent housed some eighty workers. We slept on cots in the open area of the tent. I woke up with a sharp pain in my arm from an insect bite. I thought it would soon subside, but I started to shake and shiver as if I had to contend with snow and cold, rather than heat. Fearful that I may have been bitten by a poisonous spider, the camp leader was concerned about how I could be evacuated. Fortunately, a military plane was flying overhead, and the pilot, contacted by radio, agreed to land and ferry us back to Manaus. After two days in the hospital, I was completely well.

Toby was always unperturbed. She had developed the habit of living in a sleeping bag in any place she found herself. She asked if I wanted to return to Paris, but I was determined to continue. When I asked to accompany her on this trip, I knew what the conditions would be like in the Amazon. I was not going to abandon our trip because of a spider bite.

Since Toby rarely talked about her past assignments, I had not known until I arrived in Brazil that she had explored the Amazon once before as a photojournalist. Sponsored by the Brazilian ambassador to England, she was among the first to witness the highway's construction. She accompanied the first engineers charged with laying out the road. Her living conditions were spartan, with only a curtain to allow some personal privacy, and caiman, monkey, and snake mixed with cassava and rice as her diet. For many of the natives whose lives were uprooted by the machinery and the noise, she was the first white woman they had ever seen.

Toby's next assignment, gun in hand, was to live among the gold miners of Crepuri, some 200 miles south of Manaus. As in most rough-and-tumble towns in the midst of a gold rush, its inhabitants were mostly an assemblage of lawless stakers-of-claims, killers and their victims, bar keepers, and whores. Her story was featured in a Sunday edition of the *Telegraph Magazine.*

A small boat carried us on a river drift, starting where the Rio Amazon meets the Rio Negro. We slept in hammocks on deck, swam in the river, and walked through a section of jungle so dense that the trees entirely blocked the rays of the sun from touching the ground. Toby captured these moments best in her memoir, *The Accidental Feminist*:

> Suddenly, the night was full of unfamiliar sounds . . . ? I could not always place the croaks and squeaks for here fish grunted like pigs and could do almost anything; they whistled, peeped, quaked and cawed like birds . . . [L]istening to the cacophony, I realized I was a long way from anywhere [. . . just] a minuscule part of the night, part of these black trees, of the river, the star-filled sky and the very jungle . . . I was healing and I loved my life.

A second trip together only added to the warmth of our relationship. I had become involved with a consortium constructing an oil-pipe-laying barge to be used in the North Sea. I was representing a Texas group that would help run and staff the barge once in place. One of the problems was finding welders, since workers experienced in that trade were more easily found in Texas and Louisiana than in England or on the Continent. My clients were keen to lure welders employed by Brown & Root, a large American industrial services company. I was concerned about lawsuits arising from violating its workers' contractual obligations. I flew to Houston and carefully prepared the contracts. The main difficulty was the recruits' insistence that Cajun spices and sauces be available for their meals before they would agree to leave for the North Sea.

When the barge was launched, Toby and I were invited to Aberdeen, Scotland, for a week aboard. I underestimated the financial firepower of the oil companies and the entities servicing their needs. A private plane shuttled us between Brussels and the Scottish port, while cargo planes landed there twice a day with

Fig. 28. Stanley Cohen aboard a pipeline barge during a legal work assignment.

Fig. 29. Pipeline worker's hat presented to Stanley Cohen.

supplies from Texas and elsewhere. From the Aberdeen airport, a helicopter brought us to the barge. It was a floating factory operating around the clock. Each table in the dining room had an array of Mexican hot sauces to comply with the clauses I had inserted in their contracts. Welders were positioned toward the aft of the vessel. Pipes came up from a loading platform onto a conveyor belt two feet above the deck. The welder leaned forward to bond the sections as the pipe was paused. The barge moved slowly, propelled not by motor but by two huge anchors thrown forward by catapults. Winches then rewound the anchor wires to move the barge forward, allowing the welded pipes slowly to slide off the rear deck and down to the ocean floor.

Toby had a story and photos, and I had a lesson in welding. I still have the special cap with its large visor worn by the welders to prevent sparks from smoldering in the inner ear.

31

Calder's Legacy

These trips represented a first for me: traveling with a companion. It was also the first time since law school that I had a roommate for more than a short stay. We decided to cohabit. Toby relinquished her Deià home, and I thought it best to abandon Villa Seurat and its memories of bachelor life. We moved to a grand Art Deco apartment with a large garden on Boulevard de Montparnasse, not far from where my Parisian life began.

No childhood training had prepared me to share feelings or inquire about how a loved one felt. Neither did I know how to probe for signs of distress. The same was true of Toby. She was reserved and placed no burden on me to reveal what was buried deep inside. I hinted at, but did not warn her, of my tendency to become uneasy with a pattern and then suddenly don a dress uniform in order to sit in an opera box. No ground rules governed our partnership. We were more friends than passionate lovers. My only requirement was that we have a child. Marriage wasn't required. Toby was often traveling to foreign parts, and I had legal matters that also led to lengthy trips overseas. We had what the French would call "a good table," and our evenings were often filled with friends and visitors. For years the routine calmed and suited me. Our bond has been tested but has remained firm for fifty years, even though I later became a father of a second child with a new partner.

Saché was our weekend retreat. The Calders and Davidsons were delighted with my change of status. Toby immediately became intimate with both families. Among the joys of our weekend visits were dining with a host of Calder invitees, especially Gabrièle Buffet-Picabia, a musician, journalist, and art critic, born in 1881. Divorced from the artist Francis Picabia, she had been a significant influence in the Dada movement. Here was a walking encyclopedia, nearly a century old, who beguiled us with stories about luminaries whose paintings and poems we only knew of from books and museums. She had walked and eaten and drunk with Marcel Duchamp and Apollinaire, with Picasso, Igor Stravinsky, and André Breton. The memories of those encounters were the subjects of our dinner conversation. I did not know until I read an account of her early years written by her great-granddaughters that several of those artists were her lovers.

When Sandy and Louisa spent time in Paris, they would use the guest room in our new apartment rather than stay, as they usually did, at the Hotel Madison on Boulevard Saint-Germain. Late one night, when I was away on a business trip, Sandy got up and went to our bathroom instead of the one near his room. He then sleepily entered the bed where Toby was sleeping. She didn't move a muscle. After snoring for an hour or so, he got up again to pee and found his way back to Louisa.

Calder did not seem to mind if I attended his meetings with architects who came to Saché to commission a mobile to be designed for an airport ceiling or a stabile to enhance a town square. Sandy usually started by indicating flaws in the architect's design, but if he liked the project, he quickly sketched what he had in mind. I sometimes sat at a small nearby table piled with letters and various statements. One letter I perused urged him to go to Jerusalem to install a major work. I did not know that talks on this project had been underway for several years until I received a telephone call from Yona Fischer and Martin Weyl, curators at the Israel Museum, who must have learned of my relationship with Calder. Together with the Jerusalem mayor, Teddy Kollek, they urged me to convince Calder to come to Israel for an exploratory visit. Evidently, Jean Davidson, a man of the left, believed that a visit to Israel by Calder was equivalent to his condoning how Palestinians were then being treated.

Asked by the Israelis to intervene, I spoke to Sandy and Louisa. Although they also shared Jean's views of the Palestinians' plight, they were less absolute in their reaction to the invitation. Because they were hesitant about traveling to Israel, given the unrest there, Toby and I said that if they decided to go, we would accompany them. I could not resist telling Sandy of my earlier adventure in that country. Perhaps we could go and see if the family was still waiting for me at the hotel in Herzliya. Sandy laughed. The four of us went to Israel in April 1975, despite a PLO takeover of the Savoy Hotel in Tel Aviv the month before, during which five hostages had been killed. As invitees of the government, we stayed in the Mishkenot Sha'ananim Guest House, which had opened two years earlier for eminent visiting scholars, musicians, writers, and artists. The Guest House overlooked the walls of the Old City, and the room, although sparsely furnished, was large and comfortable. Breakfast and tea were provided in a central room that allowed the residents to mingle and get to know one another. We heard music, and learned that Rudolf Serkin and Alexander Schneider were also guests there, rehearsing for a concert. They often joined us for afternoon tea.

Whatever reservations Lousia and Sandy had prior to the trip quickly dissipated because of the hospitality, charm, humor, and intellectual qualities of our guides, headed by Weyl, and the warm reception by Mayor Kollek. In addition to accompanying Calder while he inspected potential locales for a stabile, we were tourists with a full schedule to visit the classic places of interest in Jerusalem. Toby took photos of Sandy at the Wailing Wall and at the ruins of ancient synagogues. We walked the Old City souk to shop for souvenirs. I later read in Jed Perl's Calder biography that observers in Jerusalem found Sandy "tired" or "impaired." I found those comments surprising. For a man of seventy-seven, with some of the infirmities of aging, he showed great energy in striding up and down hills to find an ideal setting for a major work. I saw no more fatigue in him than what I myself felt after a day of visits to historical sites. When we strolled on King David Street, the pedestrian walk that stretches from the Jaffa Gate to the Western Wall, I was impressed by the steadiness of his gait. Bending slightly forward from the waist, as if his shoulders were burdened by a heavy weight, Sandy's arms hung motionless by his sides, perhaps a symptom of Parkinson's. He was about thirty feet ahead of me when I spied a pickpocket extracting his wallet from his back pocket. I gave chase, but the thief slipped into a crowded alleyway and disappeared.

Within a few months of his return to France, Calder submitted a preliminary model or maquette to Mayor Kollek. He was envisioning a forty-foot-high red stabile. I was surprised to learn that with all the pressure on Sandy throughout the years to accept the Jerusalem Foundation "commission," actual funding for the project was not yet available. His trip had been based entirely on speculation. But Kollek worked his magic, and by June 1976, the maquette drawing was being transformed into the final piece, which is now known as Homage to Jerusalem.

I don't know why I continued to read the documents on Calder's desk, but the accounting statements from his dealers had begun to concern me. They were somewhat vague, and when the dealers came to Saché, they scooped up gouaches and other items without making a precise list of what works or objects became part of their inventory. Noticing that a dealer had established a Swiss account in Sandy's name and was paying commissions from sales into that bank, I quickly stopped that practice and ensured that all monies were transferred to Sandy's own bank account and all taxes paid. At that time Sandy was supporting deserters from the Vietnam War, and I was especially worried about an FBI inquiry or an IRS audit.

The Calders were completely uninterested in money. Living in a simple and frugal manner, Sandy seemed to have little knowledge of how much he was being paid for his work. He had even forgotten to include a fee when he first submitted a quote for the Jerusalem work. I knew Calder often signed documents without careful scrutiny. My experience in reviewing the accounting statements from Calder's dealers led me to inquire about the provisions of his will. He gave me a copy he had signed years before. I'm sure his old-line lawyers were honest, but I saw no reason why those lawyers should be his executors. Lawyers may not be the best judges of how to preserve and enhance the reputation of an artist. I felt the Calder family members were best equipped to deal with the artist's estate, as they would have no incentive to pursue untimely sales. I had no mandate to insert myself into the process of estate planning other than my interest in helping protect Sandy and his family. I questioned him as to whether he really wanted his New York lawyer, with whom he had no close relationship, to manage his estate.

It is awkward to raise the issue of mortality with an artist of a certain age. Some years before, my firm had been hired by the Museum of Modern Art to meet with Pablo Picasso to clarify the disposition of his painting, *Guernica*. The meeting was canceled at the last minute when his secretary called with a message, "Picasso does not like to talk about his death." Calder was calm and matter-of-fact, as usual. When he requested my opinion, I told him that lawyers were less inclined than family members to be patient with an artist's heritage. Why not name his daughters and their respective spouses as executors? At least they then would have to collaborate to adopt a coherent point of view on what to do with his art. With his affirmative grunt, I prepared a codicil to his will, which he executed without comment or question.

In September of 1976, Sandy and Louisa stayed with Toby and me before leaving for New York to attend his retrospective, "Calder's Universe," that was to open at the Whitney Museum of American Art the following month. I suggested we review his entire testament when he returned. Before he left, he signed a power of attorney, granting me the right to gather documents from all sources.

He died two months later in New York. It was like losing a close family member. I knew Saché would never be the same for me.

There was much to do regarding Calder's dwelling and possessions. In addition to the contents of his house and studio, stabiles were stationed in the courtyard, and Mirós and Légers hung on the walls. All of that meant a large inheritance-tax bill. A plan was also needed to preserve his studio. The family gave me great latitude in handling these matters. If an accounting statement seemed too vague, I took the initiative and changed the estate's gallery representation. Klaus Perls, who had represented Calder for many years, was ousted and later sued by Alexander S. C. "Sandy" Rower, Calder's grandson. With the family's approval, I selected M. Knoedler Gallery. Its president, Larry Rubin, had an outstanding knowledge of contemporary art, having run his own gallery in New York and Paris. And his brother, William, an art historian and curator at the Museum of Modern Art, admired Calder.

I wanted an annual guarantee of payments for the estate, and that required negotiations with Armand Hammer, who had purchased Knoedler in 1971. Hammer, known for his trading activities with Soviet Russia since the 1930s and for his control of Occidental Petroleum as well as Ukraine's fertilizer exports, was not the easiest man to deal with. Invited to Hammer's home, I was somewhat surprised to find that he lived in a simple, renovated garage in Greenwich Village. Courteously, he explained why a guarantee was unnecessary, given both his and Knoedler's reputation. I responded, using a word I thought he would understand: *Nyet.* The guarantee was given, but the relationship was not cordial. Moreover, Larry Rubin was rarely involved, and his promise to begin working on a *catalogue raisonnée* remained unfulfilled. Later, Sandy Rower wisely and correctly changed representation of the estate to the Pace Gallery.

Unlike the estate-tax system in the United States, French succession taxes were levied against property received by an heir rather than on the estate itself. And under a French law that went into effect in 1972, by creating what is called "*dation*," an heir could pay the tax debt in the form of art objects of "important artistic or historic value" donated to French institutions. I thought the use of the dation program made sense for the Calder heirs, so I met with Maurice Aicardi, then president of the Interministerial Commission for the Conservation of the National Artistic Heritage, whose approval I needed as the first step toward this goal.

Aicardi was as non-committal as a French bureaucrat could be. He could well have been the subject of a Gilbert & Sullivan ditty. His concept of artistic merit was limited to eighteenth-century furniture, and he bluntly said he did not think the dation law applied to foreigners. I knew he was wrong, so I filed the appropriate tax returns but made no payment, indicating that discussions for the dation were ongoing. I then pressed Pontus Hulten, the distinguished museum director who had shepherded the Centre Pompidou into existence in 1977, to assist me in obtaining approval since the Pompidou would certainly be the recipient of a large Calder work. Hulten, whose exhibits at the Pompidou were brilliant and enhanced the new museum's reputation, had no desire to engage in bureaucratic infighting, and the application languished.

Two years later, Aicardi basked in the publicity after accepting Picasso works under the dation program. I believed it was not Aicardi who deserved the credit. Rather, it was Dominique Bozo, who dealt with Picasso's estate after the painter died in 1973. Bozo was a well-known curator who had spent his entire career at the Ministry of Culture, but there was no feel of institutionalism when one worked with him. As Picasso left no will, his wives, children, and grandchildren—some legitimate and some not—all wanted to share in the estate, although no one had the means to pay the taxes on a trove so large. Bozo worked it all out. The Picasso Museum in Paris was created to house the archives, donations, and dation works of art transferred to it in lieu of taxes.

When Bozo replaced Hulten as the head of Pompidou, I thus had a friend in place who could help complete the Calder dation. It was not easy to do, as several different ministries were involved. I had to wait until 1983 to obtain final approval. I then held meetings with Bozo to discuss which Calder works would be the subject of the dation. Included was a monumental piece, *Horizontal*, which was installed in the plaza in front of the Centre Pompidou.

At the last minute, Bozo compared my estimates of value for each selected work with the amount set forth in the tax return, and said to me, "Stanley, you added almost fifty per cent to the estimate for the works to be donated, amounts substantially in excess of the value contained in the tax return, an enormous saving for the estate."

The run-up in value was due to the delay in acceptance of the dation, I responded, and it was not my fault that acceptance of the dation took so long. In the interim, the Whitney retrospective had traveled to museums all over the world, so these numbers reflected present values. Before he could complain, I said, "Here is what I'll do. Let's create an Atelier Calder as a residence program for artists. I'm sure the family will make his Saché house and studio available free of charge." Bozo thought for a moment, then asked how the artists would be chosen. I suggested a committee be formed with him in charge. He finally agreed with the dation values I suggested. It was then my assignment to obtain the agreement of both the Ministry of Culture and the regional authorities. Mary Rower and Sandra Davidson, Calder's daughters, rapidly approved the plan for an atelier, as they understood that the property would be preserved in honor of their father.

It took five years to navigate the intricacies of the Ministry of Culture and the regional authorities, notably Le Centre National des Arts Plastique, which would have to pay for the upkeep of the property and for subsidies for the artists. Residencies of this nature were not well known at that time in France, and I had to invent the form for the agreement. Now in existence for more than thirty years, the program is recognized and internationally distinguished. Recipients have varied, from young artists beginning their careers to those who are well established. Among those selected have been Tara Donovan, Ernesto Neto, Martin Puryear,

Tomás Saraceno, Žilvinas Kempinas, and Sarah Sze. Of all the undertakings in which I have played a role, the Atelier Calder is my proudest achievement. The French government honored me for this work—I received the Ordre National du Mérite as well as being named Officier des Arts et des Lettres.

With taxes paid, all remaining works were to be shipped to the United States, and that required an export license from the Ministry of Culture. I needed the approval of Pierre Rosenberg, director of the Louvre. I did not think this would be a problem, as he was married to the daughter of Alain de Rothschild, and her two brothers were friends of mine. But Pierre had the habit of seeking a donation of a work of art to French museums in exchange for the export license. I refused, adding that I would summarize our conversation when I gave an interview to *Le Monde*, owing to which other artists would, of course, become reluctant to have a studio in France in the future. The export license was granted.

One other task was awkward. Calder and Miró had been good friends, and there were times when their works were hardly distinguishable. I knew Calder had sent a work to Miró before his death for the Miró Foundation, but none had been received from the Catalan artist in return. I suspect I annoyed Miró with my insistence, but now one of his paintings is with the Calder Estate.

Once the atelier was established, I suggested to Mary and Sandra that we create a Calder Prize for sculptors comparable to the Pritzker Architecture Prize. We met with Anish Kapoor to suggest that he be the first recipient. The prize would be $50,000 and would also include a residency at the Atelier Calder. Kapoor felt the residence requirement would be difficult because he did not want to uproot his family and move to Saché. The idea for the prize languished. It was finally established in 2005 thanks to

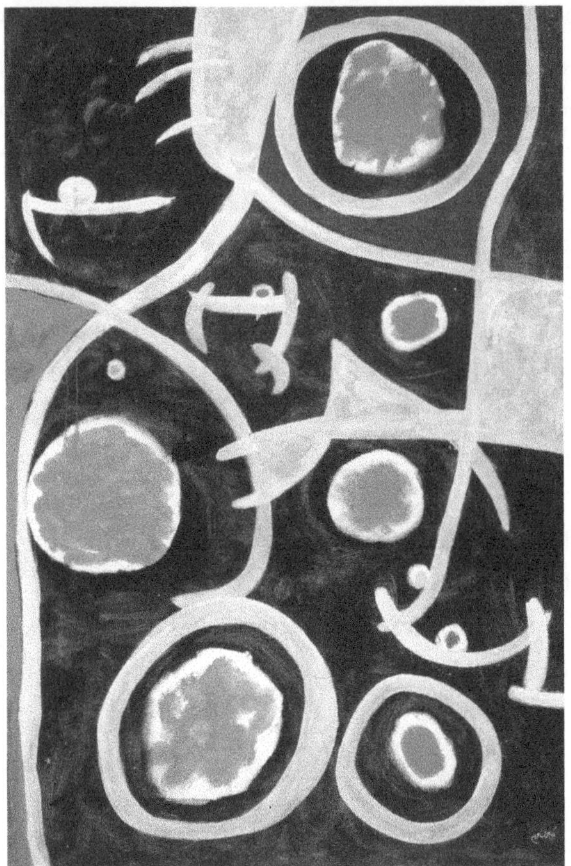

Fig. 30. Joan Miró painting intended for Alexander Calder; gift facilitated posthumously by Stanley Cohen.

Sandy Rower, who was only thirteen when Calder died. I thought of him as a kid with no interest in the artistic heritage of his grandfather. How wrong I was! Creating the Calder Foundation in 1987, he has propelled it into becoming the most prestigious organization dedicated to preserving an artist's reputation. He created an archive of his grandfather's life and works, which is the envy of museum directors throughout the world. He is intimate with all of the documents comprising the archive. He can recite without pause details of his grandfather's career, year by year. Assisting in organizing Calder exhibitions, he advises curators in placing objects in the best position for public viewing. Undaunted by the conduct of galleries that had previously represented Calder, he has recovered major works that had disappeared from inventories. Together, we fund the biennial Calder Prize. For the most part, I defer to him in the selection of the recipient.

32

A Lawyer's Life

There are moments when time seems to accelerate, when events pile on so quickly that you just want to raise your hand to force a stop. For me, the 1970s were a decade of transition, a change of momentum from my prior life of relative ease. True, I was busy with Régine, Calder's death, and the aborted Speer project, but these undertakings did not strike me as traditional legal matters. Despite the cordial partnership with Bomsel, I was still hesitant about considering myself a permanent member of the legal profession. Most of my work led to close personal relations with clients whom I also considered friends. The pace felt leisurely. Although I was nearly forty-five, I still pretended I was in the pupa stage of becoming.

Professional stress that I identified with the New York legal practice, and which I had done my best to avoid, was about to come my way. I underestimated its impact on my conduct, my emotions, and my entire way of life. A friendly English banker who was also an art collector and who knew of my relationship with Calder telephoned one day. He had a client to recommend, one Rupert Murdoch. I learned that Murdoch had inherited an Australian newspaper from his father when he was just twenty-two, and he was now engaged in an acquisition spree. After purchasing other Australian newspapers, two London-based tabloids, *News of the World* and the *Sun,* Murdoch was still eager to expand.

I had rarely handled complex commercial matters and had little experience with acquisitions, so I wondered why I was being contacted. My first reaction on meeting Murdoch for lunch was that here was a gentle soul, charming and charismatic, certainly nothing like the driven businessman the banker had described in his introductory, somewhat apprehensive, telephone call. Murdoch was interested in acquiring a series of companies that formed the leading book and record clubs not only in France, but throughout the world. The business was owned by Samuel and David Josefowitz, with headquarters in Lausanne, Switzerland. The Josefowitz complex included some thirty-odd companies organized in a manner to avoid substantial corporate tax charges. Any acquisition would require a major reorganization. A 1969 *New York Times* article referred to Sam Josefowitz as a 100-million-dollar recluse who was also the largest book printer and distributor on the Continent and one of the world's great art collectors. I had previously met Josefowitz when he came to Saché to visit Calder to buy one of his Crinklys. Sam's interest in art and the fact that he was a Jew may very well have been the reasons why Murdoch approached me rather than hire one of the major law firms with offices in Paris.

What surprised me about working with Murdoch was that he had few assistants or advance men doing due diligence on this project. He came to Europe several times, always by himself, to walk through the printing and shipping departments of the Josefowitz empire and to chat with key executives. I accompanied him, perhaps less as a lawyer than as a staff member, to discuss the nature of the business, a first for me. His questions to the executives illustrated his desire to become proficient with the details of operations. After finishing long days of visiting offices and factories, he invited me to dine, most often at Aux Lyonnais in Paris, where he indulged in its specialty—*saucisson de Lyon.*

After several months of study, Murdoch invited me to fly to New York and meet with him and his staff to decide whether to go forward with the acquisition. Here was a different Murdoch from the one with whom I dined as if he was a cordial, casual acquaintance. He sat behind a simple desk with a few employees spread around him in a semicircle. He was clearly in command, and one could sense a firmness that I had not previously detected. Speaking calmly, he weighed the pros and cons of the Josefowitz business. After a brief debate Murdoch dismissed his staff. He reflected for a moment and then thanked me for my help, but he had decided not to proceed with the acquisition. I asked him why. He responded, "None of the executives who have worked with me for years were seeking to run this enterprise and become its president. That's a danger sign." I thought that was a brilliant rationale. Murdoch had had no reason to have me fly from Paris to attend the meeting, other than his sense of politeness and consideration for my effort.

These days, when I wake up in the middle of the night cursing Fox News and its impact, I have difficulty reconciling the charm and intelligence of the Murdoch I briefly knew with the man now wreaking such havoc in his adopted country. I had missed a tell. When I attended my final meeting with him, I should have noted that Murdoch shared offices with one of his media investments, *The Star*, whose lurid headlines featured Elvis, two-headed babies, and little green men. *The Star* was later sold to David Pecker and the company that owned the *National Enquirer*. To be honest, I enjoyed the role—half-lawyer, half-businessman—that I played vis-à-vis Murdoch. But I did not know when I returned to Paris from the final Murdoch meeting that I was about to become a

New York–style lawyer plunging into meetings all day and into the night. I spent the next five years doing nothing else.

When he heard Murdoch's decision, Josefowitz invited me to his home in Lausanne. He asked me to be his lawyer. My approach to transactions, he felt, was less technocratic than attuned to developing a holistic, intuitive understanding of each party's commercial goals. I called Murdoch to be sure he wasn't having second thoughts, and if not, I asked if he had any objection to my accepting Sam's invitation. He encouraged me to go ahead.

The Josefowitz house was less a residence than a museum. Here was one of the greatest collections of Fauvist paintings, Degas and Rodin sculptures, and Rembrandt prints in private hands. His Egyptian pieces were of museum quality. As I walked around the rooms to admire what hung on the walls, Sam proved to be an expert in each of the fields represented in his collection, offering a more detailed analysis of his art than I would have found in a museum catalog. He was the first obsessive collector I knew. Business meetings were often interrupted and placed on hold if he became aware that a Pont-Aven School painting or a Gauguin (of which he had eight) might be available for sale. A portion of Josefowitz's collection was sold in 2023 by Christie's, yielding more than 100 million dollars for his estate.

Since Sam believed Murdoch had passed on the transaction because of the convoluted nature of his business structure, he asked me to reorganize his companies to better prepare them for sale. I believed that due to the complexity of their corporate structure, Sam's companies would most likely be purchased by an entrepreneur seeking to make his mark. I suggested he postpone reorganization and allow me to test my theory. I reached out to Bob Towbin, the only investment banker I knew. He presented the possible acquisition of Sam's business to Marvin Green, who ran Reeves Communication Corporation, known for introducing reality TV shows. Green had previously been chairman of Ayers Europe, an offshoot of an advertising agency considered the oldest in the world. He certainly had marketing experience, which was essential for success in the mail-order field. He quickly agreed to the acquisition.

The purchase took months to finalize. Towbin raised the money for the acquisition. A two-day closing took place in Amsterdam. I had advised Green to keep Sam involved in the business at least for six months. But he did not. That was Green's first mistake. His second was not being a Murdoch who had his hands on all the details. Instead, consistent with his leisure-loving St. Luke, Connecticut, upbringing, he built a maxi boat, *Nirvana,* to compete in the Newport-to-Bermuda race. He invited me to join him in his boat for a race in Sardinia, but seemed annoyed when I suggested that we stop for lunch. Within a few years, the Josefowitz assets were sold to cover the default on the loans.

Other acquisition work quickly followed. Régine introduced me to Tony Murray, a French Jew of North African descent—born Jacques Gaston Kalifa—who joined the RAF at the outset of World War II and plucked the name "Murray" out of the telephone book. Returning to Paris at the end of the war, he created a successful fire extinguisher company. By law, French companies were required to have extinguishers serviced at specific intervals. The cash flow from that company allowed Murray a life of ease and nights spent at Régine's.

The front-page headline of the New York *Daily News* on October 30, 1975 read, "Ford to City: Drop Dead." Even if those were not President Ford's exact words, he had denied a bailout to the near-bankrupt city. After Tony and I had had a few lunches together, he asked me to accompany him to New York. When I asked what his plan was, he responded that all cities go through turmoil and then a rebound. He then rattled off the sale prices of apartments in Paris and New York, calculating the per-square-foot value in each city. Paris was twice as high as New York. He wanted to own real estate in the United States and to buy a business there. He would find the property to acquire; my task was to find a company in bad shape that he could turn around. Twenty-two plane trips from Paris to the United States in eighteen months was my new travel record working with a single client to find an appropriate acquisition.

I learned that Holmes Protection Services, a burglar alarm company, might be up for sale. Holmes was owned by the National Kinney Corporation, a subsidiary of Warner Bros. Steve Ross had been busy reinventing himself by shedding both his wife and businesses that did not support his ambition to grow Warner Bros into a major entertainment force. Scandal-prone entities such as parking and office-cleaning divisions were spun off as a separate company, National Kinney Corporation. After a few weeks of study, Tony commissioned me to negotiate the conditions and complete the transaction. He did not want to discuss the asking price. He left all the details to me. So I arranged the needed financing from the Rothschild Bank. I was acting both as a lawyer and as an intermediary.

Holmes Protection was a hundred-year-old company that had once been part of the Bell Telephone Company. The core of its business consisted of central stations linked to its clients, primarily banks, by direct phone lines. Monthly subscriptions provided its revenue source. When Murray took over the company, he raised the rates, despite warnings that key customers might defect to competitors. Murray did not seem to care, believing that most would remain. He was right. Years later, after also buying the

National Cleaning Corporation from Kinney, Murray would sell his holdings for $140 million. He was well on his way to becoming a billionaire, the first centenarian to be on the *Sunday Times* Rich List.

In a ceremony at the penthouse of the Caesars Palace in Las Vegas, Murray married a charming woman. A few days later, he sought a divorce. Astonished, I asked him why. His wife was the host of a morning TV program. She refused to quit, insisting on continuing her work despite marrying a wealthy man. Murray could not countenance someone who would not be bound to his schedule. He was also one of those clients who wanted his lawyer as part of his full-time entourage, available to discuss anything that came to mind. He insisted Toby and I stay at his Acapulco home for Christmas and in Saint-Tropez for summer weekends. That was not our style, so we often declined, to the detriment of our relationship with Murray.

I had another matter to handle. Robert Hocq, a French war hero who had built a business in ballpoint pens and cigarette lighters, had purchased the French branch of the jeweler Cartier. He decided to also acquire the UK and US branches, which were owned separately. There certainly was a sense of satisfaction, especially for a single practitioner, to be primarily responsible for these transactions, and I understood why lawyers felt gratified by accomplishing a difficult or complex closing. But I was beginning to be weary of living on two continents and working ten-hour days, a way of life I had promised myself would not hold me captive. Due to the growing clientele in New York, I opened a small office there and hired an assistant to relieve the pressure.

But I can't leave the 1970s behind without offering a kaleidoscope of further memories of that decade.

Harry Saltzman was one of the rare film producers who made money in that field and lost it in industry, rather than the other way around. He did well by acquiring the rights to James Bond and having Michael Caine star as Harry Palmer in *The Ipcress File* and other films; but his purchase of a controlling interest in Technicolor Motion Picture Corporation was a disaster, as was his acquisition of Eclair, a French company manufacturing high-end 16-millimeter cameras. Eclair went into financial reorganization, and my legal fees were not being paid. When I mentioned this to the documentary filmmakers Albert and David Maysles over morning coffee at a Paris cafe, they called me an idiot. Did I not know the Eclair was used by Jean-Luc Godard for his film *Breathless*? I did not. Did I not know it was used for the shower scene in *Psycho*? I did not. Instead of seeking fees, at least get a camera from Eclair, they advised. So I did. I gave it to Toby, who used it to make documentary films with one of her friends.

Their film, *Memories of Monet,* won several awards. The narrative was based on the diary and letters of Lila Cabot Perry, an American impressionist artist who spent summers with Monet. Princess Grace of Monaco was scheduled to do the voiceover, but she died shortly before the film was completed. Actress Claire Bloom replaced her and did the voiceover in a single take. I sat next to her in the recording studio in New York City. When she finished, I turned to thank her. She looked at her watch; her expression instantly changed from calm beauty to fear. "Philip is waiting outside the Carlyle Hotel, and I'm late. He will be furious." She left quickly as my hand was still outstretched. I did not fully understand the tension in her relationship with Philip Roth until many years later, when her memoir, *Leaving a Doll's House,* was published.

What was I doing on a September 1976 flight to New York from London with Kenneth Tynan and Michael White on our way to view their Broadway revival of *Oh! Calcutta!*, a musical revue with some nude scenes. The title was a play on words from the French, *O quel cul t'as*—"what a great ass you have."

Tynan was a leading theatre critic for English papers and the *New Yorker*, a leading provocateur fond of erotica and free sex, unafraid of being the first to utter four-letter words on TV. White was one of the great film and theatre producers of the time. Besides *Oh! Calcutta!*, *Monty Python and the Holy Grail*, and *The Rocky Horror Picture Show*, White was noted for lunches with Prime Minister Margaret Thatcher and hip parties with major stars. When White learned that I grew up in the Bronx, he told me I could not understand his way of life. Although born to East European immigrants (his mother was a Cohen), he attended the Lyceum Alpinum, near St. Moritz. There he required enough money to live in the manner that he believed was his due, one that would allow him to remain at the center of every emerging trend. White also liked to gamble. He had borrowed money from one of my clients who had advanced funds for a theatrical production but had not paid it back because it was a low period in White's career. I visited White in London at the request of my client, who told me to "Just break his legs." Instead of betraying any fear, White suggested I attend the New York revival of *Oh! Calcutta!*, insisting the play would be a success, money would soon flow in, and the debt repaid.

During the flight, Tynan was tense, not convinced that *Oh! Calcutta!* would be a hit. He was troubled by the negative reviews in 1969 when Clive Barnes wrote in the *New York Times*, that *Oh! Calcutta!* was "witless and silly," a phrase that stuck. White, oh so cool, had no doubts—and he was right. *Oh! Calcutta!* ran for 13 years with 5,959 performances—a new record for Broadway. White not only repaid my client's loan, but he went on to produce more than thirty successful films and plays, including Louis Malle's *My Dinner with Andre*. Bankruptcy finally slowed him down.

I may have understood the reason why I was standing in the rear of the Edison Theatre with White and Tynan in 1976, but I have no recollection as to how and why I was sitting, that same year, with Norman Mailer and Gregory Hemingway, the youngest son of Ernest Hemingway, at a small table at Rao's restaurant in New York. The occasion was the publication of Gregory's book about his father, for which Mailer had written the introduction. It may have been one of my Zelig moments, since, having been ignored, I had hardly said a word. When a pause ensued, I asked Mailer, "Did you really smell her cunt?" He spoke to me for the first time, "Which one?" I was referring to that of Maria Schneider in *Last Tango in Paris*. Mailer had written a review in which he criticized the film for not having a real cock up a real cunt. "A fuse," he had written, "was never ignited." It was "a fuck film without the fuck." I explained that I had seen it in a private screening and had no expectations. Then I said, "You saw it after it was reviewed by Pauline Kael. I bet you already had the fuck sentence ready even before you had a seat in the Translux." Besides, the way Schneider was treated, I argued, was the equivalent of a fuck scene. Mailer smiled. As he may have felt there was no further reason to converse with me, he returned to his exchange with Gregory. Later, when I described that encounter to Joseph Heller and his wife, Valerie, she commented that when her husband and Mailer were together in a room, they looked like bouncers ready to pounce on an unsuspecting guest.

It was time to stop. In 1977 Toby gave birth to our daughter, Laura. I stayed close to home for the next few years. I learned to push a carriage in the Luxembourg Gardens and became familiar with the French system of crèches and education. When Toby had a photographic assignment away from Paris, I was responsible for household chores. For grade school, we started Laura at the Rudolf Steiner School, but that turned out to be a mistake. I visited a class and noted that Laura sat all by herself. We immediately flew to New York, and I arranged testing by specialists. She was diagnosed with a modest auditory-brain mismatch, a form of dyslexia. Upon our return to Paris, she transferred to the Marymount International School because it offered special exercises for this condition. Laura became an excellent student. For her baccalaureate, she performed Jean Cocteau's monologue, *The Human Voice*.

33

The Rothschilds

In 1981, François Mitterrand was elected president of France. With a left-wing majority in parliament, he was in a position to rapidly introduce the socialist policies on which he had campaigned. Topping his list of reforms was the nationalization of the domestic banking system, which included the Rothschild Bank. Due to reorganization, that family-run bank had become the holding company of other investments in various fields, including the Château Lafite Rothschild. Until that moment, my involvement with the family had been more social than legal. Éric de Rothschild, a few years younger than me, had a substantial collection of contemporary art. I accompanied him from time to time to art auctions and dined at his father's home as well as with his uncle, Elie, whom he had succeeded as manager of Lafite. Elie's son, Nathaniel, had also become a friend.

In discreet talks with members of Mitterrand's Socialist Party, we ascertained that only the bank was to be transferred to state ownership, leaving the underlying companies under the family's control. Still, Nathaniel de Rothschild invited me to Château Lafite for a planning session. It was more of a social visit than a consultation. He led me on a tour of the vineyard. The highlight of that weekend was an exceptional dinner accompanied by the house wine—vintages 1899, 1934, and 1945—as if we thought we should drink our fill before the government seized the stock.

Several family members decided to leave France for the United States. I was asked to assist with tax planning and other matters. Baron Guy Édouard Alphonse Paul de Rothschild, the patriarch of the family, whom I had never met, summoned me to his Paris residence, the Hôtel Lambert, a magnificent mansion at the tip of Île Saint-Louis. The mansion dated from the seventeenth century and was known for aristocratic balls, of which the most famous was the December 1969 Bal Oriental, hosted by Alexis von Rosenberg, Baron de Redé, Guy's friend and the mansion's former owner. I was already living in Paris when I read about that costume ball for 400 guests, replete with Indian musicians, dancers, and Africans dressed like Nubians holding torches that lit the path for invitees. And Brigitte Bardot. Remembering reading about the ball, I could never have imagined I would be sitting in the salon of the Hôtel Lambert, giving advice to its occupant.

Baron Guy was a distinguished war hero who fled France and joined De Gaulle's Free French Army forces in England. When the bank was nationalized, his open letter expressed his bitterness: "A Jew under Pétain, a pariah under Mitterrand—for me it's enough." Members of the family had been stripped of French citizenship by the Vichy government. Baron Guy felt he was being denuded once again. Although I am usually indifferent to, and not in awe of, wealth and fame, there was something unique and austere in his demeanor and dignity that captivated me.

Later, when he was settled in the United States, a rift developed between him and his rebellious son, Édouard. I became the intermediary. After lunch with the baron at Club 21, I would meet with Édouard, then aged twenty-five, and attempt to reconcile the two. More important, at least for Édouard, was my ability to convince his father to grant a larger allowance, something I was usually able to do.

Mitterrand's nationalization policy proved to be a failure. In 1986 a banking license was reissued to the family when the Socialists lost control of Parliament.

34

Joseph Heller

If there was one person whose image in my mind was accurately reflected in reality when we met, it was Joseph Heller. I had read *Catch-22* not long after my own army experience. I assumed the author was, by birth, a Yossarian, like that novel's anti-hero. I likewise believed that Heller had spent his wartime military years dealing with the equivalents of my very own Spitter.

When you meet Heller for the first time, you are either quickly eased into the position of a lifelong friend or a quick judgment determines that no intimacy will be forthcoming. Fortunately, our banter started as soon as we were introduced, and it continued until his death. At our first meeting, David Zelag Goodman, Heller's close friend and scriptwriter of *Straw Dogs* and *Logan's Run*, looked me up and down. He remarked to Heller, "This guy has a good punim!" If I was late to lunch, I heard Heller say as I approached the table, "Here comes the good punim guy."

It was only after Joe's passing, when I read his book *Now and Then*, that I fully understood the basis of our compatibility. That memoir is more than an account of Joe's coming of age and his survival during the war. It is a touching and revealing portrait of a period now gone and of places greatly changed—for Joe, Coney Island; for me, the Bronx. Heller's father died when Joe was five, and he did not grieve; mine went missing, and I did not grieve. Joe placed nickels into the Automat window to eat baked beans; so did I. He disliked eating fish; I can't abide eating them. We each obtained working papers at age sixteen and sampled so many jobs in order to stay alive that a catalog would be required to list them all. Neither of us went to a prom or dated young. He penned a phrase that I recognized all too well: "I'd been biding my time, waiting in numb hope for some unknown, defining reality finally to pop up that would clarify the course I should follow, wind me up, and start me on the way."

I would stop by Joe's writing office on Eighth Avenue from time to time when he had finished for the day, to share a martini.

Sometimes broody, sometimes brusque—and even though he insisted he was not a good parent—Heller never missed my daughter's birthday party.

Fig. 31. Joseph Heller with Stanley Cohen, Laura Cohen, and Toby Cohen.

Although he was not yet legally separated, I knew Joe had a strained relationship with his first wife, Shirley, and he sometimes had a female visitor from Santa Fe. Not long after we met, I invited Joe and Shirley to my home in Saché. They came, possibly hoping to reconcile. The trip was a failure in that regard. Nevertheless, I gave Joe a tour, explaining that our property had been traced to the fifteenth century and had served as a working mill from the seventeenth century until World War II. Even though the millwheel was gone, the wooden locks were still intact. Unaware of my obligation to maneuver the locks in accordance with river rules, I had often left them open, especially in the summertime. This allowed the river's water level to be lower than what the nineteenth-century code prescribed. For this reason, homes upstream were constructed close to the banks. An inspector from the prefecture alerted me to the requirement to maintain a steady flow, which meant raising or lowering the locks. I complied. Upstream cellars were often flooded as the water level rose, and I had to face angry neighbors. The inspector, a history buff, explained that tension between mill owners and farmers was centuries old. Indeed, a lawsuit was filed in 1789 seeking damages for untilled fields that were flooded when the locks remained shut for a lengthy period. The inspector led me to the riverbank below my house. A stone had been grafted to the channel walls in 1855 to mark the required water level.

That marble marker had been installed by Jean de Margonne, the lover of Honoré de Balzac's mother, and, undoubtedly, the father of the novelist's half-brother. Margonne had owned a good portion of the Saché commune, including the Moulin Vert, then known as La Chevrière. Balzac must have walked our grounds. Joe loved the story, and we went off to the Balzac Museum just a half-mile away, housed in the former Margonne Châteaux, where

Balzac often came to stay when he was broke and needed fresh air. His rotund body found its way there by foot, a twelve-mile walk from the stagecoach stop in Tours. Balzac wrote, "Touraine had revitalized me so much that Thursday, Friday, Saturday and Sunday I came up with the *Lost Illusions*, and I wrote the first forty pages of it." Balzac's second-floor room is preserved as it was, simple and bare—just a bed, a chair and a desk. We imagined the smell of coffee to which he was addicted and which allowed him to work fifteen hours a day.

Joe asked the curator if there was a record of what coffee Balzac drank so that we could package it and sell it to writers. Unfortunately, the curator didn't know. What Joe liked best was the room housing manuscripts with corrections in Balzac's hand. Since each correction of a proof was costly, Balzac had to pay the printer for the changes, and that was one reason he needed the patronage of Margonne. Both Balzac and Heller created character prototypes. Balzac took real characters and made them appear absurd, while Joe made absurd characters real. We returned to the mill to have a martini to celebrate the day's end and to toast the ghost of Balzac and the paths he walked. Toby was preparing dinner when Shirley insisted that she and Joe had to return to Paris immediately. I called a taxi, as Joe did not want to create a scene. Not long after, they separated, and the divorce process began.

In 1981, the grapevine spread the news: Heller was in intensive care. I was in New York City and may have been his first visitor at Mount Sinai Hospital. Joe was on his back, tubes extending ominously from his nose. Lacking common sense, I started to banter in our usual way. "What did you promise God you would do to get better?" I asked. In a whisper, he responded, "I think I'll have to go back to Shirley." That answer brought me to my senses.

This was serious. Fortunately, Joe did not remember this exchange. *No Laughing Matter*, written by Joe and his close friend, Speed Vogel, tells the story of Joe's bout with Guillain-Barré Syndrome. The book underplayed, in Heller's inimitable style, the nature of the disease and the worry shared by his friends who feared he would not recover. Valerie, his nurse, whom he would eventually marry, kept his humor up. His hospital room during the recovery period was a site for jokes and a stage for comedians' one-night stands.

When Joe was discharged, he often came to the summer house Toby and I had rented in East Hampton. He could restore his muscles by exercising in our pool. His own home was in the middle of a marital fight, with Joe, Valerie, and assorted friends in the main house, and Shirley in the annex. His 1984 divorce settled the property question. Joe retained the East Hampton house; Shirley, the Apthorp apartment in Manhattan. Joe walked well thereafter, with only a slight limp or a shaky hand serving as evidence of an illness that could have ended his life.

The following year Joe and Valerie came to Paris as part of a round-the-world trip. We dined with his French editor, François Bourin, and his wife, Shoba, to celebrate the publication of *God Knows*. Joe wanted to know why sales of *Catch-22* were substantially higher in Finland than in France. François had no explanation other than to suggest that the French had no sense of humor.

After a weekend with Joe and Valerie in Saché, Toby, Laura and I joined them in Florence. That was when I understood his reputation for eating, as described by Kenneth Tynan in a 1978 profile of Mel Brooks in the *New Yorker*. As an aside, Tynan noted the existence of the Gourmet Club, a group of mostly Jewish eaters who needed lessons in etiquette. Brooks complained that Heller grabbed the best of the food before others had raised their

Fig. 32. Joseph Heller and Stanley Cohen at a winery in Florence.

forks. Heller was quoted as saying, "I am a greedy man. I'll eat anything. I even use a fork instead of chopsticks, so I can eat faster." Neither Toby nor I enjoyed having large lunches, so we were the perfect partners for the Florence trip with Joe and Valerie. They would clean our plates with Italian bread. And as we finished, Joe would ask, "And where shall we eat tonight?"

When not dining, we wandered through the Galleria Uffizi and the Accademia. We didn't need a tour guide since Joe had been there at the end of the war and knew as much as a professional guide. As we strolled, he commented on the works of Botticelli, Caravaggio, and Titian. I asked him how he had absorbed so much about these artists. That was an opening for him to say, "God knows." Among the fond memories of that trip is sitting in the outdoor cafe of the Hotel Savoy, where Joe introduced me to the first of many Negronis we later drank together. Some would call it the battle of the noses.

A few years later, I arranged a last-minute Passover seder in New York. There were only five of us. Joe and I, Jakov Lind, Mordecai Richler, and his agent, Lynn Nesbitt. It was to be a literary seder that turned out to be a food fight. Lind, to my surprise, insisted on a serious reading of the Haggadah while Heller only thought of it as an excuse to eat an abundant quantity of food. Joe reached out for a matzo ball as Lind was easing his way out of Egypt. "I'm the simpleton," yelled Joe, and "It's time to eat." Lind tried to continue with the Passover story, but it was too late. If he

Fig. 33. Wedding of Joseph Heller and Valerie Heller at Stanley Cohen's New York residence. 1987. From left: Speed Vogel, Valerie Heller, Joseph Heller, and Stanley Cohen.

wanted any of the food, he had to hurry, or Joe would consume it all. Richler and Nesbitt were calm bystanders.

In April 1987, I hosted Joe Heller's wedding to Valerie at my home in New York.

Joe was a realist, understanding the turmoil of our nation and the need to undo the myths of American greatness when they were not deserved. *Something Happened* was a major work exposing the deadness at the heart of the "American dream." It was a book at odds with the expectations of those fans seeking an easy smile in the form of a second version of *Catch-22.* I loved to watch Joe's TV interviews because he would not be subservient to any high-powered host. When the renowned interviewer Charlie Rose tried to make a point, Heller responded, "Are you asking a question or making a statement?" Heller also understood the limits to his lifespan, especially after recuperating from his debilitating disease. *Closing Time* was an acceptance of mortality. "It has to do," noted Joe, "with a person about my age realizing not only he's way past his prime—but that life is nearing its end." Valerie wept when that title was finally stamped on the book.

When I now think of Joe, the word "enough" appears as a subtitle to his life. I knew the story of his alleged conversation with Kurt Vonnegut, Jr. so well that I'm convinced I was there when it first occurred. It was at a cocktail party at a prosperous East Hampton house, its walls hung with valuable paintings. Kurt and Heller happened to be there. Kurt asked if Heller ever felt a pang of jealousy at not having artworks of this kind. Joe responded, "I have something our host does not have."

"And what is that?" asked Kurt.

Joe replied, "Enough."

The relationship between Vonnegut and Heller illustrated Joe's lack of patience with people he did not like. Their friendship was strained by Joe's interaction with Kurt's second wife, Jill Krementz. Later, when Vonnegut briefly separated from her, he and Joe resumed a close relationship, only to disengage once more when Kurt and Jill reconciled.

At times, Joe seemed astonished by his own success. That a fatherless child such as he reached that degree of fame and even notoriety was almost unbelievable to him. I had the privilege of sitting beside Joe at a high-table dinner in his honor at Oxford University. "Just think," he said, "I am an Honorary Visiting Fellow of St. Catherine's College of Oxford University!" As a featured guest, he was mild in his comments, sitting contentedly among the academics who welcomed him. Yet he was their equal as he could talk knowledgeably about Thucydides, American presidents, Benny Goodman, or the death of Martin Luther King. He later wrote, "I have much to be pleased with . . . I have wanted to succeed, and I have."

Those words came back to me as I followed Joe's coffin to his grave.

35

Unfit for Retirement

Sometime in the 1980s, doubts about my professional life troubled me again. My principal partner, Emile-Jean Bomsel, had died as a result of a botched operation. I had always counted on his calm advice. When I was in Paris, we would have lunch every day. Our conversation ranged from legal matters to affairs of state. With his passing, I realized that there was no one in our law office with whom I wanted to dine. Bomsel's place was taken by Theo Klein, a prominent lawyer who was also the head of the Paris Jewish community, but our relationship was less personal. Besides, by then most of my work was in New York.

I knew it was time for a change when Frank Lloyd came to my office for advice. Lloyd was a highly successful art dealer who owned the Marlborough Gallery, already established in several countries. He had just purchased a home on Avenue Foch, a luxury residential area of Paris. "I'm told that you know international taxation well," he said. "I have a home in the Bahamas, and I don't pay taxes there. I have a home in New York, and I avoid American taxes. I have a home in London without any tax liability. Now that I have bought a home in Paris, can you figure out a way that I don't pay French taxes?" I thought for a moment and studied this potential client. He once boasted, "I collect money, not art." I remembered a phrase from Melville's short story, "Bartleby the Scrivener." I responded, "I would prefer not to." Lloyd was surprised, so I added, "I think you should pay taxes." He left my office without saying *au revoir*. Was there a feeling of schadenfreude when he was later indicted on charges of tampering with evidence and conflicts of interest in handling the Mark Rothko estate?

Something, however, had happened. It was more than just dissatisfaction with how I spent the day. And it was more than the despondency engendered by reading Joe Heller's novel of that title. Unlike Bob Slocum, the narrator of *Something Happened*, I did not dislike my family or my colleagues. I may have felt unfulfilled by my professional obligations, but I certainly did not resent meeting with clients. I suppose I was considered successful, given the firm I had started and the notable clientele seeking our representation. Toby and I had an apartment with one of the largest private gardens in Paris. We had a good table at home, and it was filled with friends, primarily artists and writers. How could I complain? Walking in the port of Cannes, I spied a for sale sign on a seventy-five-foot staysail ketch with a teak deck. I had no navigating skills, but I immediately purchased the boat. Finding a crew, I sent it to the Caribbean, and it became our home for a month each winter for several years until the costs became obscene.

I would later read: "A midlife crisis is a period or phase of life transition when a person begins to question the things that they have accomplished or achieved and whether those same things still provide a sense of fulfillment and meaning." According to Michael G. Wetter, a clinical psychologist, "This questioning may lead to an abrupt change in occupation, commitment to relationships, or hobby exploration." I was both irritable and irritating. A client insisted I fly from Paris to New York to attend a meeting. I did not want to go. Since I was the attorney of record, I had a fiduciary obligation and left with a grumble and a bag. The next day I woke up ornery, in the same mood I had felt during basic training when I impulsively left Fort Dix for New York City. I decided that I had had enough of lawyering and simply walked away.

Although the law firm in France owed me money, including the deposit guaranteeing the office lease, I asked for nothing, just wished them well. I was surprised that my colleagues seemed relieved at my imminent departure. I later met an ex-colleague who revealed that I was considered irritating and arrogant, and to several, imposing. Moreover, I was told—in a polite and friendly tone—that I often acted with a childish, schoolyard attitude and made disparaging remarks about the profession. In short, I had dealt with my associates as if I were Larry David in an episode of *Curb Your Enthusiasm*.

Evidently, my associates were unable to forgive one particular incident. At the end of a tense meeting on a commercial matter involving two major corporations, I was asked by both sides to prepare a memo of understanding. My secretary was ready. Instead, I first dictated a letter to my mother. My clients' analysis of my behavior took me by surprise. I had always assumed my manner to be charming, but their remarks made me realize that my attitude and comments sometimes offended rather than amused.

More difficult was a telephone conversation with Toby. We were friends and would always remain close, but our intimacy had declined. In part, this was due to my travels and restlessness, as well as to the absences caused by her photography assignments. In part, no doubt due to a traumatized childhood, she was reticent about showing deep affection. We agreed to cohabit only during Laura's school vacations and in the summer months when I had arranged a vacation rental in East Hampton. Toby accepted that I would be living in New York more often than in Paris.

Now, with age and distance, I feel uneasy reading the opening line of Elena Ferrante's *The Days of Abandonment*: "One April afternoon, right after lunch, my husband announced that he wanted to leave me." I had no plan and no companion. Would I really concentrate on making mountains into hills?

Fig. 34. Tamara de Lempicka, *The Marquis D'Afflitto on a Staircase* (1926), formerly owned by Stanley Cohen and later sold for $600,000. © Tamara de Lempicka Estate, LLC / Artists Rights Society (ARS), New York, 2026 © Tamara de Lempicka™ is a trademark of Tamara de Lempicka Estate, LLC.

A few years before, I had purchased paintings by Tamara de Lempicka for a modest sum, including a portrait of the Marquis d'Aflitto. When Madonna decided Lempicka was one of her favorite painters and featured her work in a music video, prices of Lempicka's portraits became absurd. I sold the painting to a dealer, together with a Calder gift, for an amount that made me a millionaire, sufficient money to sustain myself in an unpretentious lifestyle. I had Joe Heller's "enough." Close to fifty, I never expected to work again. But idle time, without a goal, is not as easy as it sounds.

36

More Rothschilds, the Predators' Ball, Jeffrey Epstein

Before I could even contemplate how I could replace my hectic schedule, I received a phone call from François Mayer. My foray into the financial world was destined to be short. Many would have envied my proximity to financial power. Why was I so disenchanted? I do not know. I had met François when he worked at the French Rothschild Bank before he joined Jacob Rothschild in London. He asked me to fly to London to meet with Jacob, who inherited the title of 4th Baron Rothschild, but not the chairmanship of the family bank, N. M. Rothschild & Sons. Jacob's father, Victor, relinquished that position to Jacob's cousin, Evelyn. An irate Jacob left the firm. François left with him to run the Rothschild Investment Trust (RIT), of which Jacob's friend, the financier Saul Steinberg, and his firm, Reliance Insurance Company, initially held a significant percentage. As RIT expanded, Steinberg's holding was reduced, and he eventually chose to leave the board.

François's idea was for me to take Steinberg's place on the board, subject to Jacob's approval. He thought I could be helpful to further Jacob's goal of expanding his financial conglomerate. I was just as ill-prepared for finance as I had been for Hollywood. At least then I had seen *Jules et Jim*. There comes a time when, with a whirlwind of successes in different jobs, one comes to believe one has aptitude for any task. I was soon to be firmly disabused of that notion.

In 1982, when François called, I don't believe I even had a brokerage account. Although deep down I knew accepting this was a mistake, I was flattered and could not resist meeting a Rothschild with three first names and an Oxford First in history. Jacob welcomed me with an invitation to spend the weekend at his magisterial country home. In the morning, he rode off in full hunting attire with his hounds to chase the fox while I had breakfast and conversed with his wife, Lady Serena. Breakfast included a soft-boiled egg. I was apprehensive about breaking it with the silver spoon, fearful the yellow would stain the napkin or my shirt.

When we returned to London, I was given an office at St. James's Place. Uncertain as to what I was meant to do, I sat and waited. I soon gathered that RIT wanted to expand to the United States, and François was contemplating moving to New York to seek appropriate investment opportunities. My task was to help, although the assignment remained somewhat vague. For the first time since my days as a young lawyer in New York City, I found myself subject to normal office hours. Within a few weeks, I was housed at the corner of Park Avenue and 57th Street as the chairman of Bomar Resources, a trading company formed by RIT and S & W Berisford. The latter, known for its sugar trading and other commodities businesses, was run by Ephraim Margulies, who had also successfully developed a metal trading division. A number of traders left Philips Brothers, a competitor, to join Bomar to specialize in trading rutile, molybdenum, and other metals. As chairman, I was to make sure that trading limits were not exceeded. The traders liked me, and we got on well. I enjoyed their irreverent remarks as they bought and sold metals on the phone.

Many of the traders were Jewish, some Orthodox. The latter sought my advice. A substantial portion of their income was based on profit sharing, but for religious reasons, they were unable to share in income earned on the Sabbath. "But the office is closed on Saturday as well as on Jewish holidays," I pointed out. They explained that operations overseas continued, so Sabbath profits were being booked somewhere. I could see I was in a Talmudic squeeze. "And what do you suggest?" I inquired. I was told we had to go to Monsey, New York, home to an Orthodox Jewish community, to seek the opinion of Rabbi Moshe Tendler.

And so, one evening after the office closed, we climbed into a Cadillac limousine that the Orthodox traders had reserved for the hour-long drive. First, we had to stop at a kosher deli for pastrami and corned-beef sandwiches so we would not be hungry en route. The smell lasted until our arrival. After hearing about the problem, Rabbi Tendler agreed that the traders could not share profits earned during the Sabbath or on holy days. He proposed several solutions, none of which worked for tax or other reasons. But as I listened to the religious basis of the conundrum, a solution occurred to me. Suppose, I said, we divided the trader shares into Classes A and B. Those traders who were Orthodox would receive Class A shares and profits earned from Sunday to Wednesday, and the other, less devout or non-Jewish traders would receive shares whose profits derived from Wednesday through Saturday. Fatigued by our lengthy discussions, Rabbi Tendler swiftly blessed the idea. Everyone was relieved. On the trip home, I thought to myself, how does that really work?

François suggested that I meet with Steinberg, my predecessor on the board, who was then well known as an exceptionally talented businessman as well as a corporate raider. A Brooklyn Jew, he had not endeared himself to the financial elite when he made an unsuccessful bid to take over Chemical Bank, the third-largest bank in the United States, which later, through merger, became part of J. P. Morgan Chase. That attempt brought him the sort of notoriety he may have sought all along. He was quoted in *Vanity Fair* suggesting he was comparable to Rockefeller. He said he believed he might well become the president of the United States. He later enhanced his reputation with a takeover attempt of the Walt Disney Production Company, an effort that likewise failed; but he received a substantial profit when the company paid him greenmail to go away.

Steinberg invited me to lunch at his office several times. Always in good humor, he offered some helpful background, which François had failed to do. He told me that Jacob had an interest in becoming a raider and expanding his financial enterprise, so long as it did not significantly injure his social reputation and standing within the cultural world. Saul believed that Jacob was determined to become the richest Rothschild of all and create an institution consistent with the family's historical reputation.

Jacob came to New York on one of his periodic visits. We had lunch with Arne Glimcher of Pace Gallery. This was the first time I met Glimcher. Soft-spoken and deliberate, he offered Jacob a 50 percent interest in the gallery based on the value of the inventory; no premium was required. Jacob had recently sold the Colnaghi Gallery, a gallery dating to the eighteenth century that specialized in old masters. Previously he instructed his investment trust to purchase 20 percent of Sotheby's. Both Jacob and Arne embodied what I considered to be the perfect combination of culture and capitalism. It would have been a magnificent transaction had Jacob decided to go forward, but he did not. I was too new in my relationship with Jacob to offer an opinion.

Jacob then asked me to attend a meeting in his place at the home of Sir James Goldsmith, the British financier who was seeking to raise capital for a hostile takeover. Goldsmith, handsome and charismatic, was a maverick, a nonconformist, an eccentric, known for audacious takeovers and as a lover of attractive women. He and Jacob were close friends. The gathering comprised three billionaires and me. Goldsmith briefed the potential investors about his next target company. Then he launched into a diatribe against the evils of government subsidies that were eroding hard work while promoting undeserved entitlements.

In his 1980 book *Decade of Decision,* Michael Harrington presented an analysis of the impact of corporate ideology, the successful inculcation of the trickle-down theory. Business, he wrote, was conflicted by its "allegiance to free enterprise principles . . . [while striving] to get subsidies from Washington." Remembering Harrington's words, I raised my hand. "Jimmy," I said, "I just read a newspaper article stating that you own a huge amount of timber in Georgia and you receive a cash allotment for not cutting trees." There was silence in the room. I was David Bowie just fallen to the earth. Goldsmith began to laugh as he changed the subject. And I thought: this is not going to be a career that fits my mind.

To further his goal of building a financial powerhouse, Jacob decided to merge RIT with Charterhouse, a large merchant bank, to create Charterhouse J. Rothschild. I attended planning sessions and spent a fair amount of time with the Charterhouse executives. Based on what I learned, I cautioned Jacob that a merger would be a mistake, as the Charterhouse team was conservative and more interested in traditional banking than the adventures into finance that Jacob was seeking. I had forgotten that I was dealing with royalty. Jacob responded that I did not understand his powers of persuasion and that he would convert Charterhouse executives to his point of view. A closing rapidly took place.

As I had suspected, disputes as to the future program of the merged financial institution began at once. Since the board was equally divided between representatives of both institutions, I had to attend all meetings because I had been named to this board. A trip from New York to London was required almost every other week. Fortunately, the Concorde supersonic plane was in operation between the two cities. The setting for the meetings was a large boardroom at the Charterhouse offices with a conference table big enough for the cast of twenty-four, twelve from each side. Jacob was the chairman, sitting in the middle of the throng. I was off-center, somewhat astonished that these leading members of the financial community could not resolve their differences. All were seeking success, either financially or by enhancing their reputations. I floated in the air, much as I did in fifth grade, half-listening to the debate, wondering what was really at stake as the opposing slates glowered at each other and refused to compromise on the best strategy for the combined firms. I squirmed in my seat, watching future knights and lords sitting ramrod straight, uncertain of what Jacob would propose. I hoped he would suggest a cooling-off period. Rather, in his majestic, aristocratic English tone, he announced that a de-merger should take place, and that it was a prudent course to follow.

There are times when my mouth moves too fast, completely independently of my brain. I was still upset that Jacob had not heeded my advice during the negotiating period. After all, I was a Cohen. So I blurted out that prudence required returning money to the public who had bought shares in Charterhouse J. Rothschild. As soon as I spoke, I regretted my remark as uncalled for and probably incorrect. Jacob had the right to try creating a financial powerhouse and to show his Rothschild cousins their mistake in not allowing him to become the head of N. M. Rothschild. My remark to Jacob was not meant to be offensive; I uttered it much like a criticism of a friend with whom I played basketball who had refused to pass the ball to me. With the game over, remarks, even ill-tempered ones, would be forgotten and friendship restored. But I was not in a game, nor was I to be forgiven.

My reaction at the board meeting was, at least in part, due to my questioning the goals of those who wanted more and more. I truly had little ambition other than making mountains into hills. Jacob Rothschild, Jimmy Goldsmith, Rupert Murdoch, and Tony Murray, however, had the right to increase their fortunes even if I did not see the purpose once I reached "enough." I still had not grasped that my indifference to what others coveted offended many with whom I worked. My boardroom comment was a first step in losing Jacob's respect, which I regretted since I enjoyed our cultural exchanges and his sense of humor.

When I was hired, François Mayer was being assigned to run an English public investment company primarily controlled by RIT. He planned to move to New York City to direct its activities, and I was to second him. Jacob, however, had, at my recommendation, purchased control of a brokerage and investment firm, LF Rothschild Unterberg Towbin, when the latter was having financial difficulty. I had helped structure the investment, in part, to aid my friend, Bob Towbin. François was then delegated to become its managing director. I was left alone to run an English-listed company with headquarters on Park Avenue. To direct a company in the investment field was a position for which I was unprepared and unsuited. Jacob did not believe my holding this position was in his best interest and may have thought I was neither competent nor loyal enough to assume the position of chief executive. In retrospect, he was correct. He was soon placing hurdles in my way, insisting that the company allow all shareholders to redeem their shares once per year for the first two years of my mandate. Of course, an investment company cannot properly function if its available cash is uncertain.

By then, my ego was involved. After all, I had not sought to become a member of Jacob's board nor to run an investment company. Feeling miffed, when François abruptly left me alone to join Unterberg Towbin, I formed a consortium of investors who agreed to purchase the shares of those seeking to redeem theirs. Then Jacob began an effort to convince me it would be best to relinquish full control of the investment company to RIT. I should have accepted and retreated to the beach. Instead, I responded that I had just named his cousin, Nathaniel de Rothschild, as chairman of the board, and Jacob should take it up with him. I would remain as Chief Executive. Jacob, somewhat surprised, relented. Nathaniel and I were left in peace to run an investment company with an arbitrage department and a leveraged buyout focus.

I was entering a field for which I was not suited, and that was contrary to my disposition. Why did I continue? It was not for financial gain. I was not highly paid, nor, as the head of an English-listed company, did I have substantial stock options or a large bonus based on performance comparable to American investment entities. If I were to be successful, I would have to absorb the goals and aspirations of the profession to which I now belonged, something I fought against my whole life. I should have read Gustave Le Bon's *The Crowd* and Sigmund Freud's later comment on that work, which would have served as a warning. Freud viewed Le Bon's work as pertaining to any group: by joining, an individual, despite intelligence or character, becomes part of a "collective mind which makes them feel, think, and act in a manner quite different from that in which each individual would feel, think and act were he still outside of the group." Being part of a crowd or group meant being subject to the contagion of the group's goals and adopting its standard of morality.

I had become obligated to increase the company's net asset value irrespective of any external considerations. We were, for example, minor investors with Carl Icahn when he sought control of Trans World Airlines. Our role was peripheral, but it is difficult to be only modestly involved in takeover fights since required filings identified the participants. Female flight attendants, fearing for their salaries and jobs, found my name as a limited partner. I was selected as a target of protest. A picket line formed in front of the building where our office was located. Signs in bold lettering accused Stanley Cohen of being sexist. I quietly slipped past the line.

We joined hands with Roy Disney to make a hostile bid for Central Soya, a soybean grower and processing company. I flew to Fort Wayne after our offer was accepted and became a member of the board. Despite speeches to senior management about being one happy family, termination notices were sent the following week. True, Central Soya had been badly run, and the Disney team made significant improvements to prevent the company from having financial problems, but I was uncomfortable watching pink slips arrive on the desks of long-standing executives with whom I had just dined at the local country club.

Although we were minor league players, I attended what was known as the Predators Ball, the gathering of takeover specialists sponsored and financed by Michael Milken and his firm, Drexel Burnham Lambert. Milken, a bond trader, created a new means to acquire major companies through issuing high-yield instruments known as junk bond debt. Target companies were openly shared, and would-be raiders waited for Milken to select one from their ranks to complete the task. Among those who qualified are people whose names are familiar today: Saul Steinberg, Nelson Peltz, and Ronald Perelman, among others. In addition to financial presentations, there was a frenzied party atmosphere that made headlines. I confess that I was tempted to see if I qualified to join Milken's clientele, a first step to billionaire status. We had purchased some of his junk bonds, and he cordially invited me to a breakfast meeting at his office at 5 a.m. California time. I complained that it was too early. We compromised at 6 a.m., but breakfast was no longer included. I suspect he was neither impressed by my ambition nor my drive. I knew if I were invited to accept hundreds of millions in financing together with a proposed takeover target, I would never be able to make mountains into hills. I would be bound to a world in which I had little desire to accept permanent residency. Heller's "enough" acted as a brake.

As my talk with Milken was ending, the stock market opened for trading at 6:30 a.m. California time. I watched Milken in action. Housed in the middle of the trading floor, he was a brilliant artist at work. Orders streamed in all directions. For a moment I thought the Indian god Ganesha had come alive. Milken seemed to be in a 360-degree mode, shouting prices for buys and sells, pressing those he had already helped to purchase other junk bond issues for a newer crop of acolytes. I admired the performance but had no interest in going on stage.

As our investment entity once owned shares of a company that was the object of a hostile bid financed by Milken, I had to testify before a congressional committee to prove we were not acting in concert with the raider, which would have required filing an appropriate SEC document. Not long before Ivan Boesky went to jail for insider trading, he called me to learn what deals we had in mind and most likely wore a wire during our conversation. I had kept my distance from him. Milken failed to do so. He served twenty-two months in prison until granted a Trump pardon in 2020.

I was troubled by a concept that had prevailed in that world: shareholders' value. Michael Harrington called it the "triumph of illusion." Shareholders' value justified paying lower wages and reducing staff once a takeover succeeded. But shareholders' value was just a rationale. By having extensive stock options and other perks, a class of raiders was being created and slowly embraced by the media and the public. Successful raiders now had a title all their own. It was not Sir or Lord but "Billionaire" that preceded a name in a newspaper article or a TV introduction. That was the aspirational laurel now, rather than one appropriate for a poet or a philosopher, such as I had experienced in France. My definition of "enough" was not shared by the Milken crowd.

I once visited Jeffrey Steiner, who had taken over the Fairchild Corporation with Milken's approval. Once installed as chairman, he developed the reputation of a "milkman," as corporate profits were soon being siphoned off for his benefit. Collapse of the share price and shareholder lawsuits hardly deterred him from his pursuit of cash to entertain friends and fund his opulent lifestyle. I had known him for many years. He was a charming rogue. During a visit to his office, he proposed that I listen to a conversation that would amuse me. He telephoned Carl Icahn and told him he had just spoken to Nelson Peltz. Both Icahn and Peltz were successful businessmen and corporate raiders. He told Carl that Nelson claimed he was richer than Icahn. Icahn was outraged and started to argue that Peltz was incorrect. Steiner then added Peltz to the conference call, and the debate began.

These soon-to-be billionaires, protagonists in Milken's world, were furthering an historical tendency in our society toward inequality and paving the way for a Trump to become its icon.

After two years I tried to find a graceful way out. This was awkward, as a number of investors had become shareholders as a result of personal relations with me. When Nathaniel de Rothschild suggested he should eventually be CEO as befit his name, I was relieved. I asked him to allow me to structure the change. Instead, he contacted Jacob Rothschild, who saw a way to obtain control. The affair became messy, and I sold my shares and those of my investors to Jeffrey Steiner. The Rothschilds lost control. Nathaniel was furious. Much to my regret, he never spoke to me again. There is a tendency, known as the Dunning–Kruger effect, for someone lacking competence for a specific task to overestimate their ability to perform it.

For a second time I decided that I need not work anymore. I became a concierge, thanks to Jeane Kirkpatrick, our ambassador to the United Nations. I lost that position thanks to a pedophile, Jeffrey Epstein. This is how it happened. A few months after President Carter toasted the Shah of Iran and his country as the "island of stability in a turbulent corner of the world," the 1979 Iranian revolution illustrated Washington's inability to understand how rapidly a dynasty could fall to forces beyond its comprehension and control. In November, the American Embassy was seized, and officials were held hostage. To reciprocate, Carter took control of Iranian property located in the United States. One such property was an elegant townhouse at 34 East 69th Street, in which the shah's twin sister had lived. The building had been empty for eight years. It had been proposed as a residence for our UN ambassador, but she declined. I learned that it was still vacant, and I called the State Department's Office of Foreign Missions to see if it could be rented.

A representative invited me for a tour. The townhouse had five floors, each 2,000 square feet. Built in 1929 for a wealthy owner who brought boiserie from France and marble from Greece, it had changed hands several times until it was purchased by the Iranian government in 1968. No one had been there since it was placed under American guardianship. Iranian documents were spread out on the floor; lighting fixtures were gone; bulbs dangled from the ceiling. Yet, it was, indeed, a mini palace, perfect for a shah. I berated my guide about the State Department's failure to adequately maintain seized property. I added that although it would be a burden, I would shoulder the cost of repairs if the rent were low. I moved in the following week. I was a concierge with an elevator going up and down between the floors.

At that time, Sotheby's had Wednesday-afternoon auctions, yard sales of mostly copies of nineteenth-century furniture, pianos, and other items. I filled the 69th Street house in two weeks. I also asked friends who owned galleries to lend appropriate paintings for the walls. The grandeur of the house was such that my position as a concierge was ignored. I was elevated in the minds of visitors to the status of an extremely wealthy New Yorker. Although at that moment, I was living a rather restrained life with few dinner guests or dinners, the stately nature of the house encouraged a number of institutions to ask to use it for fundraisers or meetings. I was happy to oblige.

One day, I was asked by Wendy Keys, director of the New York Film Festival, to host a last-minute celebration for Michael Moore as his film, *Roger and Me,* was being shown that evening. I only had a few hours to prepare, and I had a staff of one. According to a *New Yorker* profile, Moore and his wife, Kathleen

Glynn, remembered the night as follows: "It was our big giant night out in New York. It was like, Wow, isn't this exciting. This town house was all marble and everything, and paintings on the wall, and carpets were rolled up [. . .]." But it turned out to be a kind of radical chic—the fancy party that Leonard Bernstein threw for the Black Panthers—in reverse. Glynn was quoted as complaining, "They served beans and franks. We were from the working class, so they thought that was cool. But we knew better than that. When you throw a party, you throw a party."

I laughed when I read that report. I never told them I served franks and beans at all gatherings of a certain size. An acquaintance, Nick Pileggi, co-author of the script for *Goodfellas,* was tempted to write one entitled *The Concierge,* about how visitors treated me in that opulent environment.

Gary Keys, Wendy's ex-husband and a documentary filmmaker, whose specialty was jazz, suggested that on some Mondays when the clubs were closed, I host musicians who wanted to riff and drink and eat franks and beans. And so I did. One Monday, Michel Petrucciani came to play. I opened the door and thought there was a mistake. In the doorway stood a smallish figure no more than three feet tall with a chest almost as broad. He slipped by so readily that I wondered if he had eased his way through my legs. Without a hello, he asked, "Where is the piano?" While he struggled to climb the stairs, he added, "I only drink champagne." That was my introduction to Michel.

I later learned he suffered from osteogenesis imperfecta, known as "glass bone disease," a genetic condition that causes brittle bones. Frequent breaks governed his existence; a stumble once left his nose broken. His hands were the most normal part of his anatomy. Indeed, one jazz critic commented that among the greats, Michel had the strongest right hand. I was worried he would not be able to reach the pedals. When he played, his hands seemed to float at the level of his breast instead of his waist, the classic stance of most pianists. His energy was such that he played for hours without a break. I had to rush out several times to buy more champagne. So many fans poured in that I ran out of beans. Toward one in the morning, the last guest left, and I thought Petrucciani would as well. I thanked him in French, his native tongue, and it was as if he saw me for the first time. We chatted, and after a few minutes his impediments disappeared. I no longer feared his bones would break. He kissed his companion, who went upstairs to nap. Then he continued playing for me alone. At 3 a.m., he was hungry, had a sandwich, and his companion carried him outside.

Michel was a charmer, sometimes harsh with women, although most cradled him and were at his call. A son was born with the same genetic defect. Dead at thirty-six, Michel was buried one grave away from Chopin. The handicap for him was just an obstacle to be overcome. He was a flame burning bright, despite his everyday pain. Thinking of that evening and the hours of jazz he played for me alone, my spirit soars.

Eventually, the State Department determined I was not paying market rate. Before I had a chance to discuss a possible increase, I received a telephone call from Ghislaine Maxwell asking if I was planning to renew. She and Jeffrey Epstein had attended a charity event and knew the house. I knew Epstein slightly. He once stopped me on the street, whispering in my ear about whether I was going to get in the pants of the young woman at my side. He telephoned me sporadically asking if I knew women of my age who could be the escort for one of his clients, a Les Wexner.

I told Maxwell I had not yet decided whether to renew my lease. The next day, a representative of the State Department called. Maxwell had advised the representative that I was moving out and offered three times the rent I had been paying. I considered her conduct so outrageous that I called her to curse and shout. She later claimed that I was the only person who made her cry. She came to the house to make sure I would leave the premises. I made her promise to retain my housekeeper since she had no other place to live. As soon as I departed, the housekeeper was discharged. Apparently, Maxwell wanted no witnesses on the premises.

37

Filmmaking in Desert Hot Springs

Sandy Lieberson called from London. He had been named head of international film production for MGM/UA. He had personally acquired the film rights for a book, *The Rabbi of Casino Boulevard*, which would not fit in with the studio's slate of movies. He suggested I undertake its development. I would be doing that with Beeban Kidron, who had adapted and directed Jeanette Winterson's *Oranges Are Not the Only Fruit*, a BBC series that had received great acclaim.

The Rabbi of Casino Boulevard was the story of an uncertain and undistinguished rabbi exiled to a desert synagogue of retired Jews, close to a casino. The Rabbi, inexperienced in carnal ways, falls in love with his neighbor, Dawn, a Japanese Buddhist. The congregation becomes divided as the rabbi's faith is tested. Certain members believe their success at the gambling tables is related to the moments when the Rabbi has romantic interludes with Dawn. He is encouraged by the gamblers in the congregation to continue the affair, while others seek his ouster.

I met with the author, Allan Appel, who became a lifelong friend. Beeban and I flew to Hollywood to interview scriptwriters. I had sent copies of the book to several candidates before our arrival. All seemed enthusiastic, but no one we interviewed had read the book. I finally hired Barry Berman after watching *Benny & Joon*, a film he wrote for Johnny Depp. However, his draft for the *Rabbi* was mediocre and failed to grasp the fantasy and humor of the text. I decided to write the script. I engaged a former nun—who had written a screenplay about the conflicts of faith—to teach me the craft, and then I went to work. The ending of the book did not seem right for a film version. Allan allowed the rabbi and Dawn to marry even though Dawn refused to convert to Judaism. I did not think the fictional congregation would have accepted that resolution. My closing scene was more mysterious. The audience was left with an inconclusive ending and had to decide what the rabbi did next. Early in their meeting, Blum relates to Dawn the story of Joshua at Jericho. It was Rahab, he explained, a gentile woman who made the conquest possible. In exchange for hiding the Israelite spies, she was told, "You'll be safe if you hang a scarlet cord from your window." I wanted to use this story as the ending of my screenplay. The ending I wrote: Bloom, the rabbi, looks at Dawn's studio. It seems deserted. As the shofar sounds, Bloom stands on one leg. One arm is raised. He then rises off the ground. A scarlet cord is hanging from Dawn's window.

Did American films require a more definitive conclusion?

Sitting in a dentist's office, I came across an article about Desert Hot Springs. President George H. W. Bush called it "the dope capital of the United States." The author of the article noted that the town had the highest number of religious institutions per capita, including a synagogue where the congregation consisted mainly of retirees. So I went, seeking inspiration for the script. I drove past the hippy Hollywood hideout, Two Bunch Palms, then through open desert dotted with trailers. These were inhabited by the smokers Bush scorned. They had been camped in no-man's-land since the 1950s in expectation that Palm Springs would advance toward the north, and they could resell their small plots for large profits and grow even more pot. Instead, the town expanded west to seek the mountains' protection from winter winds.

Desert Hot Springs was a perfect eccentric setting for an eccentric film. One entered town by going past Budapest, a restaurant that, with its goulash and chicken paprika, made little desert sense. The antique shop next door, run by a defrocked priest, housed artifacts left over from the thirties. The hotels were rundown, with few guests. The town was divided into two parts. One had the choice of hot spring baths or the cool fresh water from the aquifer. I counted ten churches before I introduced myself to members of the local synagogue. I explained why I was there, which led to brisk anticipation that the congregants would soon be extras in a motion picture. The interviews were helpful; I had conversations plugged into the script. The ending still eluded me.

38

Japanese American Veterans in Israel

Attending an exhibit of photographs of Japanese Americans who had served in the US Army in World War II suggested a possibility. The exhibit was organized by Eric Saul, who had been curator of the National Japanese American Historical Society (NJAHS) and was responsible for several exhibitions that helped convince Congress to pass, and President Ronald Reagan to sign, the Civil Liberties Act of 1988 that gave an apology for incarcerating Japanese Americans in internment camps at the outset of the war. Worse than ironically, in 1943, needing additional soldiers, Nisei youth were encouraged to volunteer for military service while their families remained incarcerated in "relocation camps." The Japanese Americans of the 442nd Regimental Combat Team fought fero-ciously in Italy, Southern France, and Germany. The 442nd was the army's most decorated unit of its size.

Saul, although familiar with the Japanese Americans' heroism, was unaware that one of the units of the 442nd was the 552nd Field Artillery Battalion. A veteran of that battalion, Clarence Matsumura, learning of Saul's interest, contacted him and shared photographs and other documentation of his unit, the first to liberate Dachau. Saul, not a person to allow injustice to remain unnoticed nor heroics to go unrewarded, became determined to honor men of the 552nd for rescuing Holocaust survivors. He raised funds in order to invite veterans of the unit to Israel in 1992, where they were thanked and celebrated. Of course I went along. I first flew to Paris to scoop up my daughter Laura as she was on school vacation. I arranged to have Naomi Kaplansky, the senior documentary producer for the Israeli Broadcasting Authority, provide a news crew to follow the veterans on their trip through the country.

The photographs in the exhibit encapsulated the ironic circumstances of Japanese Americans released from internment camps rescuing survivors of concentration camps. This gave me an idea for the ending of the movie script of *The Rabbi of Casino Boulevard*. If Dawn's father was one of the Dachau liberators, Bloom's nuptials with her might be acceptable to the orthodox members of the congregation.

With Laura and the film crew in tow, we accompanied the servicemen on their trip through Israel. They were honored in parliament. They visited sites of remembrance, including Yad Vashem, where an exhibit about them, "Unlikely Liberators," was installed. They met camp survivors. During the initial part of the tour, the Japanese Americans felt ill at ease and surprisingly detached, perhaps because of the formality of the scheduled events. A change occurred at an encounter that took place in the lobby of the Renaissance Hotel in Jerusalem. Saul had placed an advertisement in the *Jerusalem Post* seeking Dachau survivors who recalled being rescued by Japanese Americans. A man called Solly Ganor responded, and Saul arranged for Ganor and Matsumura to meet and sit side by side to discuss what took place forty-seven years before. I did not expect anything but general recollections.

Ganor, a distinguished and handsome man, sat in pause mode. He was sixty-four years old, which meant he was seventeen when Dachau fell. Perhaps his initial silence allowed him to reflect on his childhood in Lithuania and the ghetto to which he had been confined when the Nazis invaded and began to kill the Jews.

Or perhaps he thought of his time at Lager X, the Dachau camp to which he and his father were sent. His mother and sister were separated and transported to a different camp where they were murdered. Those tragic memories were still unspoken. Ganor was thinking of the death march—prisoners who were just skin and bones being forced by Nazi guards to leave the camps and walk before they could be liberated by advancing Allied soldiers. It was, Ganor remembered, a "grotesque, inhuman expression of cruelty of the Nazis." What sort of men prodded those close to death to shuffle through the snow with no destination other than a grave? Ganor would later write in his 1995 memoir, *Light One Candle: A Survivor's Tale from Lithuania to Jerusalem*:

> [. . .] the last day before our liberation [. . .] we were brought into a forest, where we, starved [. . .] and exhausted, simply fell to the ground. It snowed that night, and the snow covered our bodies. For some, the snow became their grave; for us who survived, the snow was our means of survival, because the SS men who wanted to shoot us couldn't see us. The Americans were too close for them to start digging us out one by one. During the night, they ran away, and in the morning, we were freed.

In that forest, Ganor awoke to find an Asian man kneeling at his side. His first reaction was: this is a Japanese ally of the Germans tasked to murder those of us who were still alive. Instead, he was offered a Hershey bar, and he saw other survivors gently carried into nearby houses. Matsumura listened to Ganor's recital. Then he said, "I gave you that Hershey bar." The two men clasped hands, and Matsumura began to cry.

And so did I.

It was at that moment that I, secular in outlook, identified myself as a Jew, even more than when I had conversed with Speer.

Fig. 35. Former Japanese American soldier Clarence Matsumura and Holocaust survivor Solly Ganor.

I turned to Kaplansky and said, "You may continue to film for your own program, but I no longer want this footage." Perhaps I could have worked those scenes into the film, but they were out of place in a fantasy that was really a comedy, not the tragedy created by Hitler and his enablers. The film crew and I stood silent as we saw other survivors reach out to grasp the hands of veterans as they recalled what they saw when they entered Dachau.

"When the gates swung open, we got our first good look at the prisoners. Many of them were Jews. They were wearing striped prison suits and round caps," wrote one veteran. "It was cold, and the snow was two feet deep in some places. There were no German guards. The prisoners struggled to their feet [. . .] They shuffled weakly out of the compound. They were like skeletons."

At my last dinner with Kaplansky, I expressed my admiration for the Israeli nation and the dynamism of the people. "Have you ever visited the Me'a She'arim neighborhood of Jerusalem where the Haredi live?" she asked. I had not. She offered to take me to observe unchanged traditions from pre-war Europe. Naomi had previously made a documentary on that subject and was welcomed into the residents' apartments. It was my first contact with ultra-orthodox Jews. I had not realized the extent of the community nor the average size of a family, which ranged from six to twelve. I saw bunk beds in small apartments with children stacked like inventory. I expressed my surprise to Naomi. She asked me if I knew what all those bunk beds meant. I shrugged. "The children hardly study, other than to know the Torah by heart," she responded. "They do not work or do military service," she continued. And then she added, "They will be able to do something important. They will vote. In twenty or thirty years, no prime minister of Israel will be named unless he or she has the support of the ultra-orthodox community." What that would mean was a question she left unanswered.

It was time to leave. Laura and I needed a change of scenery. We flew to Egypt for a Nile cruise to visit the pyramids and tombs.

The script remained unchanged, with a rabbi floating in the air and a scarlet rope dangling from a balcony. I was invited to Disney Productions to discuss the script, perhaps out of politeness owing to my relations with Roy Disney. They said the writing was excellent, but the box office would be limited. The script, I was told, would be sent to Harvey Weinstein as it was a better fit with his type of production. I knew enough of Hollywood to realize the project was dead. I was surprised to get a call from the Andrew

Bergman team, who had *Blazing Saddles* and *Fletch* to their credit. They told me the theme and my writing conformed to their expectations for a film. My draft was a bit too Jewish, but would I like to submit other scripts? I was flattered. I retired to my room at the Château Marmont Hotel, where all prominent filmmakers stayed.

39

WordStar

The telephone rang. Fred Adler, whom I knew socially, and with whom I had once shared offices, was a well-known and highly successful venture capitalist. Among the companies he had controlled and fostered was WordStar, which had produced the first word-processing program. It had gone public in 1985 and was, at one time, the most valuable software company. Adler explained that WordStar was in decline because of the tension between him and a founder, Seymour Rubenstein. The problems, I soon learned, were much deeper than a question of relationships. Adler suggested I buy some shares from him, become chairman of the board, and shepherd its turnaround.

I should have known better, but I was arrogant, believing that he reached out to me out of respect for my talent. Instead, he knew he had found an unemployed mark, someone who knew little about computers and programming. Truly, I did not know the difference between MS-DOS and Windows, or if the code underlying WordStar allowed it to adjust to updates in operating systems. All I knew was that the company had a large subscriber base and cash almost equal to its share price, so I felt I could not lose and would learn something about a field I believed would soon dominate our lives.

I learned that Ron Posner, the former president of Peter Norton, a software company just sold to Symantec, was visiting Paris. I invited him to lunch in my garden. He was impressed with the surroundings and agreed to become president and CEO of WordStar. I bought the shares from Adler. Posner and I went to the WordStar headquarters just north of San Francisco to meet the staff of about 100, mostly programmers. They were hard-working nerds, fervently struggling to transform the product into a Windows version. WordStar, once dominant, now had less than a 5 percent market share. I questioned Posner and the top executives as to its future. The response was that because WordStar's new Windows version had received good reviews, it could compete successfully against WordPerfect, considered at that time to be the market leader.

To learn more about what I was getting into, I attended my first Comdex exposition, the Las Vegas computer trade show. I sat for hours listening to presentations by both WordPerfect and Microsoft. That was when I realized WordStar could not be saved in its present form. Microsoft was introducing a new version of its operating system and would continue to issue others. Each new version would expand the storage capacity of its product and incorporate advances to its latest word processing program. Innovation by small companies seeking a market niche would be unable to compete. Bigness would deter competition, and the public, seeking efficiency, would go for the most efficient product. But it is difficult to convince a team in place for ten years that their work has been for naught. Posner still thought WordStar could prevail, even with a smaller market share, as its base was enthusiastic and reluctant to change a well-ingrained habit. The staff insisted we could overcome WordPerfect's lead. They lived in the realm of zeros and ones, while I was off in the land of twos and threes. I responded that WordPerfect would join WordStar as a program of the past.

Fig. 36. The Water Mill house. Photograph by Marc Riboud.

I had to choose. The company would surely fail. If I were to play a role, I would have to move full-time to California. I had just bought a house in Water Mill, adjacent to the Hampton beaches. Toby and Laura would shortly arrive for the summer. With regard to WordStar, I only showed up for board and a few other meetings. I lacked the influence to force a transformation. In retrospect, I should have tried to raise additional capital to expand the company into other fields. I was captivated by email, which was just beginning to be known, and was still slow because it was tied into telephone lines. I visited a small company that had a search engine that allowed a user to tap into library files to gather general information. Putting things together, I suggested we combine WordStar with email and improved search capabilities.

Certainly that would distinguish WordStar from its competitors. One of the team members made a plaque for me, an award for "imagination." I sold my shares, and the company soon merged with other entities. I shuttled between Paris and Water Mill.

40

Betty Friedan

Once again there were no guardrails to guide me on a path. During these periods of inactivity, when I am torn between fulfilling my childhood dream of mountains and hills and finding a purpose to stall my drift toward another unfulfilled project, I reread Musil's description of Ulrich: "What he thinks of anything will always depend on some possible context—nothing is, to him, what it is: everything is subject to change, in flux, part of a whole, of an infinite number of wholes presumably adding up to a super-whole that, however, he knew nothing about." So it would not have been a surprise to Musil that I decided to attend Bill Clinton's inauguration on January 20, 1993, although I had not been invited nor had any reason to wander the streets of Washington or peer over the heads of crowds.

Betty Friedan, a warm friend from the Hamptons, was on the plane to DC. I asked her what inauguration events she planned to attend, hoping I could tag along. She shrugged and told me she was heading to Washington to meet a boyfriend and had not been invited to anything. It was a time when Betty was estranged from the feminist movement dominated by Gloria Steinem, with whom she did not get along. Feeling for her, I called a number of organizers of inauguration events, who were delighted to extend invitations to her. I became an escort. This is something I also did at Water Mill since her eyesight was not good, and she often asked me to drive her to events at night as she was afraid to drive herself.

In Washington, what I found touching was the number of young women who stopped her in the aisles and corridors, telling her how important her writing was to them. Betty did not always welcome their remarks. She was often brusque and sometimes even rude. She preferred the compliments of men.

A few months before escorting her to Clinton's inauguration, I dined with Betty as two old friends in a small Japanese restaurant in Sag Harbor. The sake encouraged me to tell stories of my life. But with Friedan, there was no small talk, just dead ahead. She always had a point of view and made little effort to withhold her opinions. The result produced both dear friends and bitter critics. Surprised to learn that I was not a one-career man, she had advice. Her book on aging was soon to appear, but I was unaware of it. It had been gestating for ten years or more. She begins *The Fountain of Age* by writing: "I realized I had to start the book with my own denial [about aging]. [. . .] When my friends threw a surprise party on my sixtieth birthday. I could have killed them all [. . .] I could not face being sixty." Betty's book touches on health concerns, the need for companionship, and dying with dignity. Many insights arose from interviews and anecdotal observations. Reviews were mixed. Christopher Lehmann-Haupt in the *New York Times* was harsh: "She seems to wish away the tragedy of being human."

Since I had frequented the Pritikin clinic where Betty also spent some time and had been started on a low-fat diet, I explained the origin of that program. Nathan Pritikin, whom I had met, had been a sickly child who spent World War II gathering statistics on deaths in occupied France. Noting that heart-related deaths declined precipitously during the war, he began to evolve a theory that exercise and diet might be reasons for the decrease, since meat was scarce and people had to walk rather than use a car.

Pritikin introduced that concept into his clinics, where food was steamed and treadmill walks started the day. Betty confirmed she lost weight from the regimen and had fewer asthma attacks. I could not resist adding that Pritikin committed suicide as his cancer advanced. God gets you one way or another.

As I had a year to go before the frightening specter of turning sixty in 1994, Betty advised me to reflect on the next stage of my life. She said I could fight it as many men try to do, holding onto vestiges of youth, or I could design a new, satisfying vocation. I nodded as if I understood. Betty then inquired about what I most regretted. I thought for a moment. After a brief hesitation, I responded, "That I never made love to Niki de Saint Phalle because a knock on the door interrupted us before we began." Betty threw her chopsticks at me.

41

Patricia Bosworth, Joyce Carol Oates

I bought a house in Water Mill, near the Hamptons on Long Island. Guests would come for weekends at the beach. Patricia Bosworth and her soon-to-be husband, Tom Palumbo, were frequent visitors. I welcomed no friend more than Bosworth. Patti exuded kindness, warmth, and friendship. When she visited, I gave her full run of the house. After a successful acting career, Patti became an extraordinary writer whose works included portraits of Jane Fonda, Marlon Brando, Diane Arbus, and Montgomery Clift. None of her books touched me more than the story of her own family, *Anything Your Little Heart Desires*. Patti spent her childhood seeking the approval of her father, Bartley Crum, whose talent made him a famous lawyer but whose absences often in the service of good causes wounded Patty. Crum advocated for Jewish immigration to Palestine and defended persons accused by the House Un-American Activities Committee. Crum's work for left-wing clients ruined his law practice, and he committed suicide in 1959. Patti's brother Bart committed suicide in 1953, when he was 18 years old. Although these terrible events hurt her profoundly, Patti also had some very good times.

As Patti had full control of my Water Mill house, it was often filled with members of the Actors Studio. Patti hosted evenings of new plays and other events. Jane Fonda accompanied Patti to a concert. When Tom Palumbo was directing Joyce Carol Oates's *Greensleeves* at Guild Hall in East Hampton, Oates paid us a visit.

She had just published *Black Water,* a thinly veiled fictional rendering of the Chappaquiddick tragedy that ended simply with "and she died." Initially apprehensive as I found Oates's works darker than I liked, I found her a perfect guest, exuding a pleasant calmness, showing an interest in the garden, and proving to be a bike-riding enthusiast. We talked about literature and the arduous task of writing. I had been told Oates worked incessantly. I expected her to arrive with a typewriter, but it was a weekend of leisure with her husband, Raymond J. Smith. I invited several Hampton writers for lunch to honor her. Invitees brought others, until we had close to fifty hungry guests, and I had a staff of one. I remained in the kitchen and helped cook. I received a kind note from Oates, to whom I had given one of my moon photos that I took with a camera placed on a high-power telescope.

Fig. 37a–b. Postcard from Joyce Carol Oates following her visit to Stanley Cohen's Water Mill home.

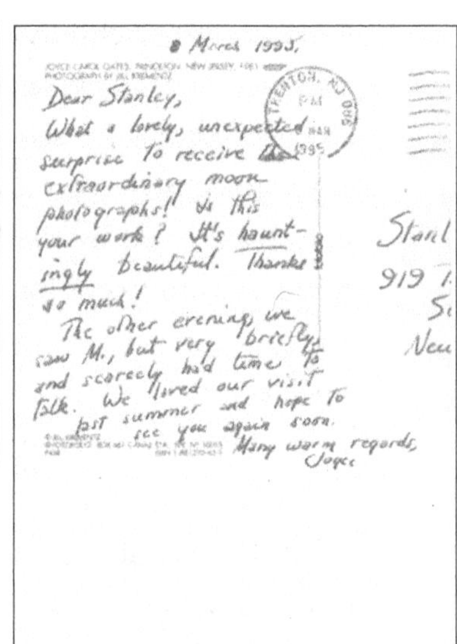

8 March 1995.

Dear Stanley,

What a lovely, unexpected surprise to receive the extraordinary moon photographs! Is this your work? It's hauntingly beautiful. Thanks so much!

The other evening we saw M., but very briefly, and scarcely had time to talk. We loved our visit last summer and hope to see you again soon.

Many warm regards,
Joyce

When Tom Palumbo died in 2008, Patti honored his memory by publishing a book of his photographs. She continued to visit me after I moved to the Hudson Valley. Alas, she was one of the early victims of Covid-19, contracting the disease before doctors knew how to cope.

42

John Calder, Jim Haynes, Ted Joans

Laura was preparing to attend college, and I wanted to ease her way. As an acting career was her goal, Farley Granger suggested she attend Sarah Lawrence College to study under his friend, Shirley Kaplan. I accompanied her to school in Yonkers, just north of New York City. And I purchased a property for Toby in Sag Harbor, not far from Water Mill. I commissioned a house to be built for her there since she eventually planned to move to the United States to be close to Laura. In the interim, Toby preferred to live in Saché. The new house was a few doors from Betty Friedan, and they eventually became good friends, sharing dinners when alone. Toby never minded isolation; Betty always needed an audience. I continued to be in and out of their respective homes.

I sometimes resided at my apartment in Montparnasse, some thirty-odd years after I first arrived in Paris. At the outset I had felt ill at ease with the freedom to wander the streets without obligations. Reaching sixty, however, I was more comfortable spending time contemplatively or meeting old friends for dinner, companionship, and talk. In particular, I was always pleased to hear the reminiscences of Jim Haynes and John Calder (no relation to the artist) as they regaled me with stories of their early days in Edinburgh. Each was a special character who made my own background seem staid.

During World War II, Jim Haynes, a friend for decades, was stationed in Scotland listening to Russian communications. He convinced his commanding officer to allow him to live in an Edinburgh cellar. He spread books across the floor, offering them to young Scots who were not yet aware of paperbacks of a certain kind. Indeed, there was no bookstore in Edinburgh selling literature appealing to adventuresome young readers. Jim's place was the first to offer *Lady Chatterley's Lover* and a coffee pot on a shelf. Readings soon began, then poetry recitals, and then plays and

Fig. 38. John Calder and Jim Haynes.

other performances. John Calder, already a publisher of note before we met, came to visit Jim when he was my guest. Among John's companions were Samuel Beckett, William S. Burroughs, Alain Robbe-Grillet, and Marguerite Duras. Before long, Haynes and Calder initiated a writer's conference. That morphed into today's Edinburgh Book Festival. Jim also helped convert a former brothel into the Traverse Theatre, now well known for its productions of contemporary plays.

Calder tested English literary censorship rules when in 1966 he published Henry Selby, Jr.'s *Last Exit to Brooklyn*. The book was first published by Grove Press in the US in 1964. Calder was found guilty in 1966 of violating the British Obscene Publications Act, but the verdict was overturned in 1968, ending the obscenity injunctions. Shortly after that legal victory, Calder's publishing house issued a "post-trial edition" that was complete and unexpurgated.

Haynes tested the limits of sexual liberation by opening the Arts Lab in London that featured X-rated cinemas, nudity, and performances by Yoko Ono, John Lennon, David Bowie, and Rod Stewart. The Arts Lab was the place to smoke dope and enjoy the sexual freedom Jim espoused. I later asked him how it ended. He confessed that he was urged by London authorities to leave the country. He went to Amsterdam, where he published the magazine *Suck* and organized the Wet Dream Festival of erotic films. Then he was invited to teach at the radical University of Paris VIII, where he stayed until his death in January 2021. He was known for his Sunday-night Paris dinners, open to all—the only ask was a small donation to keep it going. Hundreds came each week to gather and meet other alternative lifestyle devotees. His fans numbered more than 150,000, and he seemed to remember most of their names. Jim was the coolest and most relaxed

Fig. 39. Poet Ted Joans.

person I ever met. If I were tempted throughout my life to make mountains into hills, I would have to tip my hat to Jim, who made that a form of art.

When I had dinner with Jim and John, I heard stories of their affairs and tales of authors who often strayed. We also shared legendary stories about the poet Ted Joans, whose works Calder had published. Born on the Fourth of July 1928, Ted seemed to arrive at my home in Paris each year to celebrate. He walked right in and stayed a week or two. His thin, wiry, black frame was all of a sudden just there, his mouth curled into a permanent smile. Trailing the odor of garlic as he passed, he believed a clove or two or three would keep him healthy and prolong his life. My French residence was often just a waystation on his annual trip to Timbuktu, his spiritual home. Laura Corsiglia, an artist and companion, sometimes accompanied him, and they had successive marriage ceremonies performed in the Mali desert. Ted may have been the last of the Beat Generation. To be truthful, until he died in 2003, when he neglected to take his insulin, much of his life history escaped me. I was unaware he was a trumpeter, and Charlie Parker was his roommate for a while. Ted's portrait of Parker, *Bird Lives!*, hangs in the de Young Museum in San Francisco. I knew Ted hung out with Allen Ginsberg and Lawrence Ferlinghetti, but I did not know about his time with Salvador Dalí or André Breton. For the Metropolitan Museum of Art's *Beyond Borders* exhibition in 2021, Ted enjoyed a window display all his own as if mummified. He was ranked with well-known figures of his time.

Calder, Haynes, and I had dinners together at least twice a month, often joined by Calder's third wife, Sheila Colvin, a former director of the Edinburgh Festival. Jim would begin a story, which was soon interrupted by Calder, and then corrected by Sheila. Even before her marriage to Calder, she had often housed and cared for him since he went broke several times. Small-press publishing is a hazardous industry. Royalties owed to Samuel Beckett had to be forgiven or postponed to allow Calder to seek out writers who might have Beckett-like skills. I generally paid for our meals at a local Turkish restaurant in Montreuil, where Calder lived when he was not traveling to sell books from his backlist. In part, I did so because I knew he had financial problems, which obligated him to teach at the École Active Bilingue in 1995, the same year that my daughter was to graduate. This was a fact I did not disclose. In part, I was honored to settle the bill as homage to his passion and energy in bringing ground-breaking manuscripts into print, some that faltered, others that would be viewed as masterpieces. He was not an easy man; nor was he having an easy time, teaching Monday through Wednesday in Paris, then on to London for the balance of the week to keep his publishing business afloat. When he dined alone, he wrote poems "between the oysters and the wine." He penned a homage to Jakov Lind, a poem worth more than my paying for his grave:

Today I just heard
Another friend gone.
His life was all danger
But what he had done
Was survive all the terror
The Holocaust brought
And in writing about it
The reality caught.

43

The de Portes Incident Again

At this time, living alone in Paris, I often frequented Le Récamier, my table not far from where Milan Kundera sat. His admiration for Robert Musil encouraged me to read one of Musil's early works, a play called *The Enthusiast*. A character claims that "life always makes you choose between two possibilities, and you always feel: One is missing! Always one—the uninvented third possibility. And you do everything you want, and you've never done what you wanted to." That person concludes that once settled into marriage or a job, life is merely a habit, "a repetition . . . of emotions, such people are to all intents and purposes already dead." I had kept my options open as a Musil character would. And although I had enough diverse existences, certainly more than some, I had never tested whether I had the patience or aptitude to remain in place and try my hand as a writer, other than my short-lived screenplay effort.

I had once related to Joe Heller the story of recouping the de Portes jewelry and of my effort to understand whether that woman had influenced the French nation's resolve to continue its struggle against Germany. I told Joe that it was a story that had also intrigued William Faulkner some eight years before he received the Nobel Prize in Literature. Down and out in 1942, he was hired as a writer for Warner Brothers. His first screenplay assignment was the de Gaulle story and his opposition to the armistice. Faulkner began writing a draft with a great deal of enthusiasm. Briefed by many of de Gaulle's entourage, he wrote a treatment with this opening scene:

> *De Gaulle learns that the government is planning to move to Bordeaux.* [. . .] *He pleads with Reynaud to stand firm. Reynaud vacillates, but at last De Gaulle seems to persuade him to resist. Reynaud takes up the telephone to rescind the order to move to Bordeaux. Mme. de Portes enters, bows to De Gaulle, goes and takes the telephone from Reynaud's hand, and puts it back in the cradle.*
>
> MME DE PORTES. Surely you will not order this move . . .
>
> REYNAUD. Of course not. (*To De Gaulle*) I must inform you that the government will definitely move to Bordeaux.

References to de Portes were removed in later Faulkner drafts. De Gaulle's representatives felt it was undignified to insist on a confrontation between the general and the countess. The film project was ultimately canceled. Faulkner unsuccessfully tried to convince the film producer to allow him to write a fictional version. "Let us have a free hand with it. Let's accept with gratitude advice and information as to facts on all occasions but let us keep to ourselves the discretion to choose these facts." Faulkner's friend, big-wave surfer Buzzy Trent, with whom Faulkner shared quarters in Hollywood, provided details about his struggle to write the script.

> He was writing about things that he knew very little about. He knew little about the people. He knew little about De Gaulle, less about Churchill, so when he tried to write about them, they didn't ring true; they were two-dimensional, rather than three-dimensional [. . .]. You never get this feeling when you read the script. You really

> had to get under the skins of those characters, really know them to do that, and I don't think Faulkner was capable of doing that. That required a kind of research he didn't do [. . .].

Although Faulkner's effort was never made into a film, it did serve as the inspiration for *Moi, Général de Gaulle*," shown on French television:

> *Churchill walks into a bathroom, finding the Countess de Portes in the bathtub.*
>
> MME DE PORTES. Are you looking for something?
>
> CHURCHILL. A bathroom.
>
> MME DE PORTES. Use this bathtub, don't the English rule the waves?

In an offhand manner, I said to Joe Heller as we shared an early evening martini, "If the story was good enough to capture Faulkner's interest, perhaps I should do the research Faulkner failed to do and write about de Portes's role in the French collapse and the decision to seek an armistice." Joe's response was swift, "No, you won't." Then, as if to soften his sudden judgment, he added, "I want you to meet someone. I think you would get along."

He invited me to lunch with Robert A. Caro, with whom he shared a brilliant editor, Robert Gottlieb. I had read Caro's book on Robert Moses as well as his first Lyndon Johnson volume, *The Path to Power*. The second in the series, *Means of Ascent,* had not yet been published when we first met. I was flattered by Joe's offer to introduce me to Caro. I interpreted the gesture as a sign of respect and an indication that he took my suggestion seriously. The idea of meeting Caro was most appealing. *The Power Broker* is one of the greatest biographies I have ever read. Caro's ability to write about Moses creating parks, building bridges, and renovating roads illuminated how political power is acquired and deployed. It is written with the skill of a novelist, an achievement worthy of a Nobel Prize, if such a prize existed for non-fiction.

44

Archives

After that first luncheon hosted by Joe in an Amagansett restaurant, I continued to meet with Bob on a regular basis. He and his wife, Ina, visited me in Saché as Joe once had done. Since they often rented a flat in Paris for vacation time, Toby and I spent many enjoyable moments with them. He gave me a tour of his New York writing office. Bob wore a jacket and tie to indicate that it was a work environment. When finished for the day, he left no stray paper on his desk; his notes and drafts were filed in the proper place. A Smith Corona, rather than a computer, was his writing instrument. He foraged in secondhand shops to replace its aging parts.

Our conversations were not directly related to my inchoate idea of writing about de Portes and Reynaud's resignation. Nor was Bob a mentor. But it was not possible to spend time with him and not be educated about the craft required to absorb a great deal of material and render it in prose that kept a reader engaged. To appreciate Churchill's character, for example, he suggested I go to Chartwell, Churchill's home that he purchased in 1922 without realizing the repairs it would require. Caro suggested I sit and gaze at the brick wall that Churchill personally constructed with his hand-held trowel. Only then would I understand the intensity of Churchill's focus, an understanding central to an accurate portrayal of him. Bob was not giving me a tutorial; that was not his style. But I certainly grasped that no account of the story about de Portes could properly be told without an exploration of the military, social, cultural, and historical context of the period. Bob offered one key piece of advice. "If you decide to embark on the project, don't begin to write until you know the last line of the book."

With the leisure time I now enjoyed, I reconsidered whether I should write about de Portes, although I was uncertain of the form or my goal. I became obsessed with doing research to understand the historical context that led to the French surrender. I spent time in the French National Archives reading the Reynaud files, and consulted records in London, Moscow, and Madrid. The way each archive operated allowed a glimpse into national character and that nation's attempt to hide or share the past. London was always welcoming. When a file arrived, a personal beeper sounded as if to say a gift was waiting at the front desk. In Paris, French negativity turned each request into a debate; access to many files required the filing of a detailed application and a wait that could extend into months. Even a request to make a photocopy became an unpleasant task.

Since Churchill was inextricably involved in the Reynaud–de Portes saga, I journeyed to Cambridge University to study his papers. I had underestimated Churchill's tendency to control the pace and content of my effort. He was like the Ancient Mariner, and I was the wedding guest held in place before I realized weeks had passed. I attended school with him. I fought at his side in Afghanistan, South Africa, and Sudan. I was mentored by Bourke Cochran and charmed by David Lloyd George. I discovered that Neville Chamberlain's failure to grow hemp in the Bahamas may have led to his stubbornness in dealing with Hitler.

Among the surprises gleaned from my archival research was that France, despite its obligations, never expressly declared war against Germany when Poland was invaded on September 1, 1940. Instead, the French leaders merely sought parliamentary approval to increase the military budget. They wanted that vote to be held without debate since the assembly was composed of factions bitterly opposed to one another. Many believed that France was not prepared to withstand a German attack. The pacifist Gaston Bergery tried to speak but was shouted down. I wanted to review his papers and requested the single file bearing his name. After several months, permission was granted, and I rushed to the National Archives to retrieve the Bergery box. When I opened it, I was greeted by a single sheet explaining that Gaston Bergery refused to deposit his papers at the National Archives. "Ah, monsieur," said the head of the research department when I complained, "you requested the file by its number, but you never asked if there were any papers in the box."

I related that story to Lord Asa Briggs, an eminent British historian, and to Bob Caro. They agreed that something should be done to honor the "good" archivist. I decided to create an Archivist of the Year award to celebrate an archivist for his or her special effort to resist censorship or provide exceptional help to a scholar or writer. Past honorees have included Saad Iskander from Iraq and Albert Knol, who helped save the Dachau archives so survivors could trace family members who were still living. We also honored Nancy Dupree for her work in Afghanistan. Jingming Xion was thanked for preserving memories of the Chinese Cultural Revolution. Caro, Lord Briggs, Roger Cohen of the *New York Times,* and Lord Robert Skidelsky, the biographer of John Maynard Keynes, have been among the keynote speakers of these events. The award ceremony is structured as an in-depth exploration of the subject for which the archivist was selected. A joint award to Khader Salemah, the archivist of the Al-Aqsa

Mosque, and Dr. Yehosha Freundlich, the Israel State Archivist, had as its subject the difference between emotional-collective memory and knowledge based on archival research. The Archivist of the Year is now in its fifteenth year.

45

Hélène de Portes and Paul Reynaud

I had gathered many bits and pieces of history, some of which had escaped notice and did not make their way into analyses of the French collapse. I did not believe, however, that I could provide a meaningful addition to the knowledge of the period; nor did I have the temperament to spend the years that rewriting history would have required. My research, however, together with the material in my de Portes file, did provide an insight into her alleged role in Reynaud's decision to resign—an insight that escaped historians' gazes.

Some recent historical accounts assume that de Portes was more than just a "favorite" or a woman of convenience, but they provide little guidance about the passion that bound the countess to the premier. If her role was so crucial in the decision to abandon the struggle against the Germans and seek an armistice, why was there a lack of detail about her and how she attained a position of influence? I was not convinced that she had interfered in affairs of state without Reynaud's acquiescence. Reynaud, calm and precise by nature, was a no-nonsense politician, a man of numbers and statistics, who understood the nature of the German threat to France.

Hélène de Portes was best described as someone who could only speak in an aggressive tone, a woman never motionless, never silent, and, to many, extremely nervous and unstable. Relocating to Paris from Marseilles, she was determined to make her mark in the French capital. Accompanying her father, Charles Rebuffel, she was introduced to Reynaud, then a member of parliament. It was, according to a friend, love at first sight. Reynaud may have initiated the relationship because of a sexual attraction to a younger person, but he soon became ensnared by someone with a savior complex who wanted him as an instrument for her needs. From the outset, Reynaud discussed politics with Hélène, and she became mesmerized by the possibility of playing a significant role in his career.

Hélène's parents, good Catholics, urged their daughter to avoid a scandal and terminate her affair with Reynaud, who was still married. They pressed her into marriage with Count Henri de Portes, the son of a businessman, and she gave birth to two children. But, as she wrote to a friend, "I was not destined to accept mediocre horizons." Reynaud and de Portes resumed their affair after several years, and once Reynaud's daughter was married, the relationship became even more open. Reynaud convinced his cabinet colleagues to change the existing law in order to reduce the waiting period between divorce and remarriage. Hélène wrote to her mother that her husband "did not know how to completely tear from my heart the love I had for Paul despite our marriage." Her mother agreed to help her obtain an annulment. In her petition to the Vatican, she described her daughter's single and steadfast love—Paul Reynaud.

Finally, on March 21, 1940, Reynaud squeezed into office as the President of the Council of Ministers (Premier) by one vote. Reynaud's political weakness forced him to accept a compromised cabinet unsuited to carry out a coordinated war effort. Édouard Daladier, the former premier retained his post as Minister of War and National Defense. He harbored ill will toward his successor and refused to accompany the new premier to a conference in

London, where Reynaud entered into an agreement stating that neither France nor Britain would seek a separate peace without the approval of the other. That undertaking would become a major obstacle for Reynaud's later attempt to ease France out of the war without Churchill's approval. De Portes, attending the first holy communion of her son, Hervé, was absent during the frenzy of cabinet making. "Since then," she wrote to her mother, "not a day or an hour goes by that I'm not racked by remorse [. . .] for my desertion." She believed that Reynaud wanted her counsel on a full-time basis. It was a role she embraced with vigor. With no available time to tend to the children, she instructed Alice Mayer, the children's governess, to take Anne and Hervé from Paris to a family home in Arcachon.

Soon Hélène became concerned about the safety of her children in the event of a German victory. Jewelry was deposited in a safe-deposit box in Arcachon. Mayer was instructed to remove the leather case upon receipt of a coded message. In true savior-martyr fashion, Hélène wrote on the sealed package that it was to be given to Anne upon her death.

When I reached out to Anne de Vogüé to tell her of my renewed interest in exploring the 1940 French decision to seek an armistice, her brother Hervé informed me that Anne had died of cancer. She had continued her effort to shape her mother's reputation, but had never been able to craft a complete and satisfying portrait. In *What Is History,* Professor E. H. Carr seeks to define what constitutes historical facts. He gives the example of a gingerbread vendor kicked to death in 1850 and cited in a lecture some 100 years later. "Does this make it into a historical fact? Not, I think, yet. Its present status, I suggest, is that it has been proposed for membership of the select club of historical facts. It now awaits a seconder and sponsors." If the fact appears and reappears over a period of time, Carr writes, it will slip into this club or "alternatively, nobody may take it up, in which case it will relapse into the limbo of unhistorical facts about the past . . . ." Hélène de Portes is our gingerbread vendor, proposed for membership in the Select Club.

46

The Fall of France Revisited

If I were to explore the nature of the relationship between the premier and the countess, I needed a scaffold to hold the story together so a reader would not get lost in the minutiae of World War II. Recalling Caro's suggestion of sitting quietly and admiring a brick wall as a means of understanding Churchill's character, I decided to sit in Reynaud's apartment on Place du Palais-Bourbon, which he shared with de Portes.

Churchill had come there at midnight on May 16, 1940. As I reconstructed that scene, I found the scaffold. The book I have yet to complete contains material too complex to outline in detail here; risking oversimplification, I share only a glimpse. The German invasion of Belgium, Luxembourg, and France began on May 10, 1940, the very day Churchill became prime minister. German forces broke through weak French positions, swept toward the sea, and encircled Allied troops. The shooting war in France would shortly come to an end, leaving the Dunkirk evacuation as the Allied army's only escape.

As soon as the Germans invaded, Reynaud discovered that his role as premier was highly circumscribed. Authority to deal with the military and the forces in the field resided with Daladier as Minister of War and National Defense. Reynaud's primary function was to liaise with Churchill, providing him second-hand news. On May 15, Reynaud made a wake-up telephone call shortly after seven in the morning:

REYNAUD. We are beaten; we have lost the battle.

CHURCHILL. Surely it can't have happened so soon?

REYNAUD. The front is broken; tanks are pouring through.

CHURCHILL. My dear Reynaud, the battle has just begun. I remember the German Spring Offensive of 1918 and the disaster of the 21st of March. I recently wrote about it.

REYNAUD. We may have to give up the struggle.

A pause.

CHURCHILL. I'm willing to come over and have a talk.... Whatever the French might do, we should continuc the fight to the last.

REYNAUD (*in a whisper*). We will too, we will too.

In office for less than two months, Reynaud had not yet succeeded in fashioning a routine appropriate for the energetic premier he had hoped to be. He had no war room with pins and flags, no colored charts on scale maps depicting local sites, no telephones that rang incessantly to report the latest news. Instead, there was quiet, an atmosphere completely cut off from the noise and movement of German tanks and planes. Those German tanks were now approaching Paris, unopposed, while Churchill was telling tales of World War I.

Churchill hurried to France to stem the disarray. He was not yet convinced that all was lost, although he had already written to President Franklin D. Roosevelt and Benito Mussolini, Italy's dictator, that Britain was prepared to fight on alone. His staff began to explore the consequences of a French withdrawal from the war under the heading: "A Certain Eventuality." Heading directly to the British Embassy from the airport to attend a hastily arranged war council to be held at Reynaud's office at the Quai d'Orsay, Churchill seemed unaware that his French colleagues had contemplated evacuating Paris while he was en route.

Roland de Margerie, a Reynaud staff member, led Churchill to a window overlooking the courtyard to quietly confirm the French army retreat. Together, they watched confidential files being thrown into a fire below. His ally's will to fight was shattered. France was to be no more than a buffer zone. Churchill needed to delay France's exit to allow Britain time to prepare for the bombing assault on London destined to begin shortly. He returned to Reynaud's office to promise the premier that more aircraft would be made available for the battle raging in France.

Surprised to learn that Reynaud was no longer there, Churchill, accompanied by his chief of staff, General Hastings Ismay, continued to the premier's nearby apartment. Shown into the salon to await Reynaud, who had already retired to his bedroom, they sat, perhaps on the same divan on which I was now installed. Years later, when Ismay was asked in preparation for Churchill's memoir to describe the scene, he recalled "the only sign of life" was a woman's fur coat draped across a chair. Did Churchill and Ismay avert their glances, or were they compelled to stare at it? Did they wonder why the woman's coat was made of fur, although it was the warmest May in over fifty years?

That fur coat, with its warmth and richness, may have come to represent a fallen ally, its will to fight destroyed. Churchill would return to France four more times in an effort to free Reynaud from the grip of this feeling of looming defeat. I would frame the story I wanted to tell as a struggle between Churchill and de Portes for the premier's mind. That would be the scaffold I needed to relate the events leading to Reynaud's resignation some thirty days later. Like a Shakespearean play, the ending is known, but there is interest in watching the stage to see how the actors perform. The cast is large, but only three characters held my interest, each emblematic of a culture, each with a history and distinct personality whose conduct helps illuminate Reynaud's resignation.

Reynaud took the place of Daladier as the minister of war. He then named General Maxime Weygand as the new military commander-in chief and Marshal Philippe Pétain to his cabinet. Both had held high military posts in World War I. Calling up these recognized stalwarts from the past, I believe, was a shield behind which Reynaud could hide to avoid criticism for seeking an armistice. History, he knew, could only say "alas." De Portes wanted key personnel to be loyal to the premier, so Reynaud named members of his staff to the cabinet, most of whom would soon advocate for an armistice.

By May 25, a week after assuming command, Weygand knew the battle could not be won. The following day, Reynaud flew to London to meet with Churchill. He reiterated the French army's inability to withstand the German attack, hoping the prime minister would commiserate with French losses, extend a hand, and say, "You have done your best." He wanted Churchill to suggest reaching out to Hitler to settle all outstanding European questions. With his ally at his side to share the defeat, Reynaud would be spared criticism for the decision to end the war. Churchill understood. But he refused to place his nation on what he called a "slippery slope."

On June 10, without so much as a tearful goodbye or an invitation to join in the flight, the French government slipped out of Paris in the middle of the night and headed for Tours in southwest France. Reynaud neglected to say that Paris would not be defended and thus spared devastation. No evacuation plan was released. Dispatches appearing in the morning newspapers for

June 10 still reported that great battles were being fought. The following morning the government was gone, the sun was obscured by haze from the smoke of petrol depots set ablaze by the retreating military, soot coated the skin with a greasy residue, and storefronts were boarded. When the major newspapers failed to appear, everyone tried to leave Paris at the same time.

At great peril, Churchill flew into a military airport near Tours twice in four days to meet with Reynaud. Their discussions should be considered a theatrical farce. Both sides knew resistance was at an end, and yet historians narrate the meetings as if strategy was on the agenda. Reynaud sought a scapegoat and blamed the British for the lack of aid. While he insisted that, if necessary, France would fight from North Africa, he appealed for Churchill's approval to seek terms of peace. Churchill refused the request, even though he knew organized resistance in France was no longer feasible.

During this brief period in Tours, the Countess de Portes was very active. She was not a defeatist at the outset of the war, as some historians contend. She wrote to her father when the war began, "We must neither be weak nor waver." Indeed, she wanted a rifle or even a machine gun to fight German troops as they approached Paris. But with defeat evident, she became a forceful partisan for ending the war. De Portes had her point of view, less about the fate of the nation than her desire to have Reynaud continue to have a meaningful role in dealing with the aftermath of defeat. She embarked on a mission to convince anyone who would listen that fighting should cease and an armistice be sought. Unable to appreciate Reynaud's effort to preserve his reputation, she drove two hours, accompanied by her lover's principal military advisor, to confront the American representative, Ambassador Anthony Biddle, Jr. She wept and solicited his help to persuade Reynaud to follow her plan. It is difficult to believe that Reynaud was unaware of this effort, just as it is hard to understand his passionate embrace of someone whom he knew was determined to have France withdraw from the British alliance.

De Portes urged Reynaud to order General Weygand to have the military capitulate, which would have left the government in place to negotiate with the Germans. The general refused; he did not want his reputation stained. De Portes believed the general should have been forced to comply with Reynaud's order. Upset, she then counselled Reynaud to have Pétain replace him as premier in exchange for his becoming vice-chairman of the cabinet and remaining the power behind the throne. She believed Pétain was better placed than Reynaud to negotiate with Hitler. Once again, she faulted her companion for his hesitation.

De Portes opposed a possible move to North Africa. She, and most likely Reynaud, believed the exhausted and abandoned population, the long procession of panicked and starving people, would never agree to continue the struggle after their long flight to evade the German advance. And yet Reynaud still contemplated a North African stand. He dispatched General Charles de Gaulle to London to assure Britain that France would not abandon the fight and to seek help to transport troops to North Africa. But on Sunday, June 16, Reynaud resigned, due, he claimed, to the lack of support from his cabinet. Although he had lost the backing of the two aides he had recently elevated, there was scant evidence that a majority of the cabinet actually disagreed with his plan to proceed to Algiers.

On the afternoon of June 16, 1940, Churchill hesitantly telephoned Reynaud in a final attempt to convince his ally not to abandon the struggle. He proposed "an indissoluble Anglo-French Union"—no longer would France and Great Britain be two separate nations; they would be joined as a single sovereign unit. A unified war cabinet would be responsible for continuing the fight against the Germans. The declaration would conclude with a Churchillian flourish: "And thus shall we conquer." Reynaud, together with civilian and military representatives, was invited to meet at sea with a large British delegation to finalize the arrangements. Shortly after the telephone conversation, Reynaud attended a previously scheduled cabinet meeting to present the English proposition to his colleagues. And to resign.

Churchill, accompanied by key cabinet ministers and the chiefs of staff, left Downing Street for Waterloo station. A special train was ready to take the delegation to Southampton to board a cruiser at midnight and sail to a rendezvous off the coast of Brittany. But even before the train's departure, the mission was placed in doubt by news from Bordeaux. An hour later came the confirmation. Reynaud had resigned. Marshal Pétain was the premier. France would seek an armistice. "There was nothing else to do," Reynaud would later explain. They all dispersed, many with an apparent sigh of relief as if an unwanted guest had canceled a planned visit. Churchill returned to his office. When he was asked in Parliament to explain "how the Reynaud Cabinet was removed and from where the Pétain Cabinet derived its authority?" he responded, "It is a very difficult matter to understand the politics of another country." Only history, he continued, could yield a "fuller account."

My thesis, which remains to be proved, is that Reynaud decided to resign in favor of Pétain *prior* to Churchill's phone call from London. There is no other cogent reason to explain Reynaud's conduct. His apparent approval of the English offer was merely a ploy. He sought to be placed in a minority at the cabinet meeting to have a plausible excuse to resign. De Portes, I suspected, had already raised with Marshal Pétain or his aides a proposal to have Reynaud named ambassador to Washington after his resignation.

At least in the United States, Hélène would be reunited with her children and join a coterie of socially prominent women with whom she could maintain her standing. The Washington position was offered to Reynaud as soon as resigned. De Portes hurried to obtain transit visas to permit the couple to travel through Spain to Portugal en route to the United States. Two of Reynaud's aides who had left for the United States in anticipation of his arrival were arrested in Madrid. In their seized baggage was additional de Portes jewelry, state funds, and documents. That, coupled with President Roosevelt's questioning the wisdom of Reynaud becoming the spokesman of a government that might collaborate with the Germans, doomed his nomination as ambassador.

Reynaud wrote to Doriot that he and Hélène had hoped to go to the United States, but "circumstances prevented their departure." Although disappointed that Reynaud had not agreed with her to join with Pétain immediately, or had waited too long before accepting the Washington ambassadorship, de Portes still reaffirmed her love by writing in her last letter that "As long as nothing happens to him [. . .] I will never leave him." They spent the evening of June 27 in a small hotel in the town of Saint-Amans-Soult. They continued their journey next midday to Montpellier on the southern coast of France to visit Henri Pagezy.

Reynaud was driving the automobile, a two-seater Renault Juvaquatre. Its strong garnet-burgundy finish and shiny chrome contrasted sharply with the dirty vehicles lying idle along the road. The model's rarity and its deviation from the standard black conveyed a unique status. The car was weighed down by luggage in the boot and packages squeezed into the narrow space directly

Fig. 40. Automobile given by Paul Reynaud to Hélène de Portes shortly before her death.

behind the seats. On top of the packages lay a heavy suitcase, large enough to qualify as a mini-trunk. The occupants, because of their late start, did not pause for lunch, but merely shared a few pieces of fruit. Shortly after 1 p.m. they left the small village of Lapeyrade and continued on Route National 108.

There had been little conversation when the passenger turned toward the driver. "Paul," Hélène asked, "do you still love me?" Or so the story goes. Paul did not respond, perhaps uncertain as to whether she really expected a response or perhaps because he was concentrating on the road. Although he had had his license since 1904, just two years after Hélène had been born, Reynaud was not a good driver. Silence may have been due to fatigue or the monotony of the ride. "And look at me, Paul," she added, "look at me in the eyes when you answer." The National 108 spread out in front of the Juvaquatre. Although not a main highway, it was nevertheless seven meters wide with open visibility. Plane trees bordered the road, some ten meters apart. The weather was fair, the ground dry.

Paul's hands tightly gripped the steering wheel as his entire body shifted to confront her. The Renault edged to the right. The road, partially obscured by a parked military vehicle, continued straight ahead. "Hélène," he started, but before he spoke any more, the car ran off the road and smashed into a plane tree. The momentum propelled the huge suitcase toward the front seat. It struck Hélène in the left lower jaw and severed her facial artery. She was unconscious even before the impact caused the car to careen into a tree, then collide with a nearby wall, and land on its right side in a ditch. Paul ended on top of Hélène, a final embrace.

Sometime later in London, General Charles de Gaulle received news of the accident, but not of the details. He was reported to have said, "I hope she got killed, that slut."

She did, almost immediately upon arrival at the Protestant Hospital in Sète.

Bystanders lifted Paul from the car. With their help, he was able to stumble into a nearby house. He was covered with blood, his lip badly cut, his head scalped in the form of a V. He was then transported first to a military hospital. His daughter, Colette Dernis, shocked by the conditions, arranged his transfer to a private clinic in Montpellier. Reynaud's head was bandaged, but the wounds were not considered serious. "Two weeks of convalescence," advised the doctor. If he had been three inches taller, he might have been killed, rather than merely scalped. When Paul was told of Hélène's death, he said, "She was France, France was her."

The former leader of the nation did not know whether to mourn first the passing of France into its armistice or the death of his companion of many years. He felt accountable for both, but the latter, at least for the moment, was more emotionally charged; his responsibility was more direct, engendering a greater feeling of guilt. In moments of solitude, what weighed more heavily: political shame or personal grief? Reynaud had been premier for only eighty-six days, a short and dramatic stewardship during which he presided over the military defeat of France's allegedly invincible army and the failure of his nation to continue the war against Hitler.

While he was in the clinic, the newspapers carried an account of a press conference with William Bullitt, the American ambassador. Reynaud immediately wrote to him, not about France but about his personal situation, seeking assistance for Hélene's children who had just arrived in New York. They were penniless, in the charge of their governess, and awaiting word from their mother. We were soon to be married, he confessed, and now he was uncertain as to whether he should continue living, "But then this idea seized me: she would want me to live for my country." He ended the letter with, "I was, and remain, loyal to the Marshal. [. . .] I'll tell you about it when I see you." I found a copy of this letter inserted in a book in Reynaud's home in Barcelonnette. The original is in the Bullitt papers at Yale University.

Initially imprisoned by the Vichy government, Reynaud was transferred in 1942 to German control. He spent time in the Sachsenhausen concentration camp before being sent to the Castle Itter prison in Austria. After almost being killed by the Nazi SS near the end of the war, he was liberated by the American army in 1945. Reynaud's prison diary confirmed his love for Hélène. His dreams were filled with her image, and he missed her presence. Reynaud attended every session of the post-war trial of Pétain, who had been charged with "collusion with the enemy." He raised his antenna to seek any hint of his responsibility for the armistice that led to the Vichy regime. He accused Pétain of aiming to overthrow the Republic from the outset and impose an authoritarian regime in its place. Indeed, Reynaud had to sweep aside anyone's memory that he had appointed Pétain to the cabinet and had recommended him as his replacement as premier.

Archival research can reveal but cannot completely explain events of the past. Historians make judgments—guesses about what may have happened. Life was complex, Reynaud said during a post-war parliamentary investigation of the French collapse. It was up to a historian, he added, to make sense of the chaos by applying art and science to what he called a confusing period.

47

Pauline, then Paul Arrive

Although archival research was becoming addictive, I decided to give up my Paris residence and return to Water Mill. At a final garden party, Ronald Sukenick, a chronicler of the hip and a writer with a postmodern style, brought a friend he thought I might want to meet: Pauline de Grunne, an aspiring film director. We had a pleasant chat about films and dance. She had just attended a performance by Pina Bausch—a name new to me, about which I was impressed.

I was not seeking a wife, or even a relationship with a younger woman. An introduction to someone twenty-five years my junior did not make me think I could avoid the mortality that permeated Betty Friedan's book. Consistent with the indifference that so often characterized my conduct, I slid without reflection into companionship with someone whose experience was very different from my own. After several years of moving between New York and France, and with a miscarriage in the mix, too, Pauline was about to give birth to our son. The idea of having a male heir was certainly appealing. I had not proposed marriage since I had seen too many French films to believe that a signed paper was essential, but I had underestimated its importance to Pauline and her intense rage at the thought that there would be no marriage. I obediently went to the town hall to affix my signature a few days before the birth of our son. I did not yet understand the obligations that would follow. I was to be a father, unable to evade the routine a child brings in its wake. Nor did I grasp the impact on a child growing up with a much older father who might die before his son's schooling was at an end. When our son was born on June 22, 1999, we gifted him several names to prove we could arrive at a compromise: Paul Julian Alexander.

So instead of leaving Paris, I rented an apartment near the Bastille and continued writing while still engaged in sporadic archival research. Pauline seemed happy, working on her scripts. The next few years slipped by with few disturbances. Weekly chores were pleasant, including wheeling Paul in a carriage, then a stroller, while shopping at the outdoor food market on Thursdays and Sundays. I had no great urge to wander anywhere outside Paris except for summers in Long Island at my home in Water Mill. I also purchased an apartment in New York City—actually two, one for us and one, adjacent, for my daughter Laura, who used it after college before moving to Los Angeles in 2002 to have a go at an acting career. Toby was living in the waterfront home in Sag Harbor. I continued to visit her on a regular basis. It appeared I had worked everything out.

48

The Russian Samovar

I did slip off from time to time, though. Yevgeny Yevtushenko, whose Babi Yar poem criticizing Russian antisemitism had gotten him nominated for a Nobel Prize, invited me to his dacha in Peredelkino just outside Moscow to taste his Georgian wine. I had met him at the Russian Samovar, a New York restaurant, where I hung out a few years before. After a few minutes of conversation at the restaurant, drinking vodka and toasting who knows what, I knew that we would be in harmony, just as I knew after a few minutes of talk that others would be companions. I make judgments on the spot. Yevtushenko had complained of an ailing back, so I immediately brought him to my house in Water Mill for a weekend and arranged a session with a massage therapist.

I often surprised people I have just met with an offer of a Hampton weekend. Introduced at a cocktail party to the poet Quincy Troupe and his wife Margaret, I discovered the charm of their talk and that we had mutual friends. I insisted they come to stay at Water Mill. They later told me about their second thoughts. As they drove to my house, they wondered, "Who was this white guy who had offered hospitality so quickly?" Perhaps he was a racist. They then informed several friends of my address and left instructions to alert the police if they had not returned home in a day or two. Even Larry Kramer, the Pulitzer Prize finalist and AIDS activist, shepherded to my house by his friend

Sandy Lieberson for a weekend stay, may have wondered why he was there.

The Russian Samovar, owned by Roman Kaplan, Mikhail Baryshnikov, and the Nobel laureate, poet Joseph Brodsky, was frequented by an odd assortment of Russian writers who came to relive a dead period. Roman liked to drink with me—but then, he liked to drink with anyone. On each anniversary of Brodsky's death, the elaborate buffet with its odd assortment of vodka fig and cherry, cucumber and dill encouraged attendees to reminisce as if they had attended the ceremony that awarded the Nobel Prize to their departed friend, before reading excerpts from his poems:

> To a wanderer the faces of all islands
> resemble one another. And the mind
> trips, numbering waves; eyes, sore from sea horizons,
> run; and the flesh of water stuffs the ears.
> I can't remember how the war came out;
> even how old you are—I can't remember.

One evening, as I dined alone on pelmeni and kasha, I saw that Phillip Roth and David Remnick, editor of the *New Yorker*, were in conversation at a corner table. When they left, I asked Roman to change my place so that I could sit in a chair one of them had just vacated, in case they left words strewn on the floor that I could someday use. From then on, the Roth–Remnick table was mine.

49

Paul Center Stage

I may have been less involved with Laura's upbringing, but at the age of sixty-eight, when Paul first entered school, I was no longer subject to existential events that would keep me from my duties.

Paul would soon introduce me to the fragility of life. Beginning in a Paris pre-kindergarten private school, Paul, mature in looks, with a vocabulary beyond his age, was placed in an advanced section. France encourages a triage to prepare those with an intellectual bent to be trained for elite schools.

After a few weeks, his teacher alerted Pauline and me that our son had questionable motor skills and had difficulty processing abstract concepts such as days of the week. A specialist suggested that not all the requisite cells may have migrated to the right hemisphere of his brain. Was life then dependent on migrating cells? As experts forecast the problems that awaited us, we were told that mathematics, tie knotting, and shoe tying would be onerous tasks for Paul.

At last I had a mission to test my empathy and ingenuity. I wanted to ensure that my heritage of silence would not be passed on to Paul. I sought guides as competent as the ancient geographer Strabo to lead me into parts unknown. Within a few weeks, my shelves were filled with primers on the subject. I quickly found there was much about the workings of the brain that remained unrevealed even to experts in the field. Was his condition due to an old man's sperm? No one could say. Obtaining a proper diagnosis seemed remote, and I was besieged with acronyms and abbreviations like NLD and ADD and ADHD. The first step was sessions with an occupational therapist to coordinate his motor functions. If exercises begin early, I was told, Paul would develop the motor skills of a typical child. And so he did.

Since French schools are rigid in their educational approach, I pressed Pauline to move full-time to New York City. I felt Paul would be best served by the host of specialists more readily available in Manhattan than in Paris. I purchased one of those large, handsome apartments in the seventh arrondissement, a fixer-upper, so she would not feel anchored to life in America if she wished to return. I assumed Paul would attend a regular school while continuing his treatments to overcome learning difficulties. Since my experience was limited to secondary schools in the Bronx, I had not realized that an entire educational industry had developed in the intervening half century. Friends told me that I could accomplish little without the input of an expert consultant. Initially, I thought that was a joke, but I soon realized that private schools of a certain status were not used to someone walking in the door to register their child.

I had to learn which one would be most appropriate for Paul. We engaged a well-regarded advisor who spoke briefly with my son and then asked him to draw the figure of a human being. Paul's image featured sticks for arms and legs. I was proud of his minimalist tendency. The advisor abruptly ended the session by telling me that no well-known school would accept him as a student and that she could not be of any help. I was astounded. I entered Paul into a church kindergarten class close to our home. I also arranged for tests to better understand his ability to learn in a typical school environment. Those experts suggested that since Paul had attention deficit disorder (ADD), he should be enrolled in a school for the learning disabled.

Such a rapid negative classification did not sit well with me. I recalled my own early schooling years. Paul had no behavioral problems; nor did he exhibit hyperactivity. Of course, I had to be careful that my rejection of their diagnoses was not to placate my ego, but rather to do what was the best for Paul. I knew certain tasks were difficult for him. Distraction was a problem, basic organization was difficult, and procrastination a habit. But his memory was superb, as was his way with words. I tried to register him in the school run by the 92nd Street Y. Their admissions officer came to see me. She told me that Paul's conversational skill was among the best in her experience. Paul looked her directly in the eyes, was fluent in two languages, and had a vocabulary beyond his age. Nevertheless, he would not be admitted, as children and grandchildren of large donors already claimed all the available places. However, she was so impressed that she did call colleagues to ensure his acceptance in another school. But by the time Paul was in second grade, Pauline felt he should attend the Lycée Français to reinforce his knowledge of the French language. I was hesitant, uncertain that extracurricular help would be offered, but the staff assured me that tutoring was easily available.

By the age of six, Paul had to contend with another issue: growing tension between Pauline and me. When we lived in Paris, our relationship worked well. But assimilation into New York proved difficult for her. Perhaps it was the lack of a close circle of friends or a support group, though there is a substantial and vibrant French community in the city. Perhaps it was just my restless personality. Perhaps it was the long-standing mental troubles that I had not previously perceived in her. There was much I failed to understand, owing largely to my habit of not asking questions. I should have realized that a lovely young woman would not choose to live with an older man if she had not experienced some upheaval earlier in her life. She became withdrawn and silent during dinner with friends. The decorator she hired to renovate the Paris apartment claimed Pauline was unable to make decisions, leaving the work at a standstill.

Oblivious to events that had shaped Pauline's mental fragility, I approached a separation with an attitude that I now view as cavalier. I told her straight up that we were both unhappy, and I thought we should part. As she was young, there was time for her to remake her life. I would make financial arrangements that she would find more favorable than if we went to court. And we should jointly speak to Paul to explain the situation the best we could and create a schedule to share responsibility, even if she preferred to return to France. By these actions I was leaving Pauline adrift in a foreign country where her day-to-day existence was dependent on my social circle. I naively believed a straightforward explanation for our separation would suffice—as if I was bidding adieu after a one-night stand in Japan.

I moved into an apartment within walking distance of Paul's school. He would be with me on Wednesdays after school as well as every other weekend. That was an arrangement we settled with ease, but I misread Pauline's deep-seated need to relitigate how her father had treated her mother. I tried to take the blame. Her first two attorneys advised her that my offer of settlement was higher than what the court would decree. Her third lawyer promised to make my life purgatorial. And so he did, for some ten years.

I could cope, but there was something happening to Paul. He had developed facial tics, followed by seizures that caused him to faint. Once he stumbled and fell down the staircase in school. I hurried there to follow an ambulance to a hospital emergency room, then to multiple medical experts to determine the cause, whether neurological or something else. The experts gave multiple reasons. Therapists offered exercises to reduce the tics.

One Wednesday after his tutor left and while I prepared dinner, Paul seemed ill at ease. He did not respond when I asked if anything was wrong, but sat silently, moving the food on his plate back and forth. When I reminded him that we had little time before we started our walk to his mother's home, he raised his head. His eyes met mine. "I am not going there," he said. Noting the tension in his glance, I needed no verbal confirmation to understand, at last, that his relationship with Pauline was injurious to his health. I asked him if he would speak, in confidence, to Sandra Schpoont, the court-appointed lawyer who represented his interests. I knew if he revealed his fears directly to me, Pauline would claim I prompted or coached him to voice criticism of her as a tactic in the divorce. Schpoont came immediately. After an hour with my son, she advised me to keep him for the night.

I sent an email to Pauline telling her that Paul would remain at my apartment since the lessons ended late, and I would take him to school in the morning. She angrily disagreed, but I ignored her insistence that I bring him immediately to her apartment. Tears of guilt shook Paul's frame as he understood that he had just disowned his mother. I lay next to him in bed to give him assurances that all would be well. I remained there until his sobbing had stopped and he drifted off to sleep.

While Paul was at school the following day, Schpoont met with the judge handling our case. A temporary order was signed and later made permanent when the divorce was finalized,

Fig. 41. Paul Cohen, son of Stanley Cohen, at age seven.

although there was some hesitation due to my age—custody of Paul was awarded to me.

Paul did not speak with his mother, nor did he see her, for the next eight years. When no longer a minor, Paul decided to visit her in France. The meeting was cordial.

At the age of seventy-eight, I became a single parent of a twelve-year-old. That was when the carapace was shed. Memories I had refused to acknowledge, or had simply evaded or neglected, came flooding in. It was as if I had fallen from a precipice with life images placed along the path. Some caused shame, but much was revealed, certainly as impactful as years of therapy.

I fulfilled my parental chores with a seriousness that I had often not exhibited: a walk to school, playdates to be scheduled, clothing to be bought, a trip to watch the whales, a cruise to the pyramids. Due to my Archivist of the Year award program, we were invited to visit the Al-Aqsa Mosque. We were, at that time, the only infidels to visit the Dome of the Rock and the caves below. At last I found a vocation that fit my mind.

From the moment Paul came to live with me, no tics appeared, and no seizures ever disturbed his frame. There was joy in watching a child overcome the harm his parents caused. His ADD, of course, was still a burden; often I would get annoyed as he postponed or forgot his school tasks. I made lists for him to follow and attended seminars where I learned that certain struggles were there to stay and that Paul had to learn to meet them on his own. He was becoming a student in the upper middle of the class; in popularity, though, he was first.

I was not surprised when he announced, while in sixth grade, that the French lycée curriculum was rigid, with too little emphasis on American history. Since he was not returning to France, he wanted to attend a boarding school. Upon reflection, I realized it was best for him to be living with friends his age rather than watch TV with me. Unaware of the boarding-school universe, we studied lists together and began the preparation for the admission tests. Impressed by the opulence of the grounds, the mentorships available, and the quality of teachers we met, I understood why parents opted for such an environment rather than have their children remain in public schools. Such places may have fostered inequality, but all affluent parents wanted to set their child on the first step to success, which meant a college and career that they believed a boarding school would cultivate.

Paul did well in interviews. He had a choice of several schools. It came down to Kent—where my tales of a past roommate evoked a laugh—or Northfield Mount Hermon. Upon acceptance, each school suggested a final tour. Kent was initially preferred, but when the tour was over, Paul rejected the school because he learned that the headmaster drank too much and drug use was abundant. Northfield was chosen. When the time came for Paul to move in, I helped him unpack and watched him disappear down the hall, already engaged with new friends.

Whatever apprehension I may have felt about Paul's solo experience away from home, his immediate inculcation in the student body relieved any concern about his interaction with his fellow students. The tension between his mother and me did not appear to impact his relaxed charm in dealing with others.

50

Carrie Arrives

Attending the Northfield parent-orientation session, I looked around and was astonished to see, a few rows away, my moon-faced girl—the one I had left behind.

At lunch, I hurriedly pushed through parents standing in the aisles to sit next to her, hoping, after all these years, she would recall our last goodbye and forgive me for not staying to spend the night. Her name was Carrie Chen. Taiwanese-born, she lived mostly in Seattle and Hong Kong, where she had a business designing landscapes for hotels. She was recently divorced. Her daughter had a choice of many schools, but selected Northfield because it had the most relaxed feel. There was something special in Carrie's bearing and the authoritative way she walked. Our conversation seemed to begin in the middle, as would be expected of old friends renewing a talk interrupted by an unplanned absence.

Of course, with me being eighty, and Carrie, forty-four, it was absurd to think of a relationship, especially with my fixed resolution to avoid a younger woman. I had already sold my house in Water Mill, and I was looking for one not too far from Northfield so that Paul could visit for weekends. Carrie agreed to assist me. We found a splendid property with an outstanding view in the Hudson Valley, not far from Great Barrington, Massachusetts. I moved in quickly just before Thanksgiving 2014. Toby, Laura, and

Fig. 42. The Copake residence.

Paul attended that first festive dinner. They were delighted to meet Carrie, who moved in too.

Paul blossomed at boarding school. The burdens of the past faded as he thrived. He did well in his studies, qualifying easily for the college of his choice. Returning home to be with Carrie and me twice a month, despite a five-hour drive each way, he helped me with my book on France as it slowly progressed.

I was uncertain how my relationship with Carrie would develop. She may have been influenced by Ruth Ginsburg, whom we went to see when she spoke at the Glimmerglass Opera in Cooperstown, New York. Ruth took Carrie aside and gave me "a good man" label. After I loaned the Justice a Calder work, she wrote a note about how Calder and cornflakes cheered her up each morning as she watched the white and red discs move gently

Fig. 43. Stanley Cohen with Justice Ruth Bader Ginsburg at the United States Supreme Court, accompanied by family members.

in the morning breeze. Ruth hosted our family for a private tour of the Supreme Court on my eighty-fifth birthday.

Carrie and my wedding was a grand affair. Yehuda Hanani played his cello. Yumiko and Kenro Izu photographed everything.

Simon Winchester credited me for supplying him with facts he did not know. My friend Tamar Muskal sent a special song composed for our happy occasion.

And then all of a sudden, I was ninety. I had not expected to live that long. I celebrated the milestone by inviting a few friends to a small dinner party. In the middle of the revelry, I introduced

Fig. 44. Cellist Yehuda Hanani performing at the wedding of Stanley Cohen and Carrie Chen, 2019. Photograph by Kenro Izu and Yumiko Izu.

each invitee, and I realized how fortunate I was to have friends, each talented and well known in their respective fields. All were writers, artists, or museum curators. None came with the legacy of finance or law.

Carrie keeps me steady when a foul mood arises. If I'm irritable with guests that stay too long, she, always unperturbed, smooths the way. As a Buddhist, she gives care to all animals. I am just a two-legged member of her herd of goats. When I first observed Carrie walk, I felt her quiet but determined energy. But

Fig. 45. Stanley Cohen at the Copake residence.

I underestimated how quickly she would take charge of the household and make our home not only a place to live but a working farm. And she involves herself fully in the community. She drives a tractor to till the soil for planting time; she has opened an art gallery and participates in the cultural life of Great Barrington, where she is far better known than I am.

***

I wondered if all that happened to me was really chance or if there was a scheme devised by someone with a stronger hand. Am I just walking along a preordained path? If I had not found Conrad on a shelf, I would not have gone to sea. If I had not gone to sea, I would not have lived in Japan. If I had not lived in Yokohama, I would not have had the courage to abruptly move to Paris.

At this moment, I'm stretched out by the pool, an iced tea on a table adjacent to my lounge chair. Clouds move slowly through the sky, unfurling light and shadows across the countryside. The movement seems magical. God converting mountains into hills. A slight aperture appears between cloud banks. I hear a voice, muted yet clear enough to be deciphered without the need to strain: "Cohen, you don't belong here." I've heard that before, so I relax and take another sip of tea. My moon-faced girl is clipping flowers not too far away. My son will soon arrive to read my tale. Perhaps he will ask why I wrote more about others than about myself. I'll respond, "Oh, I am there, between the lines where I best belong."

Acknowledgments

Since this work has been written over an extended period of time, several different editors have assisted in improving its tone and content. In particular, I wish to thank David Ferris, Jane E. Howard, Tom Shachtman, and Hannah Hanani. Without the gracious contribution of Richard Schechner, it would have remained unfinished.

Illustration Credits

Frontispiece (p. vi) . Drawing of Stanley Cohen by Ann Geracimos, 1972. Photograph by Lisa Vollmer. Courtesy of the author.

Figure 1 (p. xii). Stanley Cohen as a toddler. Courtesy of the author.

Figure 2 (p. 6). Stanley Cohen, age eighteen, working aboard an oil tanker en route to Japan. Courtesy of the author.

Figure 3 (p. 24). Stanley Cohen's school class photograph, 1946; Cohen, top row, second from left. Courtesy of the author.

Figure 4 (p. 76). Yokohama Seamen's Club Christmas party hosted by Stanley Cohen for mixed-heritage children of American GIs and Japanese mothers. Cohen is in the second row, second from the left. Courtesy of the author.

Figure 5 (p. 80). Stanley Cohen presenting an entertainment act at the Yokohama Seamen's Club. Courtesy of the author.

Figure 6 (p. 80). Traditional Japanese dance performance at the club. Courtesy of the author.

Figure 7 (p. 88). Staff outing, Yokohama Seamen's Club; Cohen is seen in the second row, far right. Courtesy of the author.

Figure 8 (p. 110). Stanley Cohen's first Paris residence, 1 Villa Seurat. Courtesy of the author.

Figure 9 (p. 110). Villa Seurat, street view. Courtesy of the author.

Figure 10 (p. 113). Kurt Seligmann painting formerly left in Stanley Cohen's residence and later returned to the artist. Works by Seligmann are held in the Museum of Modern Art. Kurt Seligmann, *Un dimanche* (*Jubivillad*), 1938. Courtesy of the Seligmann Center at Vision Hudson Valley. © 2026 Vision Hudson Valley / Artists Rights Society (ARS), New York.

Figure 11 (p. 119). Painting by Riva Boren, who later taught Stanley Cohen French and lived in hiding during the Nazi occupation of Paris. Image source unknown.

Figure 12 (p. 130). Gertrude Stein (*right*) and Alice B. Toklas (*left*) in the salon of their apartment at 27 Rue de Fleurus, Paris, 1922. Photograph by Man Ray. © Man Ray 2015 Trust / Artists Rights Society (ARS), NY / ADAGP, Paris 2026.

Figure 13 (p. 131). Sculpture of Gertrude Stein by Jo Davidson installed behind the Stephen A. Schwarzman Building (42nd Street Library), Bryant Park, New York; installation facilitated in part by Stanley Cohen. Image courtesy of Bryant Park.

Figure 14 (p. 132). William Klein, Paris, 2016; from left: Klein, restaurant owner, Cohen. Courtesy of the author.

Figure 15 (p. 134). *Rue Aubriot* (*YSL + Nude*), Paris, 1975, by Helmut Newton. Print from the collection of the author. © The Helmut Newton Foundation / Trunk Archive.

Figure 16 (p. 136). Alexander Calder, wine-cork object. Courtesy of the author. © 2026 Calder Foundation, New York / Artists Rights Society (ARS), New York.

Figure 17 (p. 143). Alexander Calder, handwritten note to Stanley Cohen. Courtesy of the author. © 2026 Calder Foundation, New York / Artists Rights Society (ARS), New York.

Figure 18 (p. 145). Alexander Calder, gouache watercolor, modified and dedicated to Stanley Cohen. Courtesy of the author. Photograph by Lisa Vollmer. © 2026 Calder Foundation, New York / Artists Rights Society (ARS), New York.

Figure 19 (p. 146). Rug based on an Alexander Calder drawing, knitted by Louisa Calder and Stanley Cohen. Courtesy of the author. Photograph by Lisa Vollmer. © 2026 Calder Foundation, New York / Artists Rights Society (ARS), New York.

Figure 20 (p. 148). Alexander Calder delivering bread to Stanley Cohen's home in Saché, France. Courtesy of the author. © 2026 Calder Foundation, New York / Artists Rights Society (ARS), New York.

Figure 21 (p. 154). Cohen residence in Saché, France. Courtesy of the author.

Figure 22 (p. 162). Jewelry seized by the US government and later restituted. Image source unknown.

Figure 23 (p. 163). Hélène de Portes. Image source unknown.

Figure 24 (p. 184). Régine opening her nightclub in London. Image source unknown.

Figure 25 (p. 195). Architectural ruins, Turkey. Courtesy of the author.

Figure 26 (p. 196). Architectural ruins with carved tomb, Turkey. Courtesy of the author.

Figure 27 (p. 215). James Baldwin; photograph by A. Scott, a gift to Stanley Cohen on his fortieth birthday. Courtesy of the author.

Figure 28 (p. 228). Stanley Cohen aboard a pipeline barge during a legal work assignment. Image source unknown.

Figure 29 (p. 229). Pipeline worker's hat presented to Stanley Cohen. Courtesy of the author.

Figure 30 (p. 240). Joan Miró painting intended for Alexander Calder; gift facilitated posthumously by Stanley Cohen. © Successió Miró / Artists Rights Society (ARS), New York / ADAGP, Paris 2026.

Figure 31 (p. 257). Joseph Heller with Stanley Cohen, Laura Cohen, and Toby Cohen. Courtesy of the author.

Figure 32 (p. 261). Joseph Heller and Stanley Cohen at a winery in Florence. Courtesy of the author.

Figure 33 (p. 262). Wedding of Joseph Heller and Valerie Heller at Stanley Cohen's New York residence, 1987. From left: Speed Vogel, Valerie Heller, Joseph Heller, and Stanley Cohen. Courtesy of the author.

Figure 34 (p. 268). Tamara de Lempicka, *The Marquis d'Afflitto on a Staircase* (1926), formerly owned by Stanley Cohen and later sold for $600,000. © Tamara de Lempicka Estate, LLC / Artists Rights Society (ARS), New York, 2026 © Tamara de Lempicka™ is a trademark of Tamara de Lempicka Estate, LLC.

Figure 35 (p. 291). Former Japanese American soldier Clarence Matsumura and Holocaust survivor Solly Ganor. Image source unknown.

Figure 36 (p. 296). The Water Mill house. Photograph by Marc Riboud. Courtesy of the author.

Figures 37a–b (p. 302). Postcard from Joyce Carol Oates following her visit to Stanley Cohen's Water Mill home. Courtesy of the author.

Figure 38 (p. 305). John Calder and Jim Haynes. Image source unknown.

Figure 39 (p. 307). Poet Ted Joans. Image sourced from Wikipedia.

Figure 40 (p. 330). Automobile given by Paul Reynaud to Hélène de Portes shortly before her death. Image source unknown.

Figure 41 (p. 343). Paul Cohen, son of Stanley Cohen, at age seven. Courtesy of the author.

Figure 42 (p. 347). The Copake residence. Courtesy of the author.

Figure 43 (p. 348). Stanley Cohen with Justice Ruth Bader Ginsburg at the United States Supreme Court, accompanied by family members. Courtesy of the author.

Figure 44 (p. 349). Cellist Yehuda Hanani performing at the wedding of Stanley Cohen and Carrie Chen, 2019. Photograph by Kenro Izu and Yumiko Izu. Courtesy of the author.

Figure 45 (p. 350). Stanley Cohen at the Copake residence. Courtesy of the author.

Index of Names

"Jeanne Moreau, Albert Speer, Arthur Miller, James Baldwin, Rupert Murdoch, Joseph Heller—just a few of the many friends and acquaintances that people this always fascinating and surprising tale of Stanley Cohen's life and adventures. Compelling, humorous, and juicy gossip fill the pages of Stanley's autobiography . . . . Warning: once you start reading, you won't put it down!"

Sanford Lieberson

Academy Award–winning Film Producer
and Former President of Production, 20th Century Fox

"Stanley Cohen is an unlikely hero born in the heart of the Bronx, with a well-oiled moral compass that took him between the worlds of art, law, and finance. His greatest achievement came when he discovered a class of unsung heroes, archivists who preserve and protect our histories; moved by their contributions, he created an award to acknowledge their sacrifice. Though he's greatly prosperous by any metric, it took writing this memoir—a defining catalogue of achievements—for him to fully reckon the success of his life."

Alexander S. C. Rower

President, Calder Foundation, New York

"Much more than a personal memoir, this is a chronicle of a time and many places through the lens of an adventurous and daring mind. Stanley Cohen is zany, captivating, charismatic, and complex as he opens the door to a who's who of the mid- and late-twentieth-century artists, literati, glitterati, and captains of business. It offers a first-hand and intimate link to the heyday of Paris and its personages. Trying to summarize it may sound like shameless name-dropping, but the story is alive with real people and human drama and is almost cinematic as it shifts seamlessly from continent to continent and takes readers from boardroom to bedroom. . . . And in the tradition of the bildungsroman, which focuses on the psychological and moral growth of the protagonist from childhood to adulthood, Cohen's interlocking stories and dreams forge a path to finding his inner and best self. Episodic, picaresque, philosophical, and not to be missed!"

Yehuda Hanani

Acclaimed cellist, educator, and founder of the Close Encounters
With Music festival